Huzzah!

Shinin' Times at

The Fort

by Holly Arnold Kinney

Holly Arnold Kinney

Shinin' Times at

The Fort

by Holly Arnold Kinney

photographs by Lois Ellen Frank

Fur Trade Press™, LLC
PO Box 569
19192 Highway 8
Morrison, CO 80465
303-863-8803

Second edition: June, 2011

Design by Barbara Scott-Goodman

ISBN 978-0-578-05655-5
Cooking/Regional Interest

Printed in China by Imago

10 9 8 7 6 5 4 3 2

Kinney, Holly Arnold
Shinin' Times at The Fort/ by Holly Arnold Kinney- 2nd edition
Includes index
ISBN 978-0-578-05655-5

Cooking/Wine & Spirits, Regional Interest

dedication

▼▼▼▼▼▼▼▼▼▼▼▼▼▼▼▼▼▼▼▼

I dedicate this book to my guardian angel who has guided me through life,
has worked miracles, and given me so many blessings.

I also dedicate this book to my father, Sam'l Paul Arnold, who helped to create me and the Fort.

and to my husband, Jeremy Kinney, who encouraged me to change my life
and buy the Fort, as "It is in your blood…it is your destiny!"

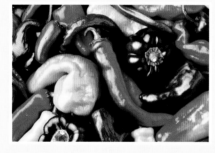

acknowledgments

▾▾▾▾▾▾▾▾▾▾▾▾▾▾▾▾▾▾▾▾

First, I am thankful to my wonderful mother, Bay, whose idea it was to build the Fort. I am also thankful for her gifts as a talented cook, animal lover, passionate gardener, and avid historian who never tired of learning about the Southwest and its people. I also happily recall her beautiful voice and skill playing the guitar; both of which were such a treat to hear. Finally, I thank her for her love for my brother Keith and me.

A big thank you to my dad, Sam'l P. Arnold, who was bigger than life itself. Dad's enthusiasm for food, history, music, and good stories were legendary. He could play the saw, mandolin, and violin, and loved both classical and folk music. He loved women, dear friends, and his children. He was enamored of his alma maters, Andover and Yale, which made him the Ivy League Mountain Man *extraordinaire*. He was sought after as a radio and television personality and by anyone who could corner him for one of his great tales of the West. Dad loved my pet bear Sissy and our German shepherd Lobo. He loved to cook and eat and made sure we tried everything from pigs' head scrapple to rattlesnake. Because he taught me much about advertising and marketing and old-fashioned hard work, I am forever grateful. He told my husband Jeremy that I was his greatest creation. I miss you and love you, Dad.

I also want to thank Aunt Mary Fox Arnold, whom I lived with when my parents divorced in 1967. She remained my best friend, champion, and advisor until she passed away in October 2005. I miss her terribly.

Thank you to my late stepmother, Carrie Shaffer Arnold, who helped my dad buy back the Fort in 1986, and then fell in love with the place and with Bent's Fort, as well. Carrie became a Mountain Woman *extraordinaire* and mother to us all. She was a remarkable artist and many of her paintings hang in the Fort as well as in private collections and the Denver Public Library. Her beautiful line drawings are featured throughout this book and now, as always, I am amazed by her talent.

I owe a gigantic thanks to my husband Jeremy for so many things, but especially for his encouragement in 1998 when I bought my interest in the Fort. At that time my fifty-six-year-old stepmother Carrie was dying of cancer and my seventy-two-year-old father had congestive heart failure. Just before she died, Carrie and Dad had found an interested buyer for the restaurant, which they deemed was too much for my father to handle. Jeremy persuaded me to take the plunge and buy the business. "It's in your blood," he said. "It's your destiny."

He was so right, although at first I was not convinced. Jeremy pointed out that if I did not step in, builders would tear down the adobe building and put up houses. "You will never forgive yourself," he reasoned. "Are you sure?" I asked, pointing out that many marriages are ruined by the restaurant business—including my parents'. Jeremy was steadfast. He owned his own business, and at the time I owned a national public relations firm call Arnold Media Services with clients from Los Angeles to New York. Jeremy reminded me that the Fort had been my home and the people who worked there were family. "You must do this!" he said. And so I did.

In 1999, I made my dad an offer to buy the Fort. He told me he would sell 49 percent to me, and keep 51 percent. I was thrilled that he wanted to stay in the business and teach me the ropes—and I had a lot to learn! Dad went on to get many awards, including the Lifetime Achievement Award from the International Association of Culinary professionals (IACP) before he died in June 2006. In December 2006, I bought the building, land, and property and his remaining 51 percent interest from his estate. The result is I am now the sole owner. I've come back home!

If it weren't for Jeremy, none of the above would have been possible, nor would I have written this book and been so optimistic and excited about our future. I would never have had the experience of working alongside

my father as a partner and witnessed his exhilaration as we brought back the shinin' times! My dad was enormously happy to witness the revival of the Fort. And so, Jeremy is my knight in shining armor and I am grateful to him each and every day. Thank you, Darling!

I also want to acknowledge my Fort family, especially those who continue to give shinin' times to our guests each night. Some of our employees have been with us for more than twenty years! Thank you to my vice president of operations, Mark Steed, who keeps the Fort running and watches every penny we spend. A big thank you to Chris Seres, who started as a busser in 1986 and is now our dining manager and who gets many compliments from guests because he never hesitates to "go the extra mile." Thank you to Mark Carpenter, who manages all the bussers and hostesses and does so much for us all. A big thanks to Executive Chef Geoffrey Groditski, Sous Chef Juan Zepeda, John Lusk, our grill manager, and Sarah Bailey, our pastry chef. Thanks to the day crew who puts hard work, love, and soul into each dish—including grilling more than seventy thousand buffalo steaks every year! Thank you to Melissa Severson, our private dining manager who continues to get awards for hospitality for her distinguished service. Thank you to our advertising manager, Wayne Lindsey. A big overall thanks to the entire Fort family which has helped me so much during the last ten years. Thanks to my personal assistant, Mary Pappas, who has coordinated meetings, photo shoots, and travel, all the while being "mom" to Jeremy and me, as well as to our pets Rita and Gilly, our garden, and our home.

Thanks to the Tesoro Cultural Center's staff, Sarah Shirazi and Carolyn Doran, who fulfill the mission of Tesoro to educate the public about the many cultures who traded at Bent's Fort. Among other things, they organize tours for thousands of school kids every year! Thank you to Tesoro Cultural Center's board of directors, advisory board, volunteers, sponsors, and fans. And thank you to historian and president of the Museum of the Fur Trade, Jim Hanson, for supplying me with "mother" heirloom seeds for an authentic fur trade garden, which I am continuing today in the courtyard at the Fort. Thank you, Jim, for donating the heirloom beans and seed packets we used for the photo shoot, and for continuing to tend to the museum's garden, with crops from the 18th and 19th centuries. Thank you to my "bro," Bill Gwaltney, his wife Trish and son Will for your love, support and passion for history.

When I decided to self-publish this book, I assembled an "A" team to help me. Mary Goodbody is our talented editor who I've known for more than twenty years through IACP. Barbara Scott-Goodman is my amazing book designer who makes sure the design is "Southampton East Coast style meets Wild Mountain Man Western style." I am deeply grateful to my good friend and fellow Dame d'Escoffier, Beverly Cox. Bev formatted all the recipes and tested many of them to insure they worked well in any home kitchen. It was great fun discussing the Fort's food in such detail with her! Thank you, Beverly! And a major tribute to photographer, Lois Ellen Frank, who is part Kiowa Indian and one of the brightest and best businesswomen I know. Lois has an amazing eye for food and scenic photography. Her assistant, Chef Walter Whitewater from the Navajo Nation, decided after a five-day shoot to conduct a blessing for the book. Thank you, Walter.

And most importantly, a thank you to all our loyal customers who visit the Fort every night. You have supported us through so many years and if it were not for you, I wouldn't be writing these words. More significantly, the Fort would not be a part of our lives. I am always so humbled by your stories, memories, and thoughtfulness. So many of you take the time to write or email me to share your wonderful memories and suggestions with the staff and me. We are truly honored to know and serve you.

Holly Arnold Kinney and her dad, Sam'l P. Arnold as partners, May 2000

foreword

In this era of franchises and formula fast food, it's refreshing to find a restaurant with an original point of view and real cooks in the kitchen. The first thing that strikes you when you visit the Fort in Morrison, Colorado, is its stunning setting. The building is nestled beside a massive red bolder and the lights of Denver shine far below. Entering the great courtyard where a bonfire blazes and the scent of piñon smoke fills the air, is like stepping back into the nineteenth century, and immediately you realize that this is not a theme park "fort" or a movie set facade, but an authentic adobe structure.

Of course, the true bricks and mortar that make a great restaurant are the people: a restaurateur with vision, a talented kitchen crew, and a hard-working wait staff who makes guests feel welcome and well cared for. That's what you'll find at the Fort.

When my friend Holly Arnold Kinney asked me to write the foreword to *Shinin' Times at the Fort*, I was honored. In this wonderfully personal book, Holly tells the story of the Arnold family in recipes and prose, and what a story it is! Her parents, Sam and Elizabeth "Bay" Arnold were western history buffs who loved good food and good times. Their fort, built with skill and love, was meant to be more than a restaurant; it was a home for their charming and creative family, including a dog named Lobo and a Canadian black bear named Sissy who liked to drink soda from a bottle!

Holly's dad, Sam Arnold, was a modern Renaissance man—Western historian, cook, cookbook author, musician, and black-powder rifle enthusiast. He could speak knowledgeably and entertainingly about most any subject, even while opening a bottle of champagne with a tomahawk. At his restaurant Sam followed what he called "Arnold's Law" or "Give people the kind of food they like," which in 1960s Colorado meant steak and potatoes. The difference was that while other Denver eateries were dishing up "Surf and Turf" with a baked potato wrapped in foil, at the Fort you could dine on a prime buffalo or beef steak with a generous side

of Fort-Style new potatoes sautéed with corn, onion, red pepper, green chiles, and crisp bacon!

In 1999 Holly joined Sam as a partner and brought her own creative vision to the restaurant. She has continued to run the Fort since Sam's death in 2006 and it seems that the food gets better and better. Holly is also the driving force behind the Tesoro Cultural Center (tesoro means "treasure" in Spanish) a not-for-profit with a mission to create community-based events and educational outreach programs that celebrate Colorado's rich and diverse history. There are interesting Tesoro lectures, dinners, and historic re-enactments throughout the year at the Fort, but two major draws are the Annual Indian Market & Powwow held in May, and the 1830s Rendezvous & Spanish Colonial Market in September. Both of these occasions bring thousands of people to the Fort.

The recipes in this book, many of which I've personally cooked to insure they would work in everyone's kitchen, are varied, delicious, and never dull. By combining Arnold family favorites, historic dishes, vintage recipes from the 1960s and 70s and cutting-edge dishes from the current menu, Holly tells the story of her family and the Fort in the most mouth-watering way. From appetizers (Sam called them Beginners) that include Duck Quesadillas, Buffalo Empanadas and a wonderful guacamole as well as more esoteric choices like rattlesnake cakes, to an outstanding selection of satisfying old-fashioned desserts including the best recipe I've ever tried for Capirotada, a traditional New Mexican bread pudding, and the Fort's memorable and addictive Chile Chocolate Bourbon cake, when you cook from this book you, your family, and friends will be in for a treat!

Great job, Holly! Let the shinin' times roll on!

Beverly Cox
Eagle Rock Ranch, Colorado
May 2010

introduction

Why Shinin' Times at the Fort?

The Fort is a very special place for me, my family, everyone who works here, and for our guests. When you walk through our impressively large, hand-carved wooden doors, you are overcome with a warm, magical, feeling—something I have experienced since I was a small girl living above the restaurant on the mountain-rimmed plains outside Denver, Colorado.

The Fort is a full-scale replica of Bent's Fort, a well-known nineteenth century fur-trading post in southwest Colorado. When my mother and father decided to build the Fort, they made sure to do so following age-old techniques for adobe buildings. The result is as authentic as you can get—a reddish brown beauty that glimmers in the setting sun and beckons hungry diners—but more about that later!

I wrote this book to honor my personal journey with the Fort, which began before I was ten years old and continues to this day. It's the story of my mother Elizabeth, known as Bay; my father Samuel, known as Sam'l; my only brother, Keith; and my stepmother, Carrie. Sadly, every one of these family members has died; my son Oren and I are the only ones left to carry on the family name and traditions—with some cheerful help from my husband, Jeremy. He is the reason I decided to partner with my father in 1999 and why I run the restaurant to this day. My mother, father, and brother are buried on the north side of the large red rock that looms eighty feet above the Fort, along with our first manager, Carlos Molina. We also buried my pet bear, Sissy Bear, and our German shepherd, Lobo, there. I like to think they all watch over the Fort, cheering us on with "Huzzahs!" every night as we give our guests some shinin' times.

The Fort's Magic

In the early 1960s, my mother told me that our gigantic red rock was a spiritual magnet that created an aura that affected every person who came in range of it. When my parents scouted locations for the adobe home they planned to build, the rock drew them in with its intense spiritual energy and strength. It's a gorgeous red color that plays dramatically with our clear blue skies and dramatic Western sunsets.

The Fort and the huge red rock nestled next to it became my home when I was just ten. While they were building the Fort, my mom and dad decided to turn the building into a restaurant, and we eventually moved into the top floor, which today houses the restaurant offices.

Since it opened in 1963, the Fort has welcomed hundreds of thousands of happy customers and its fair share of celebrities and dignitaries. In 1997, President Bill Clinton hosted an official Summit of Eight dinner there, celebrating the quintessentially American flavor of the locale and the food. The Prince of Jordan recently had dinner with us, entertained by four-star generals from the Pentagon. Governor Bill Ritter and Denver Mayor John Hickenlooper hosted a number of delegations during the 2008 Democratic Convention, because, like Bill Clinton before them, they appreciated the total experience of eating at the Fort.

As thrilled we are by such high-profile guests, our favorites are the loyal customers, many of them multigenerational, who have entered our doors since 1963. We hear from customers all the time about their own shinin' times at the Fort, whether it's a great dinner with family or friends, a holiday meal, or a preplanned and organized bar mitzvah or wedding.

We always have great fun at the Fort. Birthday celebrants are given a ceremonial headdress to wear, at Halloween the staff dresses in costumes, and in the 1960s and 1970s, my pet bear aptly named Sissy Bear was known to sidle up to the bar for a bottle of soda pop. The gentle bear "kissed" a number of celebrities and showed up in lots of photographs. We'll go to any length to ensure that dining with us is a memorable experience!

The Real Shinin' Star

As delightful as Sissy Bear was, our food is the real shinin' star at the Fort. The menu is based on the foods of the early nineteenth century when fur traders roamed the region, often using Fort Bent as their headquarters. That fort was operational from 1833 to 1849, but in those short sixteen years, it influenced much of the history of Colorado and New Mexico. At our restaurant, as at Fort Bent, game meat rules, especially buffalo, elk, and quail. Rest assured, our game dishes are prepared with the twenty-first century palate very much in mind. We are true to the spirit of our American past, but not always to the letter—in fact, our motto is "New Foods of the Old West," which I think pretty much sums it up.

Just as important as the dishes from Bent's Fort are, so are those of the Native Americans who coexisted with the traders and mountain men. We serve Taos trout, Washtunkala buffalo, elk stew, buffalo tongue, and buffalo marrow bones. Many of our dishes are based on beans, corn, and squash—three vegetables that are considered by Indians across the country as the "three sacred sisters."

Our core menu of game and heritage dishes never changes, which is reassuring to guests who make a point of visiting us whenever they spend time in Colorado, or who plan a once-a-year meal with us for a special occasion. Our talented chefs change the menu with the seasons, too, incorporating what is best and fresh from Colorado's farms and ranches, streams and woodlands. For limited times, dependent on supply, we also serve rattlesnake cakes made of snakes from Texas, and musk ox raised by the First Nations people of Canada.

On these pages you will find recipes from our standing menu as well as many others that have appeared from time to time, season to season, or for very special occasions. I also write about the traditions that have grown up around our food and events, many of them celebrating activities generated by the not-for-profit organization, Tesoro Cultural Center. The center's primary mission is to educate the public about our multicultural heritage, one that includes the indigenous people of the Southwest, through demonstrations, school tours, lecture series, and public events focused on history, art, music, dance, and cuisine.

My Family, Our Family, Your Family

My family has always felt strongly about passing on recipes from one generation to the next. This is a way to preserve family traditions, and it also maintains a link to our histories. This conviction was true on both sides of the family. Bay, my mother, was from an old southern family that settled in Georgia in the early 1700s, and Sam'l, my father, was from an equally old Pennsylvania family. I am fortunate to have old notebooks and cookbooks from both families, and in this book you will find some of my favorite family dishes.

Both of my parents believed in family and culinary history, and so they collected historic and little-known cookbooks when they researched the food that would eventually be served at the Fort. Most of these books document recipes from the early nineteenth century in Mexico and the Southwest. I have inherited this invaluable library, which now boasts more than two thousand volumes, many of which are extremely rare. My parents didn't collect all two thousand; many came from their own parents, and my father hired antiquarians to expand the collection so that during a fifty-year span, he acquired just about every book on his favorite subject.

Throughout this book I often quote or paraphrase my dad. He was a respected historian and I found writing this book an exceptional opportunity to share his knowledge and research with an ever wider audience. I learned a lot going back through his work, and I hope you will find it as fascinating as I do.

We celebrate all families at the Fort, not just mine. Because we welcome all families, large and small, many of our customers choose the restaurant for birthdays, anniversaries, and other happy occasions. I always refer to our customers as "guests" since I consider each one a guest in my home. I hope this book will be used by all members of your family. When I was a kid, my parents encouraged me to cook alongside them. Not only did I love the time I got to spend with them but it gave me confidence in the kitchen. I hope you will do the same. I promise—the entire family will have some Fort-style Shinin' Times!

The Fort's Commitment to Sustainability

The Fort uses artesian well water from a well that is more than seven hundred feet deep and we have long conserved water as a matter of practice. We also are dedicated to recycling.

The building is made from adobe bricks of mud and straw from the land on which the Fort sits. We have a full-time maintenance crew to repair the adobe. Just about weekly, workers mix mud and straw and repair the exterior walls where rain and snowmelt eat away at the structure. With this practice, we are always taking care of Mother Earth.

Whenever possible, our chefs use organic and Colorado-grown produce. We have a courtyard, just as they did at Bent's Fort, where we grow corn, beans, and squash, the three sacred sisters so vital to Native American cooking. We are working on creating an organic garden on our grounds to grow lettuces, herbs, and other vegetables.

The buffalo meat we purchase comes from ranches in the Rocky Mountains. To date, the Fort sells more than seventy thousand buffalo entrées every year, and so we are very careful about buying the meat. It has to be the best.

The Fort received the Governor's Award for being a Colorado Proud restaurant that features local Colorado food products and Colorado wines. Additionally, the Fort was recognized by the Environmental Protection Agency as a "two leaf leader" in sustainable practices during the Democratic Convention in 2008. Our commitment to being green is not only good for Mother Earth and humanity but it means our food will always taste good! Huzzah!

▼▼▼▼▼▼▼▼▼▼▼▼▼▼▼▼▼▼▼▼▼

how the fort came to exist

▼▼▼▼▼▼▼▼▼▼▼▼▼▼▼▼▼

The story of the Fort begins with a love story between two starry-eyed people who shared a lust for adventure and a willingness to explore their respective and joint creativity. My parents, Bay and Sam'l Arnold, not only built the magnificent building that houses one of the West's best and most famous restaurants but they shaped a way of life that embodied their mutual passion for history, food, and the multiethnic cultures of the American West. Because we moved into the Fort when I was barely ten years old, this means I was a lucky girl indeed: I grew up living in a real adobe fort under Colorado's bright blue skies, a building that today still speaks volumes about our country's past and its future.

Samuel Paul Arnold, known as "Sam'l", proudly sits on the rock in front of his Fort in 1963.

Samuel Paul Arnold, known as Sam'l for much of his life, was born in Pittsburgh, Pennsylvania. His parents sent him east to prep school at Phillips Academy in Andover, Massachusetts, and then to Yale, where he graduated in 1947. He was a member of the Yale Glee Club and met Elizabeth Bivens when the glee club performed at Rollins College in Florida. He always told the story of catching the eye of a beautiful young woman in the audience and falling in love on the spot. "I'm going to marry that woman," he said to himself.

After two years of courting Bay, as my mother was called, he married the southern belle from Georgia in Santa Fe, New Mexico, where the young couple set up housekeeping. My mother had refused to move north with Sam'l and he was equally adamant about not living in the South, and so the great American West was a good compromise. It turned out to be their destiny.

They loved Santa Fe. It was a thriving community where they were able to meet and become friends with physicist Robert Oppenheimer, who had headed up the Manhattan Project, artist Georgia O'Keeffe, and Mable Dodge Luhan, who is best known for starting a literary colony in Taos. My dad and I used to bring buffalo skulls to O'Keeffe in the 1970s for her to paint, and my mother told wonderful stories of parties in Taos at Mable Dodge Luhan's colony. They also were great friends with Maria Martinez, the renowned potter from the San Ildefonso Pueblo. I remember playing with her grandson Tony Da, who turned out to be an innovative potter in his own right. Sadly, Tony died in 2008.

As much as my parents loved living in Santa Fe, my father had a hard time putting his Yale education to its best advantage, and so in 1951 they moved to Denver and bought an advertising agency. The agency prospered and when my brother and I were small children, my mother convinced my father to build an adobe house outside the city in red rocks country. Here, she argued, they could raise their kids in the open air with plenty of space to ride horses.

Bay did her homework. She researched adobe buildings at the Colorado Historical Society and discovered a drawing of Bent's Fort. "Look at this!" she said to her husband. "Let's build an adobe castle like this one instead of a house."

They examined recent excavations of Bent's Fort to develop the first set of blueprints for their own structure. They hired architect William Lumpkin who was known for his work with adobe buildings, and when it was time to build, they hired local laborers who knew how to work with adobe. These skilled artisans puddled more than eighty thousand adobe bricks from our own soil and built the Fort from the ground up. My parents turned to the artists and craftspeople they had known in Santa Fe and Taos to fashion the Spanish colonial vigas, furniture, and doors so that our fort was as authentic as Bay and Sam'l could make it.

Not surprisingly, the construction project exceeded its budget. When my parents applied for a loan, the bank agreed on the condition they housed a business in the building. "You can cook," Dad said to Mom, who replied, "You can, too!"

And so, these two enterprising people began researching old diaries written by pioneers as well as the residents of Fort Bent to discover what was commonly eaten in the middle of the nineteenth century. They delved into Native American cuisine, too, and learned as much as they could about local crops and livestock. Eventually, they drafted the first menu for the Fort, which opened in 1963. Many of the dishes on that early menu exist to this day.

This led to a very busy time in our lives. Mom and Dad were advertising executives by day and restaurateurs by night. We lived above the store, literally, in the rooms that now are the restaurant offices. As a child, I thought this was heaven. I could race in and out of the kitchen and then dash up to the top of the gigantic red rock rising out of the earth next to the restaurant. We had a loyal German shepherd dog and I even had a pet Canadian black bear named Sissy Bear, which led my father to call me She Who Naps with Bear. When we discovered that a bear had also lived in the courtyard of the original Fort Bent, we were thrilled.

Life was good! Although my parent's love story eventually ended in divorce, they both maintained their affection for the Fort. Mom moved back to her beloved South, and Dad stayed in Denver to run the restaurant. I grew up to start my own public relations business in Denver and raise my son, Oren. My father married Carrie, my much-loved stepmother, who cherished the restaurant as much as the rest of us. Today, the Fort is mine alone. My parents and brother are gone and I am proud to continue what that starry-eyed couple started so many years ago, with a fond eye on the past and an inquisitive, excited eye on the future.

who was sam arnold?

Sam Arnold was my father, and I mention him often on these pages. For most of its existence, he was the guiding force behind the Fort—and in many ways behind me! I proudly entered into a partnership with him in 1999, when I assumed a 49 percent interest in the restaurant to his 51 percent, which is how we ran the business until his death in 2006. I am sure when he graduated from college in 1947, he never dreamed he would become an internationally recognized food historian, not to mention a world-class restaurateur. But that's exactly what happened to him, a boy from Pittsburgh whose life was shaped in some ways by geography. Born in Pennsylvania, he was educated in the Northeast at Yale. He married a girl from the South and the two of them moved west. The West became his true home, where he raised his family and started his businesses and where his heart joyfully resided.

Dad wrote *Eating Up the Santa Fe Trail* after intense research. It was published in 2001 and today is in its fourth printing. He pored over the diaries of the pioneers to discover what they ate as they traveled the famous trail, research that dovetailed nicely with his study of William Bent and Bent's Fort. My father lectured on these and other historical matters with deep knowledge and great delight. He truly loved his subject, and anyone who heard him talk about it could not help but be affected with his enthusiasm and passion.

He won a number of awards in his lifetime, including the Lifetime Achievement award from the International Association of Culinary Professionals. He was a radio personality and no stranger to television. In fact, he produced a ten-week PBS program called *Frying Pans West* and sold more than one hundred thousand copies of the series companion cookbook. The series aired for more than fifteen years on PBS.

But more important, Sam Arnold loved life and was never afraid to live it to the fullest. He was fervent in his love for the Fort and all it stood for; he truly appreciated good food and drink; and he celebrated his friends, his children, and his employees. My father's broad smile and ready laughter could light up a room and fill it with joy, and both are still missed—and happily remembered—at the Fort.

▼▼▼▼▼▼▼▼▼▼▼▼▼▼▼▼▼▼▼▼▼▼

an eye for the future:
shinin' times for future generations

▼▼▼▼▼▼▼▼▼▼▼▼▼▼▼▼▼▼▼▼

The Tesoro Cultural Center, a Colorado public non-profit organization, was created by my family and me in 1999 to expand the vision we had to teach the public about the many cultures that traded, intermarried, and lived at Bent's Fort, a fur-trading fort that was active in southeastern Colorado from 1833 to 1849. Today, the Tesoro Cultural Center has more than 2,500 members and has expanded both the board of directors and advisory board. The Center is supported by the community through business sponsorships, grants from the government and private foundations, media sponsors and exposure on public television. It also relies on membership dues and admission fees to various events. Today, every fourth grader in Colorado learns about Bent's Fort in their school's history curriculum.

Tesoro sponsors tours of the Fort restaurant, which is an exact replica of the original Bent's Fort, which means that over the years we have welcomed thousands of school kids and their teachers to our adobe building. These tours provide opportunities for teaching school children about their rich Colorado heritage and historic events connected to Bent's Fort. We also show them what gardens in the 1830s and 1840s looked like and talk about what people ate back in those times.

Additionally, the Tesoro Cultural Center hosts two major festivals a year.

the indian market and powwow

In May of each year, the Tesoro Cultural Center and the Fort organize a two-day festival called the Indian Market Powwow at the Fort. The market features more than 40 award-winning Indian artists who demonstrate and sell their art. We also honor American Indian veterans from as many as 60 tribes and invite them to dance in competition at the powwow. The Indian Market is juried, which draws buyers from a number of museums and galleries that collect the artists' work. Thousands of Indian art collectors and art lovers enjoy the Indian Market and Powwow every year.

the 1830s rendezvous and spanish colonial market

In September of each year, we organize another two-day festival that celebrates Colorado's mountain men and women. We recreate an encampment similar to one that these rough-and-tumble denizens of the Rocky Mountains might have inhabited back in the 1830s and 1840s, complete with black gunpowder shoots and physical competitions. We also mount a Spanish Colonial art show that features twenty top Hispanic artists during the same event. Attendees wander through the mountain man camp and then return to the 21st century by enjoying the art show.

In addition to these festivals, the Tesoro Cultural Center sponsors a lecture series that covers aspects of Colorado's history in conjunction with the Kinney/Tesoro Fellowship program. This is organized with the help of Yale University's Western Studies Department and the Howard Lamar Center for the Study of Frontiers and Boarders. Yale University is Tesoro's academic endorsing institution. Dr. Jay Gitlin, a Tesoro board member, author, and Yale professor, has commented that "Through Tesoro events, the Fort is the Bent's Fort of the 21st century, trading with the Indian tribes and mountain men and women."

For more information, visit Tesoro's website at www.tesoroculturalcenter.org.

holiday events at the fort organized by the tesoro cultural center

farolito lighting and pinecone ceremony

At the Fort, we celebrate the winter holidays in November with the Farolito Lighting and Pinecone Ceremony, which is open and free to the public. We select an honoree to light the farolitos—paper bags filled with sand and illuminated with a candle—in our open-air courtyard the Sunday evening following Thanksgiving. This is someone in the community who has inspired and illuminated our minds, hearts and souls with their brilliance and contributions to our community. During and after the farolito lighting, we sing Christmas carols that were sung in the 1830s and 1840s before beginning the Pine Cone Ceremony.

For this ceremony, everyone is given a pine cone and a piece of paper and instructed to write a message to someone who lives far away or who has died. They then tuck the message in the pine cone. Everyone participating walks single file around a bonfire burning brightly in our courtyard and tosses the pine cones into the flames. The idea is that as the fire burns the pine cones, the message is sent to the heavens.

Several hundred people gather for this ritual in the crisp Colorado mountain air, which results in a very large bonfire filled with pine cones. Tears and hugs are shared around the fire and then we serve hot cider, Mexican hot chocolate and the Biscochitos featured on page 216.

Opposite page left to right:
Powwow Dancer
Dr. Charlie Carrillo, Santero
Holly Kinney as Susan Magoffin
teaching kids

This page: Las Posadas
Native American baskets
Joseph and Mary with donkey

las posadas on christmas eve at the fort

In many small Hispanic towns in Southern Colorado and Northern New Mexico, during the winter holidays there is a multi-week-long celebration called Las Posadas. It is the re-enactment of Joseph and Mary's journey to Bethlehem, where she gave birth to the baby Jesus. At the Fort, the Tesoro Cultural Center organizes a condensed Las Posadas celebration on Christmas Eve from 4:30 p.m. until 6:30 p.m., which is open to the public and is free.

Tesoro partners with the Christian Life Fraternas, a consecrated order of lay nuns originally from Peru who represent the Hispanic communities of the Catholic Church. They select a young boy and girl, each about eight years old, to dress up as Joseph and Mary. There also are a number of young angels as well as a live donkey and a few sheep. Musicians play traditional Las Posadas songs and the onlookers sing along in Spanish as a candlelit procession follows the Fort's adobe walls. Along the way, Joseph and Mary knock on the doors of the Fort (often with diners gazing out at them), singing out in Spanish "Let us in! Please let us in! We are seeking shelter for me to give birth to baby Jesus."

The devil suddenly appears on the roof of the Fort and tries to frighten the procession away, but they persist in their journey around the building, finally arriving at the front gates where they again plead for admission. The devil dies on the roof, the gates open, and the procession, which by now includes several hundred people, enters our courtyard. There, a manger filled with hay and chairs welcomes Joseph and Mary. There is also a crib for the baby (who makes his appearance at this time). The nuns explain the true meaning of Christmas and prayers are said.

A big piñata is next raised in the courtyard for the kids in the crowd to hit while blindfolded. When the piñata breaks and spills its candy onto the ground and the children have gathered their fair share, we sing carols again, both in English and Spanish. We serve hot tamales, biscochitos, Mexican hot chocolate, and hot mulled cider. Not surprisingly, this has become a magical, cultural, and spiritual tradition for many families who join us every year to celebrate Christmas Eve.

Shinin' Times for All!

beginners

fort guacamole

Our guests love our guacamole, and for good reason. It's been voted "the best" by Denver's *Westword* newspaper, but even without the accolade we know how truly spectacular it is. We make it the way it's traditionally made in Mexico, where it originated as a way to use overripe avocados. Mexican cooks stirred *salsa cruda*—made with fresh tomatoes, serrano chiles, and cilantro—into the avocados and a glorious dish was born. In most Mexican households, neither garlic nor lime juice is part of the mix, but cooks lay slices of fresh lime on top of the dip to prevent it from oxidizing and turning brown. At the Fort, we add lime juice but never, ever use garlic or cumin. Cumin is a big no-no in New Mexican cooking, a regional conceit we follow here. • *serves 4 to 6*

3 ripe Hass avocados, pitted and peeled
3 whole Serrano chiles, seeded and minced
¼ cup freshly squeezed lime juice (2 small limes)
½ teaspoon salt
2 large, ripe tomatoes, seeded and diced
1 medium white onion, diced
¼ cup whole fresh cilantro leaves (no stems), minced

Place the avocados, chiles, lime juice, and salt in a large bowl. Mash the avocados with a fork or potato masher, leaving small lumps. Gently fold in the tomatoes, onion, and cilantro. Taste, and add more lime juice if desired. The guacamole should be spicy, so add more Serrano chiles as your taste dictates. Serve with freshly fried corn tortilla chips.

WHEN A BEGINNER IS A BEGINNING

My father, Sam'l, called appetizers "beginners," because during the 1800s that was a popular term for any small dish served before the main event. Why fool around with an unfamiliar word when an obvious one does just as well?

Our menu at the Fort offers a long list of beginners. Some have been there from the 1960s, while others were added as the years went by. I have introduced a few I particularly like and have found to be great favorites with our guests.

▼▼▼▼▼▼▼▼▼▼▼▼▼▼▼▼▼▼▼▼▼

mountain man boudies

I have wonderful memories of biting into juicy buffalo sausages seasoned with sage and herbs and dipped in a spicy, sweet chile sauce. When I was a kid living at the Fort, my parents showed travel films on Sunday evenings and served these sausages, also known as "boudies." The films satisfied their wanderlust and the food needed no introduction.

My father, Sam'l, recognized how delicious these boudies were and made them whenever possible. They are a staple at the Fort and we have any number of customers who cannot get enough of them. Sam'l wrote about their history:

"During the fur-trade period, the American West was populated by many French-Canadians making their living as beaver trappers. A favorite food was boudin, or any type of sausage, preferably those similar to the blood sausage of France. The English word "pudding" originates from the French word boudin, and the recipe for boudin generally consisted of meat and some form of cereal cooked together and pushed into intestine casings. English-speaking mountain men couldn't pronounce "dem furrin languidges," so they simply called boudin "dem boudies."

• *makes 12 sausages; serves 6*

1 cup hulled sunflower seeds
3 pounds buffalo round, brisket, or plate
1/4 pound buffalo, beef, or pork fat, see Note
1 cup uncooked instant oatmeal
2 yellow onions, finely chopped
1 tablespoon coarsely ground black pepper
1 1/2 tablespoons chile caribe
  (coarsely ground red chile)

2 cups dried bread crumbs
1 1/2 teaspoons ground sage
1 1/2 teaspoons dried thyme
1 1/2 teaspoons dried leaf oregano
1 1/2 tablespoons whole cumin seed
10 feet large pork casings (optional)

Toast the sunflower seeds in a small skillet over medium-low heat, stirring until lightly browned, 3 to 5 minutes. Allow to cool.

Fit the meat grinder with the chile plate and grind the buffalo meat with the fat. Put the mixture through the meat grinder again, so that the meat is ground twice.

The traditional way of making boudies is to mix all the ingredients except the casings together thoroughly and, with a sausage stuffer, fill the pork casings to make individual boudies twisted off every 6 inches. But if you don't want to bother with stuffing sausage casings, simply shape the mixture into patties. Grill the patties over medium-hot coals for 3 to 5 minutes per side. They can also be cooked on a griddle or in a greased pan. To be true to history, the boudies would typically be boiled and served hot. At the Fort, boudies in casings are boiled ahead of time, then grilled.

After they are boiled, boudies in casings keep very well in the freezer. When you want to eat them, defrost in the refrigerator, then grill, or cook them on a griddle as indicated. If you make patties, freeze them raw, then defrost and grill, or cook on a griddle.

Note: The fat around the kidneys is the purest, so ask the butcher for it. If you would rather not use the fat, use 3 1/4 pounds of lean beef and put it through the grinder twice. You can ask the butcher to grind the meat and fat for you.

hot sausage bean dip

Back in the day, my dad and a group of chefs took an annual fishing trip to friend Fritz Covillo's cabin in Ouray, Colorado, high in the Rocky Mountains. Fritz always served a hot sausage dip, which Dad said was "so good as to make a grown man cry!" Since then, we have served a version of the dip at the Fort and while we hope no one cries when they taste it, it's fantastic for any sort of celebration at any time of the year. I especially like to make this during football season, and it's also great heated up over a hot, smoky campfire. At the restaurant, we use buffalo sausage, but use your favorite pork or poultry sausage if you prefer. • *serves 8 to 10*

2 pounds refried beans (two 16-ounce cans)

8 ounces dark beer

¾ pound bulk hot Italian sausage

¾ cup finely chopped white onion

3 to 5 Serrano chiles, seeded and finely minced

1½ to 2 cups (6 to 8 ounces) grated Cheddar cheese

Heat the beans and beer in a double boiler to prevent burning. Meanwhile, in a large sauté pan, brown the sausage and onion over medium heat for 5 to 6 minutes. Stir to crumble the sausage as it cooks. Pour off any fat and add the chiles. Sauté a few minutes longer, then combine with the bean and beer mixture. At the last minute, stir in the cheese, which will melt nicely into the warm dip. Serve with fresh, warm, corn tortillas.

SAUSAGE MAKING

Early journals from the West tell of dicing prime parts of buffalo, salting and peppering them, adding a little onion and cornmeal and likely some red chile pepper and then stuffing the mixture into a length of buffalo gut that had been cleaned and turned inside out so that any fat was on the outside. The sausages were tied off with a whang (a short piece of rawhide), and then either broiled over the fire or boiled in a big pot. References to this culinary feat written in 1830 more often are for boiling rather than broiling.

Today, it's a lot easier to make sausage, although not too many home cooks attempt it. Heavy-duty standing mixers, such as KitchenAids, are fitted with attachments for grinding and filling casings that make short work of the process. If you don't want to stuff the meat mixture into casings, you can always form it into patties and pan-cook them.

It is important to grind the meat for boudies coarsely. We grind it twice through the chili plate, which has larger holes than the plate used for most ground meat. If you don't know which is the "chili plate," use the plate with the largest holes. And if you don't have a machine, ask your butcher to grind the meat for you.

▼▼▼▼▼▼▼▼▼▼▼▼▼▼▼▼▼▼▼▼▼

buffalo eggs

We serve this little beginner at the Fort made with tiny, pickled quail eggs wrapped in spicy buffalo sausage and then deep fried. It's our version of Scotch eggs and it's served with a tangy sauce that completes the dish as beautifully as hollandaise does eggs benedict. The little eggs are more full flavored than chicken eggs and have the added benefit of being easy to pop in your mouth whole.

This dish is an outgrowth of my dad's appearance on *The Today Show* in the 1980s when weatherman Willard Scott mentioned how much he liked Scotch eggs and asked Sam'l why the Fort didn't serve them. This was all my dad needed to hear before he hightailed it back to the kitchen to develop his own version of the classic dish. Naturally, I think he surpassed it! • *serves 6*

Canola oil, for deep frying
1 dozen pickled quail eggs (not canned quail eggs; if you can't find them in a jar,
   use 1 dozen small hard-cooked hen eggs instead)
1¾ pounds buffalo sausage or bulk hot Italian sausage
½ to ¾ cup all-purpose flour
½ to ¾ cup milk
1½ to 2 cups crushed white or yellow corn tortilla chips
Sweet Red Chile Sauce, page 75, for serving

In a deep fryer, heat the oil to 350°F. Rinse the eggs and pat them dry. If you are using hen eggs, cut them in half, either lengthwise or crosswise. Divide the sausage in half and roll or pat it out on a floured surface to a ³⁄₈–inch thickness. (If you have enough counter space, don't bother dividing it.)

Wrap each egg with about 2 level tablespoons of sausage, then roll it in the flour, dip in the milk and roll in the tortilla crumbs. Fry a few at a time until golden brown, 4 to 6 minutes. Drain the eggs on crumpled paper towels and keep warm in a preheated 300°F. Allow the heat to return to 350°F between batches. Serve with Sweet Red Chile Sauce.

buffalo empanadas

We only recently added these empanadas to our menu when Chef Geoffrey Groditski developed them to honor the memory of his grandmother. According to Geoffrey, she made the best empanadas ever and so he produced these light, flaky pastries filled with buffalo meat and served with two sauces: Sweet Red Chile Sauce or just plain Red Chile Sauce. The minute they were on the menu, they were an instant hit. You cannot eat just one!

• *makes 18 empanadas; serves 6*

1½ tablespoons canola oil

¾ cup chopped yellow onion

3 Anaheim chiles roasted, peeled, and diced,
   or ½ cup canned mild green chiles

¾ pound lean ground buffalo

1 tablespoon minced fresh garlic (2 cloves)

4 teaspoons dried Mexican oregano

4 teaspoons Dixon chile powder (or other
   medium-strength New Mexican chile powder)

1½ teaspoons ground cumin

1½ teaspoons ancho chile powder

Salt and freshly ground black pepper

1 to 2 tablespoons all-purpose flour

One 17.3-ounce package frozen puff pastry
   sheets, thawed

6 ounces shredded Cheddar cheese

Canola oil, for frying

Sweet Chile Sauce, page 75,
   or Sweet Red Chile Sauce, page 75,
   for serving

Place the oil in a large skillet over medium heat. Add the onion and cook until translucent, 4 to 5 minutes. Add the chiles, buffalo, garlic, and spices. Continue to cook, stirring, until the meat loses its pink color and the chiles have softened, about 10 minutes. Season the meat mixture to taste with salt and pepper and set aside to cool.

On a lightly floured surface, roll the puff pastry sheets to about a ⅛-inch thickness. Using a 4-inch cutter, cut 9 rounds out of each sheet. If needed, reroll the pastry scraps, after stacking them and gently pressing them together. Refrigerate the pastry rounds, removing a few at a time to form the empanadas.

Preheat the oven to 300°F. Place 1 rounded tablespoon of the meat mixture and about 1½ teaspoons of cheese on each puff pastry round. Moisten the edges of the dough with water, and fold in half to enclose the filling. Use the tines of a fork to decoratively seal the edges. Empanadas may be made ahead to this point and refrigerated or frozen.

Deep-fry the empanadas in small batches at 375°F, or fry them in ½ inch of hot oil in a cast-iron skillet, turning occasionally, until golden brown. Drain the empanadas on crumpled paper towels and keep warm in the oven until all have been fried.

roasted buffalo bone marrow

At the Fort, we have been serving roasted buffalo marrow bones for more than twenty-five years. Both Julia Child and famed Italian chef Lidia Bastianich ordered the bone marrow as an appetizer and savored every bite. Most of our guests who have the curiosity to try it order it again and again.

When my dad, Sam'l, who was a respected food historian, first read about buffalo bone marrow in his research, he talked to our buffalo suppliers and convinced them to cut the knobs off the femurs (the front legs), split the bones in half, and sell them to us. Once cooked, we sprinkle them with a little salt and pepper and serve them stacked like "Lincoln Logs." Paul McIlhenny of the Tabasco company family is a good friend who suggested we put a few drops of green jalapeño sauce on the roasted bone marrow. As we tasted the combination, we were sold! This is an amazingly popular beginner at the Fort and I eat it whenever I can. You can scoop the marrow, sometimes called prairie butter, from the bone with a fork or search for surprisingly dainty marrow spoons at antiques stores. • *serves 4 to 6*

4 to 6 buffalo or beef femur bones
Freshly ground black pepper, to taste
1 baguette
1 tablespoon olive oil
Hawaiian red clay sea salt or other coarse sea salt
Cilantro sprigs or Italian parsley, for garnish
Tabasco Green Pepper Sauce, optional

Saw the femur bones in half lengthwise or cut them into 1½-inch thick discs. You might want to ask the butcher to do this for you.

Preheat the oven to 450°F. Arrange the marrow bones on a jelly-roll pan or baking sheet with sides and roast on the middle shelf of the oven for about 14 minutes. Watch the marrow as it cooks, as you want it cooked, but still gelatinous in the center. If overcooked, the marrow will liquefy.

While the bones are roasting, thinly slice the bread, brush lightly with olive oil, and arrange on a separate baking sheet. Place in the oven for about 5 minutes, until lightly toasted.

Arrange the marrow bones on oval serving plates. A sprinkling of Hawaiian red clay sea salt around the plate is very tasty and represents the Hawaiian fur traders hired by the American Fur Trade Company in the 1820s. Garnish with sprigs of cilantro or parsley.

Remove the marrow from the bones with marrow spoons or butter knives. Spread the marrow on the toasted French bread. If desired, top with a dash of green pepper sauce.

AN ODE TO BUFFALO

Buffalo, or bison as they are also called, have roamed our continent for tens of thousands of years. Ancestors of today's bison existed nearly 120,000 years ago and by the time the first Europeans arrived in the 1600s, estimates are that there were upward of sixty million buffalo living in what today is North America.

The Plains tribes relied on the animals for food, clothes, shelter, and trade, and before the Spanish, French, and Americans brought guns, the Indians had any number of ways to kill enough bison to satisfy their needs. They used arrows, of course, but also would drive a herd off a cliff. The indigenous people respected the buffalo, admiring its strength, intelligence, speed, and character, and they believed that anyone who ate the flesh of the animals would gain some of the same attributes. Not surprisingly, Native Americans developed a number of rituals surrounding killing these magnificent animals and always honored the source of food for the tribe.

Between 1830 and 1860, nearly all the buffalo were slaughtered by Americans trying to meet the hunger for bison hides and bison tongues in Europe and the Eastern states. Thousands upon thousands of bison were killed, some for profit and many for sport, so that sadly, by the 1890s, barely three hundred buffalo were left. That they were nearly extinct troubled President Theodore Roosevelt a few years later and prompted him to urge Congress to establish wildlife preserves. Gradually and with careful husbandry, our bison herds have flourished so that today there is a sustainable number of them. More than four hundred thousand bison make up private herds as well as those that graze on government lands. A number of Indian tribes raise buffalo in an effort to re-establish healthful eating habits on the reservations. I work with the Intertribal Bison Cooperative, a nonprofit Indian organization that is a co-op for all the tribes that raise buffalo. Currently, the co-op sells meat to the Smithsonian Museum of the American Indian and donates it to member reservations. Because we sell more than seventy thousand bison dinners every year at the Fort, we cannot partner with the co-op yet, as it does not have enough meat, but I am looking forward to the day when we can serve native-raised bison meat. Spiritually, the comeback of the bison for the tribes is powerful.

In the 1840s, when some young adventurous Americans traveled the Santa Fe Trail from St. Louis to New Mexico, the buffalo were a common theme in personal diaries. Seventeen-year-old Louis Garrard kept such a diary in 1846 that later became a book, *Wah-To-Yah and the Taos Trail*.

"We never eat but twice a day, very often but once in 24 hours, at which scarcity of food, of course, there was grumbling," writes Garrard. "Darn this way of living, anyhow; a feller starves a whole day like a mean coyote and when he does eat, he stuffs himself like a snake that's swallowed a frog, and is no account for an hour after."

▼▼▼▼▼▼▼▼▼▼▼▼▼▼▼▼▼▼▼▼▼▼

After experiencing his first buffalo hunt, Garrard watched the more experienced men skin and butcher a "fine fat young male." He observed that the men ate the liver raw. "[They ate it] with a slight dash of gall by way of zest, which, served á la Indian, was not very tempting to cloyed appetites; but to hungry men, not at all squeamish, raw warm liver with raw marrow was quite palatable. Before the buffalo range was half traversed, I liked the novel dish pretty well!"

Other accounts describe "prairie butter," which is broiled buffalo bone marrow. This was considered a delicacy. Trappers and hunters took the hip and leg bones of the buffalo, split them and roasted the marrow over the campfire. They sopped it up with good, hot sourdough bread, which explains why they called it butter.

Both Indians and trappers considered marrow an important food. While it usually was spread over bread, it also was used in soups and stews, and some frontier desserts included marrow with berries.

Europeans have long treasured beef marrow, and these days Americans are recognizing its succulence. It's showing up at the best restaurants in New York, Chicago, and Los Angeles—and buffalo marrow has been on the menu at the Fort for years.

▼▼▼▼▼▼▼▼▼▼▼▼▼▼▼▼▼▼▼

buffalo tongue with caper sauce

I can still recall boiling buffalo tongue in water and Bay spices in the kitchen of the Fort with my mother. Even as a young girl, I was surprised at how large the tongues were but even so I realized they were smaller than beef tongue. After we boiled them, my mom and I peeled off the outer skin so that the tongues were edible. I was always taught to revere the buffalo tongue, which was considered sacred meat by the Indians, used in religious ceremonies. I was told to be grateful to the intelligent animal who sacrificed his life to nourish our stomachs and our souls.

My dad, Sam'l, wrote about the history of the buffalo tongue:

"Buffalo tongue was thought by many to be the greatest gourmet delicacy of the American 19th century. Considered holy meat by Native Americans, it has a delicate flavor and fine texture and is far superior to beef tongue, which has a coarser quality. The demand for buffalo tongue was a major reason for the wholesale slaughter of the bison. Tragically whole herds were killed for their hides and tongues, the latter which were smoked, salted or pickled and sent east in fully loaded railroad cars. Such fine restaurants as Delmonico's in New York City reportedly served it to the likes of President Ulysses S. Grant and singer Jenny Lind, the Swedish Nightingale. Today, in limited numbers, buffalo tongues are once again gracing gourmet palates, for in addition to the herds that still roam on federally protected land, bison are thriving on ranches in all 50 states." • *serves 8 to 12 as an appetizer*

TONGUE
1 small yellow onion, coarsely chopped
1 bay leaf
1 tablespoon freshly ground black pepper
1 buffalo tongue (about 2 pounds)

CAPER SAUCE
1 cup mayonnaise
1 tablespoon capers, drained
1 tablespoon prepared horseradish
$1/8$ teaspoon dried oregano
$3/4$ teaspoon freshly ground black pepper
Italian parsley, for garnish

Bring a large pan of water to a boil with the onion, bay leaf and pepper. Add the tongue and reduce heat to low. Poach gently for $2^{1}/_{2}$ to 3 hours, until tender and cooked through.

In a mixing bowl, whisk mayonnaise, capers, horseradish, oregano and pepper until well blended. Cover and chill the sauce until ready to serve.

When the tongue is cooked, remove it from the poaching liquid and allow it to cool slightly. While still warm, peel off the light outer skin with a knife. Preheat the broiler. Slice the tongue into $1/2$-inch thick pieces across the grain. Assemble on an ovenproof platter and heat briefly under the broiler. Place a bowl of the caper sauce on the platter and garnish with parsley.

crispy citrus lamb riblets

When Dad hungered for crispy lamb ribs, also known as Denver ribs, he asked Chef Dave Woolley to create a recipe for them. Dave spiced the ribs with a buffalo wing-style sauce, and today these little riblets are one of our most popular beginners. The Lamb Council features them often, too. Because lamb riblets, sometimes called Denver ribs, are sometimes hard to find, I suggest you try these with babyback pork ribs. You won't be disappointed.

• *serves 4 to 6 as an appetizer*

LAMB
1 ½ racks lamb spareribs
   or pork baby back ribs (about 18 ribs)
2 large carrots, diced
2 stalks celery, diced
2 medium onions, diced
8 cups chicken broth

SAUCE
½ cup hot sauce (Frank's Hot Wing Sauce)
⅓ cup Thai sweet red chile
2 teaspoons tamarind syrup or Worcestershire sauce
2 teaspoons honey
⅛ to ¼ teaspoon tangerine oil
Canola oil for deep frying

TOPPING
Black sesame seeds
Chopped Italian parsley
Chopped cilantro

Preheat the oven to 400°F. Place the ribs, carrots, celery, onions, and chicken broth in a shallow roasting pan. Cover tightly with lid or aluminum foil and place the pan on the middle rack of the oven. Reduce the oven heat to 325°F and braise the ribs for 2 hours or until tender.

Remove the ribs from the liquid and allow to cool. With a sharp knife, cut the rack into individual ribs and pat dry with paper towels.

In a saucepan, combine the hot sauce, Thai sweet chile, tamarind syrup, honey, and tangerine oil. Warm the sauce over medium heat, stirring occasionally, until heated through.

In a deep fryer, heat the oil to 350°F. Fry the cooked ribs in small batches for 3 to 5 minutes, until browned and crisp.

Remove the ribs from the oil, and drain on a wire rack. While the ribs are still hot, toss with the sauce. Sprinkle the black sesame seeds, chopped parsley, and chopped cilantro on top. Serve immediately.

duck quesadillas

The smoked duck filling is the result of two of our chefs perfecting a dish that has become a signature of the restaurant. Former executive chef Dave Woolley created a tasty barbecued coffee-smoked duck filling in 2002 that he mixed with aged Mexican cheese before filling the quesadillas. Our current executive chef added his own touches for rehearsal dinners and weddings, and I have found the quesadillas to be perfect for cocktail parties of any kind. My husband Jeremy and I like a few for dinner with nothing more than a fresh green salad. • *serves 4 to 8*

DUCK
1 whole duck, about 5 pounds
2 quarts chicken broth
1 carrot, peeled and chopped
1 celery stalk, chopped
½ yellow onion, sliced
3 cloves garlic, peeled,
  and crushed with the side of a knife
2 to 3 bay leaves
¾ cup Coffee BBQ Sauce, recipe follows

QUESADILLAS
Eight 8-inch flour tortillas
2⅔ cups duck mixture
12 ounces (about 3 cups) shredded Panela
  or Monterey Jack cheese

Preheat the oven to 350°F.

Remove the giblets and neck and reserve for another use. Rinse the duck inside and out with cold water and place in a braising pan. Cover with broth, and add the carrot, celery, onion, garlic, and bay leaves. Cover the pan tightly with a lid or aluminum foil. Place in the oven and braise for about 2 hours, until the duck is cooked through and tender. Remove the duck from the braising liquid and cut into quarters. Smoke the quarters with hickory for 20 minutes, see Note. After smoking, allow the duck to rest for about 10 minutes. Remove the skin and discard. Remove the meat from the bones and finely chop. Mix the duck with about ¾ cup of Coffee BBQ Sauce.

Place a flour tortilla on a medium-hot griddle. Top with ⅓ cup duck mixture and ⅓ cup cheese. Remove from the griddle when the tortilla is slightly crispy and fold in half. Cut into triangles and serve with your favorite salsa and crema or sour cream.

Note: Look online and in grocery stores for foil smoking bags used to smoke in home ovens or turn to page 240.

coffee bbq sauce

- *makes about 2 cups*
1 tablespoon olive oil
½ cup diced yellow onion
1½ teaspoons minced garlic (1 clove)
1 tablespoon coarsely ground coffee
1 (9.3-ounce) jar (¾ cup) hoisin sauce
1 cup ketchup
⅓ cup cider vinegar
⅓ cup brown sugar
¼ cup chicken broth
2 teaspoons Worcestershire sauce
1 teaspoon New Mexican chile powder
½ teaspoon kosher salt

In a large saucepan, over medium heat, heat the oil. Add the onion and sauté until translucent, 3 to 4 minutes. Add the garlic and cook for 1 to 2 minutes. Stir in the coffee and cook for 1 minute. Add the hoisin, ketchup, vinegar, brown sugar, chicken broth, Worcestershire, chile powder, and salt. Bring the sauce to a simmer, stirring occasionally. Allow the sauce to cool, then puree in a blender. Strain the sauce to remove any excess coffee grounds.

rattlesnake cakes

The rattlesnake meat we serve at the Fort is USDA-inspected and comes from Texas (see To Cook a Rattlesnake, page 42), and because it's a seasonal meat, it's not always available. My dad created the recipe for these cakes, which are very similar in taste and texture to crab cakes. If you can find rattlesnake meat, you will love these, but they are also good made with chicken. • *makes 12 cakes; serves 6*

1 ½ pounds boneless rattlesnake fillet
   or skinless, boneless chicken breasts
¾ cup finely diced red bell pepper
½ cup finely diced red onion
1 ½ tablespoons olive oil
⅓ cup panko bread crumbs
1 ½ teaspoons kosher salt
¾ teaspoon ground cumin

½ teaspoon freshly ground black pepper
½ teaspoon ground Dixon chile
   (or other medium New Mexican chile)
¼ cup mayonnaise
2 large eggs
2 tablespoons fresh lime juice
6 tablespoons clarified butter, see Note

Steam the rattlesnake (or chicken) in a steamer for 30 to 45 minutes, rotating it every 15 minutes to ensure even cooking. The snake should be firm but not hard to the touch when done. Allow to cool.

Place the meat in a food processor with very sharp blade. Pulse two to three times until it reaches a crab cake-like consistency. Do not process too long or the cakes will be mealy when done.

Sauté the bell pepper and onion in the olive oil until all the moisture evaporates. Place the vegetables on a sheet pan to cool.

Combine the panko and spices in a large mixing bowl. Place the mayonnaise in a mixing bowl and whisk in the eggs one at a time. Add the lime juice and whisk until smooth.

Stir the cooled vegetables, mayonnaise mixture, and chopped meat into the panko and spices. Press the mixture into a 9-inch square pan, cover with plastic wrap, and chill in the refrigerator for at least 1 hour.

Form the mixture into cakes using a 2-inch round biscuit cutter. The mixture must be tightly compressed to hold its form during cooking. The cakes should be about 1-inch thick when finished.

Preheat the oven to 400°F.

In a large skillet, over medium-high heat, sauté the cakes in the clarified butter until golden brown, 2 to 3 minutes per side. Transfer cakes to a cookie sheet lined with baking parchment and finish in the oven, about 5 minutes.

Note: Clarified butter has had the milk solids removed and so keeps about three times as long as other butter. It's great for cooking because it can be heated to relatively high temperatures. To clarify it, melt about 1 cup (or more—but not less) of unsalted butter over low heat and let it simmer for about 20 minutes. Do not stir it during this time, as the moisture will evaporate and the white milk solids will sink to the bottom of the pan. Carefully pour the butter from the pan and leave the milk solids behind. (You can use a sieve if you prefer.) Use right away or cool and refrigerate for up to 3 months.

TO COOK A RATTLESNAKE

My father first cooked rattlesnake in 1975 at a historic Denver festival, where he also prepared more than four thousand buffalo burgers and three hundred pounds of Rocky Mountain oysters. He also prepared one hundred twenty pounds of rattlesnake, which he cut into chunks and dipped in tempura batter before deep frying them. Delicious!

When I was about nine years old and had recently moved to the Fort, my older brother Keith and I caught a four-foot-long rattler down the hill from the restaurant. We killed it and brought it home with plans to skin it and make hat bands, as our mother had shown us. That evening a customer complained that we had no rattlesnake on the menu. We had buffalo and other game, he said, but no snake. My brother, who was bussing tables nearby, ran to fetch our trophy. He held the long, bloody creature in front of the customer and asked him which section he would like. We called his bluff and didn't have to cook the rattlesnake, but we did get some pretty cool hat bands that always reminded us of our catch.

Nowadays, rattlesnake is always on our menu when it's in season. We get the boned snake meat primarily from Texas, where folks in the western part of the state participate in rattlesnake roundups. It seems that every so often, Texans get together to collect the numerous snakes slithering hither and yon on the prairie and turn the event into a contest, with prizes awarded for the longest, heaviest, and oldest snakes. Once the snakes are rounded up, meat purveyors take over.

We used to get the snakes skinned, heads removed, and frozen. They were tightly coiled and when the cold snakes were submerged in boiling water, they unwound so that some of our younger cooks feared they were coming to life!

My dad had a thing or two to say about rattlesnakes — of course! Here they are:

"Let them eat snake!" yelled the host of a small dinner party one night at the Fort. Much to his own amusement, the dish was brought to his table. For years, the Fort served a rattlesnake cocktail when it was in season. Today, we make a rattlesnake cake, similar to a crab cake. Each night, our guests ask for rattlesnake. If it isn't in season, and we don't have it, they are sorely disappointed. It is truly delicious.

The longest snake I ever saw was seventy-six inches long, but in New Mexico there are stories of much larger snakes. The larger, the better, as you can feed more guests. If you have caught a rattler and want to prepare it for cooking, first cool it in the refrigerator or freezer. It will go to sleep and will be safe to handle. Using a cleaver, or hatchet, cut off the head low enough down on the neck so that it may be freeze-dried and made into a hat ornament. Next, stretch it out on a table and, using a razor blade, an X-Acto knife, or a very sharp skinning knife, slice the skin of the belly lengthwise, starting at the neck and continuing down the snake. Remove the organs,

and wash well under running water. Use a pair of pliers to pull off the skin. It should be easy to remove since there is some fat between the skin and the muscle. Try not to damage the skin, for it may be rubbed on the underside with a little salt and then stretched onto a board and tacked down to dry for display as a monument to your bravery and culinary skills.

Once the snake is cleaned and skinned, braise it in a pot with onion, bay leaf, and peppercorns. After 90 minutes of gentle boiling, the snake is done. Allow to cool, and then strip the meat from the bones by hand. Arrange atop a bed of lettuce on a serving platter or in cocktail glasses, and serve with a sweet red chile sauce.

There are many rattlesnakes around the Fort and up on our Red Rock, so be careful walking around. We want to be sure you bite the snake before he bites you!

▼▼▼▼▼▼▼▼▼▼▼▼▼▼▼▼▼▼▼▼▼

six shooters of acapulco shrimp

This easy shrimp beginner is the outcome of a trip Sam'l and Dave Woolley, who at the time was our executive chef, took to Mexico in 2003 with Rick Bayless. Rick is the owner of several Mexican restaurants in Chicago and is recognized as one of our nation's leading authorities on the cooking of that sunny land, and both Dad and Dave were excited about the journey. When they returned home they were itching to add a shrimp ceviche made with bay shrimp, avocado, celery, and serrano chiles to the Fort's menu. I came up with the idea of turning the ceviche into shooters, served in shot glasses on a wooden plank with tortilla chips. At the Fort, you can down your six-shooters and shout "Huzzah! • *serves 6 (12 shot glasses or 2 for each person)*

SHRIMP
1 pound cooked and peeled small shrimp,
   see Note
1 cup diced celery
2 ripe avocados, peeled, pitted,
   and cut into 1-inch cubes

SAUCE
½ cup mayonnaise
1¼ cups tomato juice

1 tablespoon plus 1 teaspoon ketchup
2 teaspoons prepared horseradish
½ Serrano chile, seeded and minced
6 to 8 cilantro leaves
Juice of 1 lime (3 to 4 tablespoons)
Dash of Worcestershire sauce
3 to 4 tablespoons small capers, drained (optional)
6 sprigs cilantro
6 lime slices

Rinse the shrimp in very cold water. Combine the shrimp and celery; this can be done well ahead of time. Add the avocados at the last minute to keep them from becoming discolored.

Combine the mayonnaise, tomato juice, ketchup, horseradish, minced chile, cilantro leaves, lime juice, and Worcestershire in a blender or food processor. Pulse on and off making sure the mayonnaise is fully incorporated. When ready to serve, toss the sauce with the shrimp, celery and avocados. Spoon into shot glasses and garnish each glass with a few capers, if desired, a sprig of cilantro, and a slice of fresh lime.

Note: We use Icelandic bay shrimp, but any quality shrimp will work. Try to choose fresh shrimp, rather than frozen.

rocky mountain oysters with panko

Even as a little girl, I worked in the Fort's kitchen as a prep cook, and peeling and cleaning Rocky Mountain oysters was a routine job and I barely gave it a second thought. One day I invited my sixth-grade school friends to the Fort and before they arrived, I prepared a large bowl of lightly seasoned, deep-fried Rocky Mountain oysters. "These are delicious! What kind of sausage popcorn is this?" one friend asked as she and the others happily downed the little tidbits.

"You are eating buffalo bull testicles with a light breading and salt and pepper," I answered.

They looked at me with disbelief, but didn't stop munching them. To this day, they still tell this story with much delight. Now they bring their friends and children to the Fort and surprise them with the same dish ordered off our menu. Calf fries—another name for testicles—are smaller and more tender than bull fries, so ask your butcher for them.

• *serves 6*

6 calf or veal testicles (or turkey fries—testicles—may be substituted)
1 cup panko bread crumbs
1 teaspoon black pepper
¼ teaspoon cayenne
½ teaspoon salt
Canola oil, for deep frying
Sweet Red Chile Sauce (page 75), for serving

With a sharp paring knife, cut and peel the skin away from the testicles. They will peel and slice much more easily if they are slightly frozen.

Cut the testicles into 1-inch pieces. In a shallow baking pan, combine the panko, black pepper, salt, and cayenne. Heat the oil to 375°F and preheat the oven to 200°F. Fry the breaded "oysters" for 3 minutes, until a light crust forms. Drain on crumpled paper towels and keep warm in the oven. If you are serving them as an appetizer, skewer each one on a toothpick. Serve with Sweet Red Chile Sauce for dipping.

Note: To make these with panko, the light, feathery Japanese bread crumbs so wonderful for breading, peel and slice the oysters as described above. Roll them in a mixture of panko, salt and pepper rather than in the seasoned flour.

spirits & libations

bent's fort hailstorm julep

Since the day my father and mother opened the Fort in 1963, this has been a signature cocktail. My dad explains its origins: "Back in the 1830s at Bent's Fort in southeastern Colorado, the favorite hot weather drink, especially on the Fourth of July, was the hailstorm. Enjoyed by trappers, voyageurs, Mexicans and Native Americans alike, it is the earliest known mixed drink in Colorado and was described in a number of journals of the early west. It was originally made with either Monongahela whiskey from Pittsburgh or a wheat whiskey from Taos, three hundred miles south of Old Bent's Fort. At the Fort we use a variety of whiskeys or cognac for this bestselling drink." • *serves 1*

3 ounces bourbon, Scotch, or Cognac
2 teaspoons confectioners' sugar
2 sprigs fresh mint
Crushed ice to fill one widemouthed pint Mason jar or julep cup

Put the alcohol, sugar, and mint in the jar and fill with ice. Secure the lid and shake vigorously 50 times. (If using a julep cup, muddle it with a silver spoon, crushing the mint against the ice and the walls of the jar.) I like to do a little chant to the god of mint during the shaking.

The ice will bruise the mint so that it releases its flavor and the ice will melt a little and dilute the drink. When well shaken, remove the lid and drink from the jar.

THE FORT'S FAMOUS MOUNTAIN MAN TOAST

This toast was a favorite of my father's, and I have carried on the tradition he started by encouraging its recitation at every conceivable opportunity. On just about any evening at the Fort, you will hear it, getting louder as the toast progresses and those gathered around the table get more "into it."

The toast is not old but was written in 1988 when Dr. Peter Olch, his wife Mary, my dad, and my stepmother Carrie were invited to Bent's Fort to give lectures. Dad later wrote: "Peter gave his famous speech on 'Bleeding, Purging, and Puking', or medicine on the western frontier. I gave a talk on the culinary delicacies of the mountain man [dried buffalo lung with congealed blood pudding among them]. And then, after a long and hot day, we retired to a Mexican restaurant for dinner. All four of us were writers with a good command of early nineteenth century words and phrases. It was only a matter of adding a very large pitcher of margaritas before the Mountain Man Toast was born. Since, it has traveled the world over, been printed and reprinted and has gained a life of its own."

The toast teaches history in such an entertaining way—and our guests are rewarded with a free drink if they memorize the words and hand gestures—that it has become something of a ritual at our restaurant. It's best said with a large group. My dad's good friend Julia Child loved it so much, she said it while wearing a ceremonial headdress! Here is the toast (with translation following):

"Here's to the childs what's come afore (glass in right hand, held at shoulder)
And here's to the pilgrims, what's come arter (glass in right hand, arm extended)
May yer trails be free of griz (left hand over glass, making clawing motion with fingers)
Yer packs filled with plews (left and right arms extend out, making a circle)
And fat buffler in yer pot! (glass extended, left hand rub/points at your belly)
WAUGH! (extend hand with glass)

Translation:
Childs: What the mountain men called one another
Pilgrim: Lightly derisive term used by mountain men for the "sod-busting"
   covered wagon migrants traveling west
Arter: After
Griz: Grizzly bear, a major cause of death for mountain men
Plews: Large beaver pelts, originating from the French word "plus,"
   pronounced PLU. Extra large pelts were marked with a plus sign and were called "plews" by the Americans
Fat buffler in yer pot: Fat, tasty buffalo in your belly
Waugh: Historic Mountain man exclamation, meaning "cheers" or "right on"

shrub

The shrub was also drunk at Bent's Fort in the 1830s and '40s. Today, many day trappers and traders still make it for the holidays and it is prized as a Christmas drink. Essentially, it's dark rum with sugar and citrus juices. Over the decades, all types of fruits, including cherries, were added to the rum to further make its name authentic. This is a very old recipe. • *serves 4 to 6*

1 pound granulated sugar
2 cups water
1 cup fresh orange juice
Juice and grated zest of 1 to 2 lemons
1 quart dark rum

In a large pot, mix the sugar with the water and bring to a boil over high heat. Reduce the heat to medium low and cook for about 5 minutes or until the syrup is clear. Set aside to cool.

   Put the orange juice and the juice and zest of 1 lemon into a half-gallon jar. Add the rum and syrup, stir, taste, and add more lemon juice and zest if needed. Cover the jar or jug and refrigerate the punch for 3 days.

the last roundup

These cocktails are close to lethal so that we warn guests that no one can order more than two, unless they arrive and leave on horseback. And even in that case, the horse has to know its way home! • *serves 1*

1 ounce Demerara rum
1 ounce white rum
1 ounce Puerto Rican gold rum
1 ounce Jamaica Mount Gay rum
½ cup fresh orange juice
6 tablespoons sweet-and-sour syrup
2 tablespoons Falernum (almond syrup)
1 tablespoon grenadine
Sparkling water, to top
Orange slice and maraschino cherry, for garnish

Combine all the liquid ingredients except the sparkling water and garnish with ice in a widemouthed pint Mason jar. Stir or shake the jar. Top with carbonated water and garnish with the orange slice and cherry.

real georgia man mint julep

My mother, Bay, was from an old Georgia family that claimed Sir Francis Marion as an ancestor. Marion was also known as the Swampfox, who helped the Patriots win the Revolutionary War. Her heritage gave her rights to creating a genuine Georgia mint julep. My dad captured the rich history of the drink:

"In the pre-Civil War South, mint juleps identified a distinct way of life. Business was done on the veranda with a julep or two. Courting, also on the veranda, involved juleps and Thomas Jefferson designed a special julep cup that is still made today. There are numerous rules for making juleps, from how fine to crush the ice and how much sugar to add, to how big the silver goblet should be, if a cup should be used instead, and how many mint leaves to add. Further refinements address whether the mint should be spearmint or peppermint, and whether spirits other than cognac or bourbon can be added. Every southern colonel had his favorite recipe, but this version, served in Mason jars in a tradition begun at the Kentucky horse races, is so good that you'll feel like a hog in hickory nuts. The perfume of the peach makes it especially wonderful." • *serves 1*

1 teaspoon cold water
1 teaspoon confectioners' sugar
12 sprigs fresh mint leaves
3 ounces Cognac
3 ounces peach brandy or whiskey
Crushed ice to fill a widemouthed pint Mason jar or julep cup

Place the water in the jar. Add the sugar and stir to dissolve. Add the mint, Cognac, and peach brandy and fill the jar with ice. Stir with a spoon but do not crush the mint.

TOMAHAWK THE CHAMPAGNE

At the Fort, we "tomahawk" Champagne bottles instead of sabering them as they do in France. We slice a tomahawk down the neck of the bottle and then flick it across the neck. The neck is the weakest point of the bottle and the bottle is pressurized, and so the top of the bottle pops off and the Champagne spouts from it for each guest to catch in a glass. Be sure to wrap the bottle in a cloth before tomahawking it, because there could be a weak spot other than the neck that could crack in your hands. This is rare, but an ounce of protection is better than the cure.

My dad taught his pal Julia Child how to tomahawk a bottle of Champagne, and later that week she taught Jay Leno how to do so when she was a guest on *The Tonight Show*. She gave my dad all the credit, which turned out to be something of a backhanded compliment as the bottle Julia used was weak and broke all over the set! Although she grabbed a second bottle and tomahawked it perfectly, NBC decided to use the broken bottle take to promote the show.

▼▼▼▼▼▼▼▼▼▼▼▼▼▼▼▼▼▼▼▼

jim bridger

To explain the origin of this drink, I will let my dad do the talking: "We created this drink in 1964 and named it for the great frontiersman Jim Bridger. He was a fur trapper who made a name for himself in the Wind River area of Wyoming as well as other parts of the West. As far as we know, he never came as far south as Bent's Fort, but Alfred Jacob Miller painted Ol' Gabe Bridger (his real name was Gabriel) on horseback in Wyoming wearing a British armored breastplate, a gift from the western sojourning Scottish lord Sir William Drummond Stewart. One hundred and fifty years later, a descendant of Bridger visited us and enjoyed the drink. She disclosed that Jim had been a teetotaler and would not have added the rum!" • *serves 1*

2 tablespoons frozen apple juice concentrate
2 tablespoons fresh orange juice
2 tablespoons sweet-and-sour syrup
2 tablespoons fresh lime juice
1 tablespoon grenadine
1 dash orgeat syrup or Falernum (almond syrup)
3 ounces Jamaica golden rum
Crushed ice to almost fill a widemouthed pint Mason jar
Orange slice and maraschino cherry, for garnish

Combine all the ingredients except the garnish in the jar. Stir or shake the jar. Top with the orange slice and maraschino cherry.

bear's blood

When my parents first started serving this drink at the Fort in 1963, they served it in custom-made, yellow ceramic bowls with bright red interiors and brown bear handles on either side. Our customers loved them, of course, but we quickly discovered how impractical they were because they could not go through our industrial-sized dishwashers without breaking or dulling. We continued to serve Bear's Blood cocktails in the bowls until 1967, offering the bowls for sale to everyone who ordered one. When they all were sold—and it didn't take long!—we served the drink in a more conventional glass. Just a few years ago, I got a letter from someone in Rhode Island who had bought one of these old bowls at an antiques store and, noting the Fort's name on the bottom of it, contacted me and included a picture. Happily, Bear's Blood bowls live on! • *serves 1*

6 tablespoons orange juice

3 ounces light rum

1 tablespoon grenadine

Juice of ½ lime

Dash of orange flower water

Dash of sweet-and-sour syrup

Crushed ice to half fill a widemouthed pint Mason jar

Sparkling water, to top

Mint leaf, for garnish

Combine the ingredients except the sparkling water and mint leaf in a widemouthed pint Mason jar. Stir or shake the jar. Top with carbonated water and a mint leaf.

SISSY BEAR, IN SAM ARNOLD'S WORDS

How do you teach a bear to drink from a bottle? You take a bottle of the bear's favorite drink—root beer or Kool-Aid, in Sissy's case—hammer a nail through the bottle cap in three places to make small holes, and then give the bottle to the bear. She'll worry it and worry it, first licking the cap, and when she realizes where the sweet bubbly liquid is coming from, she'll suck at the cap. Soon you can give her an open bottle, and she'll hold it up and guzzle the sweet stuff down. It was great fun to take Sissy into the barroom. Hermann, the bartender, filled up a bottle with fountain cola, Sissy would belly up to the bar standing up like a man and swill it down just like anyone else. Some bar patrons were sure they had reached their drinking limit when Sissy showed up.

▼▼▼▼▼▼▼▼▼▼▼▼▼▼▼▼▼▼▼▼▼▼▼

trader's whiskey

During the Temperance movements of the early nineteenth century, there was a lot of underground contraband liquor sold across our young country. If you cut the liquor with water and other flavorings, handsome profits were to be made. My dad explained it best: "The alcohol that came west, despite federal efforts to limit or eliminate it, was plentiful. It was referred to by many names, among them 'great father's milk,' 'Taos lightening,' 'belly wash,' and 'whistle belly vengeance.' Traders often watered it down to as little as 3 percent alcohol to extend its profitability. Many strange additives were used to give an interesting taste: red chile, tobacco, or even a liberal pinch of black gunpowder (sulfur, charcoal, and saltpeter). Some said the sulfur was good for a spring tonic; the charcoal kept teeth bright. When ordinary whiskey was later made available to the Indians, they rejected it because it didn't have the good, old-fashioned flavor they were used to. Having read about this concoction [described below] in early trappers' journals, I tried it and found it surprisingly good. We began serving it in 1964, and it has remained on the menu ever since. Modern consumers find it both tasty and smooth and many prefer it to regular raw whiskey." • *serves 36 as shots*

1 cup water
2 tablespoons cut tobacco (Virginia Burley is best)
4 small dried red peppers, such as piquines
1 liter Old Crow or similar bourbon whiskey
½ teaspoon old-fashioned black gunpowder (do not use modern, high-speed powder; it is poisonous!)

Make a tea by boiling the water, tobacco, and red peppers together for 5 minutes. Strain and add the tea to the whiskey, little by little, to taste. Add the gunpowder.

The drink should have a gentle nip from the peppers and an herbal taste from the tobacco. The small amount of saltpeter in the black powder will have no effect. Damn!

1732 philadelphia fish house punch

My dad first tasted this punch in his home state of Pennsylvania when he attended friends' weddings and it was the drink of the day. Without a doubt it packs a punch and while the citrusy drink slides down very easily, it's good to remember that a little goes a long way. We were both excited when, in 1994, we came across a recipe for the punch in *Jerry Thomas' Bartender's Guide,* which was published in 1887. Always on the lookout for historic recipes, we immediately added this to our repertoire.

This may well be the oldest punch to be served in America. According to author N. E. Beveridge (a pseudonym!), who wrote Cups of Valor in 1968, it is thought to have originated in the 1600s in London as a farmers' club punch, after which it traveled to the New World and was served at the renowned Fish House Tavern in Schuylkill, Pennsylvania, near Philadelphia. It is also sometimes called Decatur Punch. Be warned: This tastes so smooth that some of your guests may not be aware of its power. If you serve it from an unattended punch bowl, post a warning sign. • *serves 4 to 6*

1½ pints sweet-and-sour syrup
¾ pound sugar, dissolved in a little water
½ pint Cognac
¼ pint peach brandy
¼ pint Jamaica rum
1 pint cold water
Ice

Combine all the ingredients with ice and serve.

original santa fe 1848 gin cocktail

My father wrote a few sentences about this cocktail. I think his words say it all! "At the United States Hotel on San Francisco Street in Santa Fe, New Mexico, travelers in 1848 found that their host was a New Englander who went by the name of Long Eben (short for Ebenezer). He served a concoction called a Gin Cocktail. This slightly sweet but powerful gin drink is a dandy!" • *serves 1*

3 ounces gin
Dash of Peychaud bitters
2 dashes maraschino liqueur
2 dashes dry vermouth
2 small cubes of ice
Small lemon slice, for garnish

Stir all the ingredients but the lemon slice together with the ice, strain, and serve garnished with the lemon slice.

PILOT'S COCKTAIL

"Since airplane pilots may not drink alcohol for many hours before flying, we developed the Pilot's Cocktail, which is close to an alcoholic drink in taste but without the alcohol. We simply fill a wide-mouth Mason jar with ice and our favorite mineral water, and then add a good squirt or two of Peychaud bitters. The tiny amount of alcohol in the bitters is insignificant, yet the bitters flavor provides a wonderfully refreshing drink that's not sweetened with sugar. It's excellent for diabetics, calorie counters and restaurant owners." —*Sam'l Arnold*

hot buttered rum

In the words of my dad, nothing beats hot buttered rum on a blustery, cold day. "In Colonial America, rum was plentiful due to trade with the West Indies. Newly made rum was often shipped from Jamaica and other British Colonial islands to the London docks where it rested to age. Some of it, though, was shipped to America, where it was often drunk pretty raw, with just a bit of sugar and water to ease its way down. Even today, nothing in the world tastes better when you've been out on a cold, snowy day than a real hot buttered rum. I like the taste of heavier Jamaica Mount Gay or Demerara rum in this drink, though not a really dark one, like Myers." • *serves 1*

¾ cup water
1 rounded teaspoon Hot Buttered Rum Batter, recipe follows
2 ounces dark rum
1 cinnamon stick
1 pat of butter

Pour the water in a bar mug and bring to a boil in the microwave. Stir in the batter and rum. Garnish with the cinnamon stick and top with the butter.

hot buttered rum batter

• *makes enough for about 30 drinks*
1 cup (2 sticks) unsalted butter, softened
1 cup dark brown sugar
1 teaspoon ground cinnamon
¼ teaspoon grated nutmeg

In a blender or food processor fitted with the paddle attachment, whip the ingredients together and store, covered, in the refrigerator. The batter can be refrigerated for up to 3 days and can be frozen, wrapped well in plastic wrap, for up to 1 month.

yard of flannel

While this holiday libation may be an acquired taste, once you acquire it you will be in love. It marries the hoppy taste of beer with the warmth of rum-based eggnog and, as my mother used to say, will "warm the cockles of your heart" on a snowy evening. When Dad researched the cocktail, here is what he discovered: "A fine colonial winter specialty in taverns, this hot ale drink takes its name from its lovely soft texture. The Yard of Flannel is a wonderful holiday drink that used to be a favorite among coachmen, outriders, and wagoneers. Coming out of the tavern, bartenders would hand up a yard-long glass of this to freezing coach drivers perched high above. The recipe sounds far more complicated than it is, and is worth the effort in the resulting warmth of body and soul." • *serves 4*

1 quart good ale
4 large eggs
4 tablespoons sugar

1 teaspoon powdered ginger
4 ounces Jamaica dark rum
Grated nutmeg, for sprinkling

Heat the ale in a saucepan. In a blender, beat the eggs with the sugar. Add the ginger and then the rum and blend well. When the ale is almost boiling, slowly combine the two mixtures, alternately pouring the hot ale, a little at a time, into the egg mixture and blending well, to prevent curdling. Pour back and forth between the saucepan and the blender until the drink is silky or as soft as flannel. Serve in a large glass sprinkled with nutmeg.

BEER AT THE FORT

The Fort was the first American establishment to serve Carta Blanca beer imported from Mexico. This was in 1963, when we opened, and yet the most popular beer we had on draft was Coors. At that time, Coors was only sold in Colorado and was a cult brew. Made with Rocky Mountain spring water, it was so refreshing that Coloradoans were known to smuggle it out of Colorado for friends in other states.

Coors was brewed in the nearby town of Golden, Colorado, and the Coors family has been coming to the Fort since we first had their beer on tap. They have always appreciated a Herman Joseph or golden Coors with our game meat. The family asked my dad to be their spokeperson for an historical cookbook they published and so in 1982, Dad traveled the country talking about, among other things, Pete Coors' great grandmother's recipe for sauerbraten. During Pete's run for Senate, we hosted a dinner for him and served recipes from the book, including his great grandmother's. In the small world department, Pete's uncle, Bill Coors, was part of Jeremy's parents' wedding party and was also one of my father's close friends.

As well as Coors, we serve a wide selection of microbrews. This is not difficult, since Colorado is a leader in the microbrewing industry and we have our pick of truly great beers.

▼▼▼▼▼▼▼▼▼▼▼▼▼▼▼▼▼▼▼▼▼▼▼

prickly pear margarita

On summer evenings, our guests like to sit on our patio, enjoying the cool air of the foothills as they gaze down on the city lights of Denver or watch a dramatic sunset. We play classical music, or Erik Manywinds, our Blackfeet musician, plays an Indian flute and many people sip one of these margaritas, either on ice or frozen. Shinin' times for all!
• *serves 1*

2 ounces tequila
Juice of ½ large lime
1 teaspoon confectioners' sugar
1½ ounces triple sec
3 tablespoons prickly pear syrup, see page 241
½ cup cracked ice
Salt, for the rim of the glass
1 slice of lime, for garnish

Put all the ingredients except the salt and lime slice in a mixing glass. Add ice cubes and stir. Strain and serve straight up in a salt-rimmed glass garnished with a slice of lime.

old-fashioned santa fe margarita

This recipe is made with the simplest and best ingredients—including only fresh lime juice. The result is one of the best margaritas you'll ever drink. • *makes 4 servings*

½ cup fresh lime juice
Salt, for the rim of the glass
6 ounces tequila
2 ounces premium triple sec

Rub the rim of a cocktail glass with lime juice and dip it in salt. Shake the rest of the ingredients with ice, strain into the glass, and serve.

fort coffee

Be careful when you order a Fort Coffee. Yes, it's truly delicious but it's punched with alcohol. Some of our guests have this instead of dessert. • *serves 1*

¾ ounce Bailey's Irish Cream
½ ounce Frangelico hazelnut liqueur
¾ cup plus 2 tablespoons hot, brewed coffee
Freshly whipped cream, for topping

Stir the Bailey's and Frangelico together. Pour this into the hot coffee, stir once or twice, and serve topped with whipped cream.

bear hunters' tea

When Chris Seres, who has worked at the Fort for more than twenty-three years, noticed that I had a heavy cold during one of our weekly manager's meetings, he suggested I have a Bear Hunter's Tea. The hot toddy made with tea and honey liqueur cured what ailed me! • *serves 1*

¾ cup plus 2 tablespoons water
1 bag orange pekoe tea or other black tea
1 tablespoon plus 1½ teaspoons Barenjager honey liqueur
Lemon slice, for garnish

Bring the water to a boil in the microwave or in a teakettle. Steep the tea in the water for 2 to 3 minutes. Remove the tea bag and stir the Barenjager into the tea. Garnish with the lemon slice.

salty dog with saddle leather

We put this cocktail on our menu in 1963 when we opened and it's been popular ever since. The "saddle leather" is a stick of buffalo or beef jerky garnishing each glass. • *serves 4*

2½ cups grapefruit juice
6 ounces gin or vodka
1 teaspoon salt
4 sticks buffalo or beef jerky, for garnish

Pour all ingredients over ice cubes in 4 highball glasses. Stir well, garnish with jerky and serve.

1809 stone fence

My father wrote about this potent cocktail. However, we still don't know where the name comes from! "In early nineteenth century America, drunkenness was rife. Congress passed many laws trying to limit the manufacture and sale of spirits. Rum and whiskey were two major offenders, but the biggest problem was applejack, which nearly everybody could make. Apple cider, once fermented, can be frozen and the alcohol poured off; you don't even need a still. One food historian suggested that the famed Johnny Appleseed, who traveled the countryside planting apple trees, might well have been the publicity man for the distillers' league. Temperance groups literally decimated the apple orchards of early America in an effort to slow alcohol consumption. Fortunately, they didn't succeed in wiping them out. This drink, from *Jerry Thomas' Bartenders Guide* published in 1887 is a Fort favorite." • *serves 1*

1 wine glass of bourbon or rye whiskey
2 or 3 small cubes of ice
Apple cider

Combine the bourbon and ice in a small bar glass and fill with sweet cider.

strawberry sangaree

Fruit sangarees were popular in the days of Bent's Fort. Fruit syrups were combined with red wine and ice for a cool, refreshing drink. Made the same way today at the Fort, they're in high demand during the hot summer months • *serves 1*

6 ounces red wine
½ cup frozen strawberries in syrup
⅓ cup cracked ice

Blend the wine, strawberries, and ice in a blender and serve in a tall glass.

colanche cooler

This refreshing drink originated in Mexico and is nothing more exotic than fresh lemonade with a splash of prickly pear syrup and lime juice. Delicious! • *serves 4*

1 cup prickly pear syrup, page 241
1 cup orange juice
1 cup cranberry juice
½ cup fresh lime juice
½ cup fresh lemon juice
Sparkling water, for topping
Lime wedge, for garnish

Pour the syrup, orange juice, cranberry juice, lime juice, and lemon juice into a half-gallon container. Add enough water to fill the container and stir well.

Pour the cooler into tall glasses with or without ice. Top with sparkling water and garnish with the lime wedge.

WINES AT THE FORT

The Fort served Robert Mondavi Wines when he first opened his Napa Valley vineyard in 1965. My dad and the Mondavis were good friends, and I believe they taught each other a lot about their respective spheres of interest. Dad wanted the Fort to have one of the top wine lists in Colorado and set out to achieve it. He knew a lot of good French wines from Pauillac and Medoc, as well as French Champagne, which had been traded along the Santa Fe Trail, and he stocked our cellars with similar vintages. Additionally, we supported wines made in Colorado and New Mexico. New Mexico, believe it or not, became a serious wine region as early as the mid-1800s.

Nowadays, my husband Jeremy and I travel to Napa Valley and stay with Jack and Dolores Cakebread of Cakebread Cellars. While in California, we taste a lot of wine with an eye to stocking our cellars. We visit with the Duncans who own Silver Oak Cellars and are also buffalo ranchers. We see Kate McMurray and Janet Trefethen of Trefethen Family Vineyards, and Joseph Phelps of Joseph Phelps Vineyards. Joseph is a Colorado contractor who was a friend of my father's.

When I joined my father to run the Fort in 1999, we had lost our competitive edge with wine. The industry had become so sophisticated over the years and the Fort had simply not kept up. I was determined to turn this around quickly. I wanted to earn a Wine Spectator Award and designation for the restaurant.

We asked our dining manager, Chris Seres, to expand his position to include managing our wine program. Chris contacted a master sommelier and got to work. They swapped out the mediocre wines for best-selling vintages. They bought little-known but great wines from boutique vineyards and never spent more money than was allocated to our inventory. I was unaware of all Chris was doing and so was surprised and gratified when he announced that he was applying for the Wine Spectator's coveted award. We got it! I was so proud of Chris, and I am still proud that we have earned this distinction every year for the last six.

Today, Chris organizes a wine tasting each month, which is attended by 100 to 150 guests. Our staff and customers love the wine program and our exciting, extensive wine list. We like to offer a fair value for our wines. It is our philosophy that if you give good value on good wine with a smaller markup than is standard, your customers will come back and order more wine. This attitude has benefited us and our customers well for more than forty-seven years. And let's face it. There is nothing better than a good bottle of Cabernet, Shiraz, or Pinot with a juicy buffalo steak!

chiles & sauces

jalapeños stuffed with peanut butter

Lucy Delgado, who was well known in the 1960s as a traditionalist New Mexican cook, taught my father to stuff peanut butter into peppers. "These are the best appetizers I know," she told Dad during one of their recipe swaps. "But if I show you how to make them, you have to promise to try them." Peanut butter-stuffed jalapeños?

"I vowed I would taste them even though they sounded stranger than a five-legged buffalo," Dad commented. When Lucy prepared them she had a last word of instruction, "Pop the entire pepper in your mouth so you're not left with a mouthful of hot jalapeño and too little peanut butter." Sam'l gamely took the little morsel by the stem and in it went. Miracle! Delicious!

In the 1980s, NBC's *Today Show* came to Denver and Sam'l was a guest. He served Bryant Gumbel our jalapeños stuffed with peanut butter, who devoured all eight Dad had prepared for the show. The TV host couldn't stop eating them! I was amazed he could still talk with his mouth full of pickled jalapeños and gummy peanut butter.

At the Fort, we pickle fresh jalapeños and stir a little mango chutney into the peanut butter. The hand-pickled chiles are far better than canned ones, but if you don't have time to pickle your own, buy Faro brand jalapeños from Mexico. • *serves 6 to 8*

1 pound Fort-Style Pickled Jalapeños, recipe follows, see Note
¾ cup peanut butter (smooth or chunky)
2 tablespoons mango chutney

Slice the pickled jalapeños in half lengthwise not quite all the way through, leaving the 2 halves attached at the stem end. Using a knife or spoon, remove and discard the seeds and ribs. In a small mixing bowl, combine the peanut butter and chutney. Stuff the chiles with the peanut butter mixture and press the halves back together. Arrange the stuffed jalapeños on a platter and serve.

Be sure to warn guests to put the whole chile (except the stem) in the mouth before chewing, to get 70 percent peanut butter and 30 percent jalapeño. A nibbler squeezes out the peanut butter which changes the percentages and makes it very hot indeed.

Note: You can substitute a 12-ounce can of pickled jalapeños for the homemade ones. When handling hot chiles, be sure to wash your hands thoroughly before touching your eyes or face.

fort-style pickled jalapeños

• *makes 12 to 16 jalapeños; about 1 pound*

1 pound small to medium-size fresh jalapeños (12 to 16)

3½ cups cider vinegar

1¾ cups water

½ cup sugar

2½ teaspoons salt

2½ teaspoons sesame oil

1 teaspoon pickling spice

¾ cup coarsely chopped yellow onion

¾ cup coarsely chopped carrot

3 cloves garlic, peeled, whole

Rinse the jalapeños and trim off the woody ends from the stems.

In a 4- to 6-quart stainless-steel or enameled pot, combine the vinegar, water, sugar, salt, sesame oil, and pickling spice. Add the jalapeños, onion, carrot, and garlic. Cover and bring to a simmer over high heat, stirring occasionally. Reduce the heat to low and simmer for 5 minutes. Remove from the heat.

While still hot, transfer the jalapeños and pickling juice to a sterilized 2- to 3-quart canning jar or other glass container. Cover tightly with a lid or plastic wrap and refrigerate for at least 1 week before using.

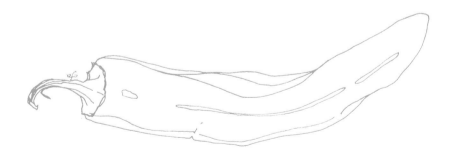

CHILES, CHILES, AND MORE CHILES

No one loved chiles more than my dad. He started the Colorado chapter of the International Association of Green and Red Chile, which in its heyday boasted more than fifteen hundred members and the motto, Up your Pod! As a recognized food historian, Dad wrote about the little vegetable that conquered the world. Here are his words:

"In the Middle Ages, Europeans enjoyed a 'long pepper,' brought to them from India. It was mild but with a discernible undercurrent of heat and cooks loved the zest and life it gave to their dishes. This was the pepper that Christopher Columbus sought when he set sail to find the Spice Islands. When he arrived in the West Indies in 1492, the local people served him foods he'd never before encountered—much less imagined. One was a pod pepper, hotter than the long pepper and much more easily stored and transported. The pod pepper had actually originated on Mexico's Yucatán Peninsula, and on his second voyage to the New World Columbus returned to Spain with its seeds. This chile (or capsicum, as it's also called) spread across the western world to Africa and Asia and today figures prominently in the cuisines of any number of countries around the world. From the remotest Americas through Europe, across India, around Asia, and everywhere in between, chile pods—long, short, thin or fat, red, yellow, green, brown, and purple—have traveled to tantalize man's soul and his palate.

"It seems to me that much of the chile's popularity worldwide stems from its ability to make otherwise unexciting cuts of meat and many kinds of starches (rice, pasta, potatoes) both flavorful and pepper-hot. And, of course, one needn't be rich to enjoy it.

"It's very versatile, too. The Thai spoon a bit of chicken or pork cooked in a chile-heavy curry sauce over large bowls of rice. The Mexicans add chile-flavored meats to cornmeal tamales. I use it in just about everything. Eating a very hot chile imparts a certain euphoria and for many (including me), it's a virtual addiction."

▼▼▼▼▼▼▼▼▼▼▼▼▼▼▼▼▼▼▼▼▼

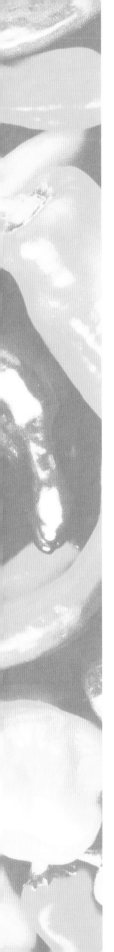

holly's ristra chile sauce

This is one of my favorites and when I make it I always leave a few seeds in the pods because I like my chile sauce medium-hot. Chiles can surprise you; ones that you expect to be mild are incendiary while the hot-looking ones end up being mild! However, the number of seeds you leave in the pods determines, to some extent, the heat of your finished chile sauce. • *makes 3¹/₂ to 4 cups*

¼ cup olive oil
¼ cup all-purpose flour
2 tablespoons dried Mexican oregano
3 cups chicken broth
6 dried red New Mexican chile pods
6 cloves garlic, peeled and roughly chopped
Salt

Place the olive oil in a large saucepan over medium heat. Stir in the flour and 1 tablespoon of the Mexican oregano. Cook, stirring constantly, for 2 to 3 minutes, until the flour turns golden brown. Slowly whisk in the chicken broth. Continue to cook, stirring, for about 1 minute, until the sauce begins to thicken. Set the sauce aside while preparing the chiles.

Rinse the chile pods under lukewarm water wearing rubber gloves. Break off the stems, and open the pod and wash the inside of the chiles. Inside the pod is an oil sack that is connected to the seeds. This membrane and the seeds contain the heat.

In a blender, combine the chiles, 1 cup boiling water, the garlic, the remaining 1 tablespoon of oregano, and ¹/₂ teaspoon salt. Put the lid on and puree. Press the puree through a coarse strainer into the chicken broth–based sauce, and stir until well combined. Simmer the sauce, stirring often, for 20 to 30 minutes, adding water to thin it, if necessary. Add salt to taste.

Variation: You can use fresh red chile powder in place of the peppers by adding 1 teaspoon of fresh chile powder for every pepper. Do not use the commercially made chile powder for use in Texas bean chili. Only use the pure ground chile powder.

sweet red chile sauce

My dad liked this sauce with our Buffalo Eggs (page 30) and Rocky Mountain Oysters (page 45), and it's good over other meats, poultry, and eggs. Surprisingly, it's not made with New Mexico chiles but from commercial sweet red chile sauce. Easy! • *makes about 1½ cups*

¾ cup chile sauce (found in the ketchup aisle)
¾ cup hot mango chutney, such as Major Grey's
1½ tablespoons yellow mustard seeds

In a small mixing bowl, combine the chile sauce, chutney, and mustard seed. Chill the sauce for at least 6 hours to give the flavors a chance to mellow and mingle.

COLORFUL CHILE RISTRAS

Both ancient and current-day residents of New Mexico and Colorado dried chiles to preserve them for use throughout the winter. More often than not, ripe chiles are gathered in the fall and worked into full, colorful ropes or strands called ristras. These are hung in the kitchen and the fiery little dried chiles are plucked from it once the cold weather sets in to flavor stews, rubs, and egg dishes — just about anything and everything.
If you buy a ristra, be sure it isn't shellacked, which means it is meant only for ornamental use. Beautiful chile ristras come in many shapes and sizes, but the most common are the red Anaheim peppers worked into strands ranging from three to six feet long. In New Mexico and Colorado, you find these at roadside vegetable stands in the fall. When you buy one of these, it's advisable to hang it outside for two or three weeks to air it out and make sure it's completely dry before you bring it inside. Otherwise the chiles could mold.

▼▼▼▼▼▼▼▼▼▼▼▼▼▼▼▼▼▼▼▼▼▼▼▼▼

chopped green chile sauce

Everyone seems to have a preference when it comes to chile sauce. For example, my husband Jeremy likes green sauce more than red, but lots of folks prefer red chile sauce, in part because of its cheery color. I like both sauces equally and sometimes spoon both red and green sauces on my plate, regardless of what else is on it! At the Fort we make a hot green chile sauce and a mild one, such as this one. It's wonderfully versatile and can be served on the side or spooned into a pocket cut in a thick steak, as we do in the recipe for Gonzales Steak on page 156. • *makes about 2 cups*

10 to 12 New Mexican green, Anaheim, or California green chiles, roasted and peeled
  (canned will do, but fresh are best)
½ teaspoon salt, to taste
2 large cloves garlic, peeled and minced
¼ teaspoon dried Mexican oregano
1 to 2 teaspoons olive or canola oil

Slit the chiles to remove the seeds. With a large chef's knife, chop the chiles into fine dice and mix with the salt, garlic, and oregano. Drizzle with the olive oil. Serve as a topping or filling for a grilled steak or other grilled meats, or use to make Green Chile Enchilada Sauce (page 82).

red chile sauce

Serve this smooth sauce with chicken, quail, pork, beef, buffalo steaks — you name it! • *makes about 2 cups*

6 tablespoons canola oil
4 tablespoons all-purpose flour
1 cup Red Chile Puree, page 78
1 to 2½ cups chicken broth

Place the oil in a sauté pan over medium heat. Add the flour, and cook stirring for about 2 minutes until the flour turns golden brown. Turn off the heat, and add the chile puree. Return to the heat and cook for 30 seconds, stirring constantly. Gradually add 1 cup of the broth, whisking the sauce until smooth. Simmer over low heat for 8 to 10 minutes, stirring often, and add enough broth to make a medium-thin sauce.

red chile puree

We serve this classic red chile puree at the Fort. My dad does the best job of explaining how our family first discovered it.

"Way back in 1949, when I owned a toy store in Santa Fe called La Boutique Fantasque, local artist Will Shuster painted a jack-in-the-box sign for the top of a tall pine pole that had been cut and draw-knife peeled by Taos wood carver and furniture maker Elidio Gonzales. Elidio, a small, thin man with soulful eyes, looked as I imagined Don Quixote might. My wife and I became great admirers of his craftsmanship, and as time passed, his Spanish Colonial furniture was sought by the likes of author Leon Uris and actor John Wayne. Many years later he carved the Fort's doors and our first chairs.

"One Thanksgiving, Elidio invited us to his home. Atop his big carved table were laid a roast turkey, salad, hot flour tortillas, and mashed potatoes that were topped with red chile puree instead of gravy! What a wonderful discovery this turned out to be. In addition to spooning this thick, red sauce over mashed potatoes, we use it with our tamale pie as well as many other dishes. It's also the base for our versatile, smooth, and spicy Red Chile Sauce, which we love with pork chops, steaks, enchiladas, and just about anything else fit to eat!" • *makes about 1 cup*

12 dried New Mexican red chiles, rinsed, lightly oven-toasted,
   stems broken off and seeds shaken out, or ½ cup pure New Mexican ground red chile
   (medium to mild; Medium Dixon is best)
1 clove garlic, peeled
½ teaspoon salt, to taste
½ teaspoon dried Mexican oregano
1 to 1½ cups hot water

Place the chiles, garlic, salt, oregano, and hot water in a blender and pulse on and off until pureed. The mixture should be loose and pourable. If needed, add a bit more water. Press the puree through a coarse strainer into a bowl.

adobada marinade
for pork, chicken, or beef

This marinade is delicious with almost any meat, poultry or even fish you want to soak in a full-flavored brew. When you marinate food, use a nonreactive dish—glass or ceramic are best—and marinate meat and poultry for at least 4 hours. When you marinate fish, don't leave it in the marinade for longer than 35 to 45 minutes or it will turn a little mushy. • *makes about 1 cup*

½ cup medium red chile caribe (coarsely ground chile)
1 cup chicken broth
½ teaspoon dried Mexican oregano
2 cloves garlic, peeled and minced
½ teaspoon salt

In a nonreactive (glass) dish large enough to hold the meat or fish, combine the chile, chicken broth, oregano, garlic, and salt. Use the marinade right away or cover and refrigerate for up to 2 days.

Note: For pork, chicken, or beef, marinate for at least 4 hours. For any fish, marinate only 35 to 45 minutes.

IS IT SPELLED CHILE OR CHILI?

In my research, I discovered that the ancient Capsicum genus, or chile, has been domesticated for more than seven thousand years. Between 5200 and 3400 BC, Native Americans grew chile plants to use for cooking and medicinal reasons. This places chiles among the oldest cultivated crops of the Americas. By 1600, it was commercially grown in the United States by the Spanish colonists who settled in the Rio Grande Valley of northern New Mexico.

The word *chil* is derived from the Nahuatl (Aztec) dialect and refers to plants known as capsicum, and the aji or axi comes from the extinct Arawak dialect of the Caribbean. The correct spelling of chile, with the "e" at the end, is the authentic Hispanic spelling of the word. English linguists have changed the spelling from ending in an "e" to an "i." In fact, the word chili refers to the bean-based dish most famous in the state of Texas, and not the pepper.

▼▼▼▼▼▼▼▼▼▼▼▼▼▼▼▼▼▼▼▼▼▼▼▼

samoren sauce

In the 1980s when my son Oren was about 10, he was in the habit of walking over to his grandpa's house on Sundays to cook with GrandSam. Together they came up with this incredible jalapeño sauce, which quickly found its way to the Fort to become one of our favorite sauces for meat with its sweet bite of ginger and mustard mixed with the jalapeños. When it came to naming their creation, neither was shy about using both of their names: Sam and Oren, Samoren! This recipe is easily doubled. • *makes 6 half-pint jars*

2 pounds fresh jalapeño chiles, stems, seeds, and ribs removed
½ pound fresh ginger, peeled
2 cloves garlic, peeled
2 pounds sugar
4 cups white distilled vinegar
2 cups water
1 tablespoon black mustard seeds
1 tablespoon salt
1 tablespoon pectin

In small batches, puree the jalapeños, ginger, and garlic in a food processor and remove to a large nonreactive (enameled) pot or saucepan. Add the sugar, vinegar, water, mustard seeds, salt, and pectin. Bring to a boil over medium heat. Reduce the heat to low and boil gently, stirring frequently, for 35 to 45 minutes, or until the mixture thickens and the sugar reaches the soft-ball stage when dropped in cold water.

Wash the jars, lids, and screw bands in hot soapy water and rinse well. Sterilize the jars by submerging them in boiling water for 10 minutes, then keep them in hot water until ready to fill. Treat the lids and screw bands as directed by the manufacturers. Use tongs to lift the jars out of the hot water and place top down on a clean dish towel to drain. Fill the sterile jars with hot sauce, leaving ¼-inch headspace. Wipe the jar rim with a clean cloth, and close with a treated canning lid and screw band.

Place the filled jars on a rack in a canning pot filled with boiling water. The water should cover the jars by at least 1 inch. Bring the water back to a boil, and boil gently for 5 minutes. If you are at an altitude of 1,000 feet or more, add 1 minute to processing time for each 1,000 feet of altitude. Remove the processed jars to a protected surface and allow to cool. Allow to sit undisturbed for 12 hours. Check the seal, remove the screw band, label and store the sauce in a cool, dry, dark place. After opening, store in the refrigerator. This sauce makes a marvelous gift!

chipotle sauce or marinade

I love the fact that many sauces can double as marinades, and this is one of the most versatile. I particularly like this with seafood—it's amazing with shrimp—but it's also terrific with meat. Serve as a sauce for Shrimp en Appolas (page 206), or as a condiment or marinade for seafood, pork, or poultry. • *makes about ⅔ cup*

½ cup olive oil
1 clove garlic, finely minced
Juice of 1 lemon
3 dashes of chipotle sauce or ½ teaspoon mashed chipotle pepper in adobo sauce
1 teaspoon honey or sugar (optional)

In a small nonreactive (glass) mixing bowl, combine the olive oil, garlic, lemon juice, chipotle, and honey, if using.

CHILES AND THE FORT

"A day without chile is a day without sunshine!" said Elidio Gonzales, who, in the early days of the Fort, was the brilliant wood carver we employed to craft our chairs and other furniture. He even carved the Fort's front door, much admired by everyone who passes through it. We agree with Elidio: At The Fort, we cook with what we consider the very best New Mexican chiles, which grow in certain valleys in New Mexico and Pueblo, Colorado.

Like the grapes that are blended into fine wine, chile varietals grown in certain places have distinctive qualities. Hatch, Chimayo, or Dixon are the chiles that are grown near towns of their namesake. Most of the chiles we use in our cooking at the Fort come from Hatch and Dixon. I often go through Chimayo to buy the wonderful chipotle chile and green powder sold there, which I use this to create extra layers of flavor in sauces, soups, eggs, and rubs for beef and pork.

Our menu is rich with chile: you will find them in the recipe for Gonzales Steak on page 156, the dipping sauce for the Buffalo Empanadas on page 31 and in many of the other Beginners. In this chapter, you will find some good, basic chile recipes and learn how to make homemade chile sauce from peppers hanging on a ristra and how to roast Anaheim peppers in your oven. These techniques are easy and add tremendous flavor to many dishes.

▼▼▼▼▼▼▼▼▼▼▼▼▼▼▼▼▼▼▼▼

green chile enchilada sauce

This sauce can just as easily be made with red chile sauce. At Christmastime, we serve red and green chile sauces together. If you want both sauces on the plate for a dish such as huevos rancheros or grilled steak at any time of the year, just say you want them "Christmas style." Everyone in New Mexico and southern Colorado will know what you mean. • *makes about 3 cups*

1 recipe (2 cups) Chopped Green Chile Sauce, page 77
2 to 3 cups chicken broth, divided
1 tablespoon unsalted butter
1 tablespoon canola oil
2 tablespoons all-purpose flour
Salt and freshly ground black pepper, to taste

In a blender, puree 1 cup of the green chiles with 2 cups of the chicken broth. In a sauté pan, melt the butter with oil over medium heat. Add the flour and cook, stirring for about 2 minutes, until the flour turns golden. Add the chile puree and cook, stirring, until the sauce thickens. Stir in the remaining chopped chiles and enough chicken broth to make a medium-thick sauce. Taste and season with salt and pepper.

HOW TO CHAR GREEN CHILES FOR SAUCE

Start with 12 fresh Anaheim chiles, each about 6 inches long and 2 to 3 inches in diameter. Lay the chiles on a broiler pan and broil for 3 to 5 minutes or until you see the skin blistering and charring. Turn the peppers to char all sides. I turn each chile a quarter turn at a time and cook them until the skin bubbles and turns black.

Using tongs, lift the peppers from the broiler pan and transfer the chiles to a gallon-sized plastic bag. Seal the bag and let the chiles stand for about 10 minutes. This is called "sweating" the peppers. Run the peppers under cool water and peel off the blackened skin. The peppers are now ready for chopping. They can be used to make a sauce or draped over any broiled meat. If you don't use them right away, store them in a zipped plastic bag in the refrigerator or freezer. I keep several bags in my freezer all winter and use them as I need them.

▼▼▼▼▼▼▼▼▼▼▼▼▼▼▼▼▼▼▼▼▼

soups

▼▼▼▼▼▼▼▼▼▼▼▼▼▼▼▼▼▼▼▼

bowl of the wife of kit carson

In the spring of 1961, two years before opening the Fort, my family and I took a road trip to Mexico in a tiny English Morris Mini Cooper S. When we reached Durango, some six hundred miles south of the border, we were told that the best place to eat was the drugstore. The next morning, we watched as a stream of young children came in from the fields to fill family lunch buckets with a special soup sold at the store. It smelled so good, we knew we had to try it.

The bowls we were served held a heady, spicy broth of chicken with nice bites of white meat, nutty garbanzo beans, rice, a touch of oregano, chunks of avocado, and bite-sized pieces of soft white cheese. The secret of the amazing flavor, though, was the chipotle chile. This is smoked jalapeño and gave the soup a distinctive bite and delicious smokiness.

Caldo Tlalpeño is the soup's proper name and when the Fort opened, it was squarely on the menu. No one could pronounce its name or knew what it meant and despite its innate deliciousness, the soup did not sell. One day Leona Wood, the septuagenarian who ran our gift shop-trade room on weekends, told us that she remembered "my grandmother serving us this dish!" We were thrilled to hear this. Miss Wood happened to be the last granddaughter of frontiersman Kit Carson, and with a little genealogical figuring, we dubbed the soup Bowl of the Wife of Kit Carson. It has been a bestselling signature dish ever since. • *serves 4 to 6*

2 whole boneless, skinless chicken breasts (about 2 pounds)
4 to 6 cups chicken broth
¼ teaspoon dried Mexican leaf oregano, crumbled
1 cup cooked rice
1 cup cooked, dried garbanzo beans (chickpeas), or canned garbanzos, rinsed and well drained
1 chipotle chile (canned), packed in adobo, minced
4 to 6 ounces Monterey Jack or Havarti cheese, diced
1 to 2 ripe avocados, peeled, pitted, and sliced
4 to 6 sprigs fresh cilantro (optional)
1 fresh lime, cut into 4 to 6 wedges

Place the chicken breasts and broth in a large saucepan. Bring to a boil over medium-high heat, skimming off and discarding any foam that rises to the top. Turn off the heat, cover, and allow the chicken to poach gently for 12 minutes. Remove the chicken from the pot and cut into strips, about 1½ inches long. Return the chicken strips to the broth and add the oregano, rice, garbanzos, and chipotle.

Divide the cheese among 4 to 6 deep soup bowls.

Return the soup to a boil, then ladle it into the bowls. Garnish each portion with avocado slices, cilantro, if using, and a wedge of lime. Serve with hot tortillas as an appetizer or Duck Quesadillas (page 38) as a main course.

POSOLE AND ITS POSSIBILITIES

Posole (sometimes called *Pozole*) is a stew made of hominy, pork, green and/or red chiles, garlic, Mexican spices, and meat broth. Every Southwest Indian and Hispanic family has its own recipe for posole, which is considered "comfort food" and is usually prepared for major feast days, such as Christmas. In New Mexico, more pork is sold for posole during the winter holidays than turkey, ham, roast beef, or goose.

Posole is also the name of the particular corn used in the stew. Nowadays, I rely on frozen posole for most uses, but when I can't find it, I soak dried posole overnight and then boil it according to the package directions.

European settlers in the New World observed the Indians pouring water through the ashes from their fires to make a caustic solution. They boiled dried kernels of corn in this ash water solution until the hard outside covering of the kernels loosened and floated to the surface. The skins were discarded and the remaining soft corn kernel was cooked or dried and ground into meal. The partially cooked kernels are what people in the Southwest and Mexico call posole.

When the Spanish settled here, they brought horses, sheep, pigs, and many foods unfamiliar to the Indians. Over time, the indigenous people adopted the domestic animals and used them as an additional food source, which explains why so many posole recipes include pork or other meats and poultry. Today's recipes commonly include garlic and onions from the Spanish and hominy corn, chiles and Mexican oregano from Native Americans.

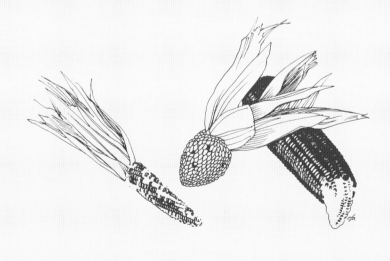

holly's posole

During our Indian Market Powwows at the Fort, held each May, we make this dish for the visiting artists. They love it, and I am not surprised they do, as it's my personal favorite. When I need a little comfort in this complicated world, this is what I crave. With each bite, I experience the tastes of the ancient ones as they weave a rich tapestry with those cultures that followed.

I nearly always make this with frozen posole, which is sold with other frozen Mexican food in many supermarkets. If you cannot find it, use dried posole, soaked overnight and then boiled according to the package directions.

• *serves 8 to 12*

2 to 3 tablespoons olive oil

1 large white or yellow onion,
   peeled and chopped (about 2 cups)

3 cloves garlic, peeled and crushed

1 pound lean boneless pork shoulder,
   cubed for stew

1½ to 2 tablespoons dried Mexican oregano,
   crumbled, to taste

1 large bay leaf

2 pounds frozen posole, defrosted, see Note

1 gallon of liquid—equal parts water,
   chicken and beef broth, see Note

½ pound fresh medium to mild green chiles, peeled,
   seeded, and chopped, or frozen chiles, chopped

Salt, to taste

GARNISH

2 cups grated Monterey Jack cheese

6 Serrano chiles, seeded, and minced

3 limes, cut into wedges

Place the olive oil in a Dutch oven over medium heat. Add the onion, garlic and pork. Cook, stirring occasionally, until the pork is browned and the onion caramelizes. This may take up to 15 minutes. Do not stir too often, as you need the onion, pork, and garlic to brown well. This process adds flavor! Add the oregano and bay leaf.

Stir in the posole, 12 cups of the broth mixture, and the green chiles. Bring to a boil, then reduce the heat to low and simmer, covered with a lid, for at least 3 hours, stirring occasionally, and adding more liquid as necessary. Taste, and add salt if needed.

Ladle the steaming hot posole into bowls and garnish with grated cheese, minced Serrano chiles, and lime wedges. Serve with warm flour tortillas.

Note: When buying frozen posole make sure that the ingredients listed include corn, lime, and salt. One package weighs 2 pounds.

I use a concentrated chicken and beef bouillon, which I add "to taste" for rich flavor. I do not recommend the cubes of stock sold at supermarkets, since they don't give enough richness of flavor. If making your own stock, reduce it to a concentrate for the best flavor.

heirloom bean soup

During an excavation at Mesa Verde, the ancient Indian Anasazi ruins in the Four Corners region of Colorado, archaeologists discovered small, colorful beans still in pots dating from AD 1200. When cultivated, the beans sprouted and now Anasazi beans are sold commercially—literally having been rescued from oblivion. Other ancient beans have been revived as well, such as the Zuni Golds and the brown Teparary beans.

I make this soup in a micaceous clay soup pot, which I bought from Debbie Carrillo after seeing her demonstrate the art of micaceous clay pot cooking at Tesoro's Spanish market. Debbie is one of the notable artists who visit the Fort during our Spanish market and while I was amazed by the pot, I was not surprised that she recognized and harnessed its properties. The clay is composed of more than 60 percent shiny mica, a mineral, and when formed into pots, the handles stay cool while the minerals distribute the heat evenly and cook the beans perfectly when set directly over the fire. It's easy to get a sense of the ancient Indians cooking these same beans in a similar pot, smelling the same aromas and anticipating the meal as eagerly as we do today. I love the connection. You don't have to use a micaceous clay pot for this recipe. Instead, use a good, stainless-steel bean pot, or any heavy pot that distributes heat evenly. If your pot is made of cast iron, be sure it has been well seasoned so that the iron does not flavor the soup. • *serves 4 to 6*

½ cup brown Teparary beans, see Note
½ cup Anasazi beans, see Note
½ cup Zuni Gold beans, see Note
2 small ham shanks (I prefer the smoked ham shanks to the hocks, as there is more meat and less fat)
2 tablespoons olive oil
1 large yellow onion, peeled and diced
3 medium celery stalks with leaves, chopped

2 cloves garlic, peeled and minced
1 to 2 tablespoons ground mild to medium New Mexico red chile, to taste
1 teaspoon ground sage
Salt, to taste

GARNISH
⅓ cup toasted sunflower seeds
Fresh cilantro or sage leaves

Pick over, rinse, and soak the beans in cold water to cover. (Some cooks soak beans overnight and others cook dried, rinsed beans and simmer for a much longer time.) At high altitudes, you will need to cook the beans for at least an additional hour.

Drain the beans and place in a heavy-bottomed soup pot along with 7 cups of cold water. Bring to a boil over medium-high heat, then reduce the heat to low.

Meanwhile, place the olive oil in a large deep skillet or sauté pan over medium heat. Add the onion, celery, and garlic and sauté until the onion is caramelized and the garlic is light golden brown, 3 to 5 minutes.

Add the sautéed vegetables, ground chile, and sage to the beans. Simmer until the beans are tender, 2 to 3 hours.

Season the soup to taste with salt. Remove the ham shanks. Cut the meat off the bones and return it to the soup. Ladle the hot soup into bowls. Garnish with toasted sunflower seeds and fresh cilantro or sage.

Note: To buy these heirloom beans, turn to page 241 where we have listed some sources.

buffalo vegetable soup

There is nothing particularly unusual about this soup, unless you think buffalo is out-of-the-ordinary! For us at the Fort, buffalo is as common as a beautiful sunset over the Rocky Mountains, but for many folks, it's exotic. While you can make this with beef, if you can find buffalo—also called bison—you will be rewarded with lean meat that is low in cholesterol and high in iron. We make this popular and hearty soup with organic vegetables so that it's not only one of the tastiest on the menu but one of the most healthful, too. It can easily be a main course, served with nothing more than freshly baked Bannock Bread with Dried Western Fruit (page 138) or Jalapeño Cornbread (page 142).

• *serves 4 to 6*

1 cup diced zucchini

½ cup diced yellow onion

½ cup diced red bell pepper

2 tablespoons canola oil

2 cups diced leftover buffalo or beef roast

8 cups chicken broth

½ cup shelled edamame (frozen)

½ cup corn kernels, fresh or frozen

1 cup roasted tomatoes, fresh or canned

1 tablespoon tomato paste

1 tablespoon minced fresh garlic (2 large cloves)

1 teaspoon dried thyme

Salt and freshly ground black pepper, to taste

GARNISH

3 to 4 tablespoons minced fresh cilantro
or Italian parsley

In a large heavy-bottomed soup pot, over medium-low heat, sweat the zucchini, onion, and red bell pepper in oil for 3 minutes. Add the buffalo and cook for 5 minutes. Add the broth and bring to a boil over medium-high heat, stirring occasionally. Add the edamame, corn, roasted tomatoes, tomato paste, garlic, thyme, and salt and pepper.

Simmer the soup for 35 to 45 minutes, skimming any foam or fat from the top. Garnish with minced fresh cilantro or parsley and serve.

chile con carne new mexican-style

My dad made this dish when my brother and I were kids and it's always been a family favorite. Not surprisingly, when Dad opened the Fort in 1963, he put the chile on the menu for special occasions.

"When I first lived in Santa Fe in 1948, I learned from restaurateur Luis Salazar how to make real New Mexican chili con carne," Dad wrote. "Mr. Salazar came from a long line of Santa Feans and at his Original Mexican Café on College Street, everything was made from scratch. He boiled the blue kernel corn in huge kettles with slaked lime to make posole and the masa for corn tortillas. He dried ripe red Espanola Valley chiles and then stemmed, cleaned, and cooked them to make red chile con carne, which translates to mean 'chile with meat.'

"Mr. Salazar's chile con carne recipe reflects the cuisine of the little villages north of Santa Fe, which is very different from those in southern New Mexico, Texas, and Arizona. It contains no beans, no tomato, no onion, no cumin, and only a slight touch of garlic and Mexican leaf oregano. Twice-cooking the pork, first to poach it and then to brown and caramelize it, gives the chile great depth of flavor. The longer you simmer it, the more tender the pork will be and the thicker the chile. Additional cornmeal will thicken it, too.

"This dish is easy to digest because it contains no tomatoes, which are acidic and contribute to indigestion. Once you taste it, you may never go back to the tomato-and-kidney bean-based recipes." • *serves 4 to 6*

2 pounds bone-in pork shoulder (pork butt), trimmed and cut into fist sized pieces
2 tablespoons vegetable oil or rendered pork or bacon fat
¼ cup cornmeal (blue, yellow, or white)
¼ cup cold water
½ cup Red Chile Puree, page 78
½ teaspoon dried Mexican leaf oregano
Salt, to taste

For best results start this recipe a day ahead to give the broth time to cool completely so it can be thoroughly defatted.

Place the pork in a heavy-bottomed soup pot, and add enough water to cover. Bring the water to a boil over high heat, then reduce the heat to low, cover, and simmer the pork gently for 1½ hours. Remove the meat to a large bowl and place the broth in the refrigerator. When the pork is cool enough to handle, cut the meat away from the bone and dice into ¼-inch cubes. Store in the refrigerator until ready to use.

Skim off the fat from the top of the chilled pork broth. Bring the defatted broth to a simmer. Heat the oil in a deep skillet until smoking. Dry the reserved pork cubes with a paper towel and sear in the oil until thoroughly browned. Add the browned meat to the broth. Add ½ cup of broth to the skillet, and stir to loosen and incorporate the browned bits.

Stir together the cornmeal and water. Add this mixture to the broth in the skillet, stirring well to thicken. Remove about ½ cup broth from the soup pot and set aside in case the chile needs thinning after it has simmered. Pour the broth and cornmeal mixture into the pot and add the Red Chile Puree. Adjust the seasonings with oregano and salt. Simmer for 20 to 30 minutes to blend the flavors, then serve piping hot.

CUSTOM-MADE FURNITURE AT THE FORT

Antonio Archuleta from Taos, New Mexico, has custom made Spanish Colonial-style furniture for the Fort since we opened in 1963. He is also a master builder and brilliant wood carver and much of our furniture displays his artistry—as does some of the furniture in my own home, I am pleased to say that a king-sized master bedroom bed, guest beds, and a beautiful *trestero* with intricate carvings make me smile every day. In my opinion, there is no finer artisan making traditional Spanish Colonial-style pieces than Antonio.

Antonio learned his craft from Elidio Gonzales in the 1950s, and in the ensuing years has won more awards at the Santa Fe Spanish Colonial Market than anyone can count. He always called my father his "gringo daddy"; I am *mi hermana* (my sister) and Jeremy, my husband, is *mi hermano* (my brother). Antonio makes all the Padre Martinez chairs at the restaurant without nails and instead relies on tongue-and-groove construction. We serve more than 350 customers a day, and so over the years Antonio has made perhaps thousands of chairs for us. Visitors to the Fort also take note of Antonio's beautiful benches and cabinets— all spectacular!

simple shiitake mushroom soup

Even before my parents built the Fort, they were intrigued with the foods of the West, and so each fall we hiked into the mountains to forage for mushrooms. When we found fresh morels, chanterelles, and boletas, we photographed them for identification and then stowed them away in anticipation of supper. When it was time to eat, my mother sautéed them in butter in a soup pot set over the campfire. She added chicken stock and cream, a little tarragon and chervil, and sometimes deglazed the pot with a splash of dry vermouth. If she had it, she sprinkled a little nutmeg on top. The resulting soup was like a first kiss!

This recipe, designed to be made in a kitchen and not over a campfire, relies on a blender or food processor to puree the soup. I am sure if my mother had had a food processor on the trail, she would have used it! • *serves 4 to 6*

1 pound fresh shiitake mushrooms or 2 to 3 ounces dried shiitake or other wild mushrooms
3 to 4 cups reduced-sodium chicken broth
1 pint (2 cups) heavy cream
2 teaspoons minced fresh tarragon or ½ teaspoon dried tarragon
1 teaspoon minced fresh chervil or ¼ teaspoon dried chervil
Salt and freshly ground black pepper, to taste
Fresh tarragon or Italian parsley sprigs, for garnish

Trim off and discard the woody or discolored stem ends from the fresh mushrooms. Separate the stems from the caps, then wipe stems and caps with a damp cloth. If you are using dried mushrooms, reconstitute them in hot water to cover and don't use the stems because they'll be too tough. Save the broth; strain out any dirt and grit by pouring the liquid through a coffee filter. Substitute this liquid for some of the chicken broth.

Place the mushrooms and 3 cups of broth in a large saucepan. Boil the mushrooms in broth over medium-high heat for 10 minutes. Allow to cool slightly, then puree in a food processor or blender. Return the puree to the saucepan and stir in the cream, tarragon, and chervil. Season with salt and pepper. If the soup seems too thick add the remaining chicken broth. Simmer for 15 to 20 minutes.

If you prefer a perfectly smooth soup, pour it through a conical sieve (chinois) to filter out any remaining solids. Ladle the hot soup into warmed bowls. Garnish with fresh herb sprigs and serve with hot crusty bread.

navajo zucchini-jalapeño soup

Chef Juan Zepeda at the Fort recently was inspired by how the Navajo, or Dine, as they are also called, use chiles, corn, and squash. To highlight Navajo methods, he developed this masa-based soup, which rapidly became extremely popular with our guests. The masa, or cornmeal, thickens the soup and the chiles provide enough bite without being hot. The toasted pepitas add nuttiness and a wonderful sense of ancient comfort food. Chef Juan told me that in his native Mexico, soups are usually the main course and not just a first course. This soup could easily serve that function with the Quinoa Salad with Fresh Garden Mint (page 102) and the Pumpkin-Walnut Muffins (page 146).

• *serves 4 to 6*

1 pound zucchini (2 to 3)
½ pound russet potatoes (1 to 2)
½ cup chopped yellow or white onion
½ cup diced mild green chiles
1 small jalapeño chile, peeled and seeded
¼ cup fresh cilantro leaves
1 teaspoon minced garlic (1 clove)
3 tablespoons minced fresh shallots (1 medium)
6 cups vegetable or chicken broth
1 cup fresh, frozen, or canned corn niblets
Salt and freshly ground black pepper, to taste
⅓ cup corn masa harina
⅓ cup cold water
½ cup lightly toasted hulled pumpkin seeds (pepitas) or sunflower seeds, for garnish
Fresh cilantro sprigs, for garnish

With a vegetable brush, scrub the zucchini and potatoes under cold running water. Slice the zucchini and peel and coarsely chop the potatoes. Place the zucchini, potatoes, onion, mild chiles, jalapeño, cilantro, garlic, and shallots in a heavy-bottomed soup pot. Stir in the vegetable broth. Bring to a boil over medium-high heat, stirring occasionally. Cover and reduce the heat to low. Simmer, stirring occasionally, for about 30 minutes, or until the zucchini and potatoes are tender when pierced with a knife.

Allow the mixture to cool slightly, then puree in a food processor or blender. Return the pureed soup to the pot and stir in corn. Bring the soup to a boil over medium heat. Season to taste with salt and pepper.

In a large measuring cup, stir together the masa harina and water. Gradually whisk the masa mixture into the soup. Simmer, continuing to whisk until the masa is incorporated into the soup has thickened. Taste again and adjust the seasonings. Ladle the hot soup into bowls and garnish with the toasted pepitas and cilantro.

curried butternut squash soup

Inspired by the familiar squash soups found throughout the Southwest and flavored with East Indian curry—traded at Bent's Fort in the nineteenth century—this delicious soup appears on our menu with happy regularity as a soup special. It is perfect served on a cold evening with cornbread and a green salad. • *serves 4 to 6*

1 large butternut squash (about 3½ pounds)
3 tablespoons butter or vegetable oil
2 large leeks (white and yellow parts only),
    rinsed thoroughly and chopped
4 teaspoons peeled, minced, fresh gingerroot
1 tablespoon curry powder, preferably Madras
⅛ to ¼ teaspoon cayenne pepper, to taste
4 to 6 cups chicken or vegetable broth
Salt, to taste

GARNISH
2 to 3 tablespoons minced Italian parsley
4 to 6 tablespoons crisp, crumbled bacon
4 to 6 tablespoons mild goat cheese
3 to 4 tablespoons hulled squash seeds (pepitas),
    lightly toasted (optional)

With a large, sharp knife, cut the squash in half lengthwise. Scrape out the seeds and stringy inner portions.

To cook in a conventional oven: Preheat the oven to 350°F. Place the squash halves cut side down in a baking pan and add enough water to come 1 inch up the sides. Cover the pan tightly with aluminum foil and bake for about 1 hour, until the squash is tender when pierced with a knife.

To cook in a microwave oven: Place the squash halves cut side down in a microwave-safe dish with ½ inch of water. Cover the dish with microwave-safe plastic wrap and cook on "high" for 12 minutes. Allow the squash to sit in the microwave without removing the plastic for 10 to 15 minutes, until it is cool enough to touch.

When the squash is cool enough to handle, use a large spoon to scoop out the pulp and set aside. Discard the skin.

Place the butter in a heavy-bottomed soup pot over medium-low heat. Add the leeks, ginger, curry, and cayenne and cook, stirring, until the leeks are softened, but not browned, 5 to 7 minutes. Stir in the squash and 4 cups of broth. Season to taste with salt.

Bring to a simmer over medium-high heat. Reduce the heat to medium-low and cook, stirring and breaking up the squash with a spoon, for 20 minutes. Carefully transfer the mixture to a food processor or blender and puree until smooth. Return the puree to the pot, and if the soup seems too thick, add additional broth. Taste and add more salt, if needed. Bring the soup to a simmer over medium heat, stirring, until heated through. Ladle it into warmed bowls and garnish each serving with parsley, crisp bacon crumbles, and a tablespoon of goat cheese placed in the middle of the bowl. Toasted squash seeds, if desired, are also a very good garnish for this soup.

Note: Curry powder may discolor wooden and plastic utensils and food processor blade.

holly's root vegetable soup

Honestly, when I was trying to lose some weight, I made a basic vegetable soup but quickly discovered I wanted more flavor and substance to fill my belly. To satisfy my hunger, I started using primarily root vegetables and caramelizing the onions and other veggies before adding them to the broth. Now, I make a large pot of this nearly every Sunday and portion it into small plastic containers. I refrigerate two or three and freeze the rest. There's lunch or even supper! Delicious, nutritious, and filling. I confess, this soup has never made it onto the menu at the Fort, but I couldn't write a book without including it. It's that good and tastes even better on the second day—you will never go back to canned soup again. If you're not trying to cut as many calories as possible, serve this with Bay's Southern Spoon Bread (page 143), the Quinoa Muffins (page 145) or the Pumpkin-Walnut Muffins (page 146). • *serves 4 to 6*

1 small yellow or white onion

1 celery stalk

1 small turnip

1 small rutabaga

1 carrot

1 small sweet potato

2 tablespoons olive oil

10 fingerling potatoes,
    washed but not peeled, and cut in half

1 small fresh fennel (anise) bulb,
    trimmed and diced

2 cloves garlic, peeled and minced

2 to 3 teaspoons herbes de Provence

1 bay leaf

6 cups chicken or vegetable broth

1 can (6 ounces) tomato paste

1 cup shredded cabbage (optional)

GARNISH

4 to 6 tablespoons mild goat cheese

4 to 6 sprigs Italian parsley sprigs

2 to 3 slices bacon, cooked crisp and crumbled

Peel and dice the onion, celery, turnip, rutabaga, carrot, and sweet potato.

Place the olive oil in a heavy-bottomed soup pot. Add all the vegetables and herbs and sauté over medium heat, stirring every 2 to 3 minutes, for 4 to 6 minutes, or until the edges of the onion, celery, and fennel begin to caramelize. Continue to cook over low heat, stirring occasionally, until all the other vegetables have softened, 15 to 20 minutes. This browning adds flavor!

Add the broth, tomato paste, and shredded cabbage, if using, and bring to a boil over medium-high heat. Reduce the heat to low and simmer, stirring occasionally, for 30 minutes.

Ladle the soup into bowls and garnish each serving with 1 tablespoon of goat cheese, a sprig of parsley, and a sprinkling of crumbled bacon.

holly's tarragon gazpacho

Although the Rocky Mountains that surround the Fort are snowcapped year round, it gets hot and dry in the high country in the summertime and nothing hits the spot more deliciously than this refreshing cold soup. I love to use summer's best tomatoes, cucumbers, and scallions from the farmer's market and fresh herbs from my small garden. Gazpacho is a Spanish soup and seems to fit perfectly into our southwestern lifestyle. • *serves 4 to 6*

1 ½ cups peeled, diced, fresh plum tomatoes or one 14 ½-ounce can diced tomatoes
½ cup peeled, chopped cucumber
½ cup chopped scallions (2 to 3)
2 tablespoons tarragon vinegar
1 large clove garlic, peeled
2 cups spicy Clamato juice (or V8), chilled
3 tablespoons minced fresh tarragon
½ teaspoon hot pepper sauce, if you can't find "spicy" Clamato or V8 (optional)
Salt, to taste

GARNISH
½ cup homemade croutons, fried in olive oil
½ to ¾ cup sour cream
4 to 6 sprigs fresh basil
1 to 2 ripe avocados, peeled and sliced (optional)

Place the tomatoes, cucumber, scallions, vinegar, and garlic in a food processor or blender. Pulse on and off until the vegetables are chunky. Pour into a large bowl. Stir in the vegetable juice, tarragon, and pepper sauce, if using. Salt to taste. Cover and refrigerate until well chilled.

Garnish with croutons, 2 tablespoons of the sour cream placed in the center of each bowl, and sprigs of fresh basil. As an alternative if you wish, slices of avocado are also a beautiful garnish.

from the
gardens & fields

quinoa salad with fresh garden mint

This salad is similar to a Middle Eastern tabouleh because it relies on tomatoes and fresh garden mint. It is one of the Fort's favorite side dishes, particularly because we use full-flavored, juicy heirloom tomatoes. Our customers love it with the Herbed Lamb Chops (page 188) in the spring and summer and also as a complete protein salad served with our Three Sacred Sisters Tamale Pie (page 193) or any of our soups. • *serves 4 to 6*

1½ cups (8 ounces) quinoa
1 cucumber, peeled, seeded, and diced
⅓ cup fresh mint leaves, minced
⅓ cup minced Italian parsley
⅓ cup fresh lemon juice
⅓ cup olive oil
Salt and ground black pepper, to taste
2 ripe tomatoes (preferably heirloom varieties), seeded, and diced

In a large fine-mesh strainer, rinse the quinoa under cold running water and drain well. Place the quinoa and 2½ cups of water in a large saucepan and bring to a boil over high heat. Reduce the heat to low, cover, and simmer until most of the water has been absorbed, 15 to 20 minutes. When done, the grain appears translucent, and the germ ring will be visible. Drain the cooked quinoa and spread it out in a shallow baking pan to cool.

After the quinoa is completely cool, place it in a salad bowl, and add the cucumber, mint, and parsley. In a small mixing bowl, whisk together the lemon juice and oil. Season the dressing to taste with salt and pepper. Drizzle the dressing over the quinoa, add the tomatoes, and toss gently. Taste the salad and adjust the seasonings.

quail salad with damiana vinaigrette

When my dad dined at the Fort, he always ordered this salad as a special request. He also reveled in telling our customers that Colorado's population had grown over the last forty years due in large part to the Fort serving the Mexican herb, damiana, in our salad dressing. It is supposed to be a potent aphrodisiac! • *serves 4*

4 cups mixed salad greens

1 ripe avocado, peeled, pitted, and cut into narrow wedges

1 tablespoon small capers

1 tablespoon beni-shoga (kizami-shoga) red pickled ginger

¼ cup cubed jicama

1 small jar marinated artichoke hearts, cut into small pieces

1 to 1¼ cups Damiana Vinaigrette, page 112

8 partially boned quail (see William Bent's Teriyaki Quail, page 172)

GARNISH

1 medium tomato, cut into wedges

8 large radish crowns

½ cup toasted cashews

4 lemon wedges

Toss the greens, avocado, capers, beni-shoga, jicama, and artichoke hearts with the dressing. Place the salad on individual plates or 1 large platter and arrange the quail on top. Garnish with the tomato, radishes, toasted cashews, and lemon wedges.

MY DAD DISCOVERED QUINOA IN PERU. HERE'S HIS STORY IN HIS OWN WORDS

In the mid-1970s on a trip to Peru, I learned of the grain called quinoa (KEEN-wah). The individual grains are tiny balls and have a texture similar to black lumpfish caviar. Quinoa takes on the flavors of the foods with which it's mixed, but its most significant feature is that it contains more usable protein than any other grain in the world, including amaranth, rice, and spelt. Dr. John McCamant, a former professor at Denver University and one of the country's experts on quinoa, says that it is close to being the perfect food.

Archaeological evidence shows that quinoa was cultivated as early as 5000 BC in the Ayacucho Basin in Peru. It was a staple of the Andean peoples and was held sacred by the Incas, who called it the mother grain.

I was so excited about it that I immediately wanted to begin importing the grain to the United States until I discovered that a man named Stephen Gorad in Boulder, Colorado, was already importing and selling it to specialty grocers. Eventually, he sold his company to a conglomerate in California and today quinoa enjoys sales nationwide. It will never compete with grains such as wheat because it lacks gluten for making yeast bread and because it is difficult to grow, but it's becoming better known all the time.

Quinoa's native environment is near the equator, which means a long growing season high in the Andes at altitudes ranging from 7,000 to 13,000 feet above sea level. This means cool temperatures. After many years of research and experimentation, in the 1980s quinoa was finally cultivated successfully in the Rocky Mountains. Today, White Mountain Farms, high in Colorado's San Luis Valley, grows (in addition to excellent potatoes) several strains of what has been dubbed the super grain of the future. White, tan, and black varieties of quinoa are available, but the original black grain, from which the others have derived, is by far the best. In Peru, it's called *coital quinoa*, although I haven't been able to find out why.

The preparation of quinoa is easy. The plant grows to about six feet and has a large seed-covered head coated with a natural soap to discourage animals and insects from eating it. This is rinsed off in the commercial milling process, but the grain should be rinsed again at home before using. It's important not to overcook quinoa because the moisture inside the tiny balls will cause them to explode. When this happens, the grain becomes an uninteresting, flat shell. Cook it similarly to rice, with a liquid to grain ratio of 2:1. Usually, depending on altitude, it cooks for 12 to 15 minutes.

▼▼▼▼▼▼▼▼▼▼▼▼▼▼▼▼▼▼▼▼▼▼

smoked duck breast salad

When we first served this lovely salad at the Fort, we made it with smoked pheasant but now use smoked duck which is a little easier to come by—unless you know a good pheasant hunter with a smoker. The duck is especially succulent and works beautifully with the other ingredients. If jars of quail eggs are not available, substitute 4 hard-cooked hen's eggs, cut into quarters. Don't use canned quail eggs because the quality is poor. • *serves 4*

About 2 cups chicken broth

2 (6-ounce) Smoked Duck Breast Fillets, recipe follows

4 cups mixed greens

1 recipe Bayou Salado Dressing, page113

2 cups sliced pickled beets

4 hard-cooked large eggs

4 tablespoons lightly toasted pine nuts, for garnish

4 tablespoons currants, for garnish

8 fresh onion rings, for garnish (optional)

16 hard-cooked pickled quail eggs

12 radish crowns

In a wide skillet, bring the chicken broth to a simmer over medium heat. Add the duck breasts and cook gently for 5 to 10 minutes or until warmed through. Drain and slice the meat into ¼-inch-thick slices.

Toss the mixed greens thoroughly with the Bayou Salado Dressing, then divide equally among 4 dinner plates. In the center, overlap 6 slices of pickled beets to make a ring and place a whole hen's egg in the middle. Arrange the slices of smoked duck breast on the beets, leaving visible the white top in the center of the hard-cooked egg. Garnish the salad with toasted pine nuts and currants. A few rings of fresh onion are a nice addition, if desired. Arrange the quail eggs around the edge of the plate with the radishes.

smoked duck breast fillets

• *serves 2 to 4*

1 tablespoon brown sugar

1 tablespoon kosher salt

3 tablespoons hot water

2 (6-ounce) boneless duck breast fillets

1 applewood or hickory aluminum foil smoking bag, see page 240

Mix the brown sugar, salt, and hot water until the salt and sugar are dissolved to make a brine. Place the duck in a shallow pan and add the brine and enough cold water to cover the duck. Let the duck sit covered overnight in the refrigerator.

Preheat the oven to 250°F. Remove the fillets from the brine and place in the smoking bag. Fold the end of the bag to seal. Place the bag on the middle rack of oven and smoke 35 minutes for rare, 40 minutes for medium, and 45 minutes for well done. Let the duck rest in the bag for 5 to 10 minutes. Open the bag carefully to avoid being burned by the hot steam. Remove the skin from the fillets, and discard. Slice the breasts and serve.

PICKLED DEVIL'S CLAWS

We used to eat these at home and at the restaurant, but alas, our supplier, Dexter Hess, no longer can provide them. This story from my dad gives you insight into how much history and a sense of adventure inspired my family. Here's what Dad wrote:

"In the summer of 1845, Lieutenant James Abert, a West Point grad, spent some time at Bent's Fort and kept a journal documenting the flora and fauna. Several entries concern a plant with large seedpods called Myrtinia proboscidia, or devil's claws. He wrote that when pickled, these pods resembled pickled okra and were good to eat.

"In the late 1980s, a retired botanist named Dexter Hess read these journals and went in search of devil's claws on the prairies south of La Junta, Colorado. Picking the seedpods at just the right time of year wasn't an easy task. Early August is a hot time in Colorado; the plant is not much more than two feet tall, and more than a few rattlesnakes inhabit the plains. But Dexter and his wife gathered enough for some experiments. Pickled, the little pods were delicious, and I commissioned him to pick and pickle devil's claws for the Fort.

"They should be picked in late July or early August when the pods are young and before the antennae have formed and hardened. Using a long pin to probe the pods before picking is the best way to check for a tender tip. If hardened, the sharp hook (the devil's claw, no doubt) may cut your mouth. Still, it's a good idea to eat them carefully because it's nearly impossible to tell if the pods will be soft all the way through.

"Pickled devil's claws have a slightly crunchy, sour pickle taste and the seedpod and antennae are tasty as well as fun to eat. I keep a secret store of them to feed adventurous eaters."

fort green salad

My dad loved all the flavors and textures found in this salad, as do I. We have made it for years and serve it with every meal at the Fort as part of the price of the entrée. It's never extra, although we keep adding "extras" to the mix to make this salad the best there is. The last flavor delight my dad added was in 1999 when he discovered peppadew peppers, introduced to him by our close foodie friend Suzanne Roser. • *serves 4 to 6*

2 cups cubed herb bread
2 tablespoons olive oil
⅓ cup grated Parmigiano-Reggiano cheese
1 tablespoon raw or roasted hulled pumpkin seeds (pepitas)
6 cups mixed fresh salad greens (mesclun)
1¼ to 1½ cups of your favorite Fort salad dressing
½ cup finely diced jicama
12 slices tomato or 24 cherry tomatoes, halved
3 teaspoons beni-shogi (kizami-shoga) red pickled ginger
12 pickled, hard-cooked quail eggs (sold in jars; the canned Asian ones are not very good)
4 to 6 peppadew peppers, diced (small sweet/hot pickled red peppers sold at olive bars in grocery stores)
2 (6-ounce) smoked duck breast fillets, sliced ¼ inch thick (optional), page 106

Preheat the oven to 350°F. Toss the bread cubes with the olive oil. Arrange in a single layer in a baking dish. Bake for about 8 minutes, until golden but not dry, then toss with the cheese. Set aside.

If you use raw pepitas, roast them in a dry skillet over medium heat, shaking it periodically until they begin to pop.

To make the salad, toss the greens with the salad dressing and divide among chilled salad plates or shallow bowls. Add, in order, the jicama, pepitas, tomato, beni-shogi, quail eggs, and peppadew peppers. Sprinkle the croutons on the top. To make this an entrée salad, top with sliced smoked duck breast fillets.

heirloom three sacred sisters salad

The ancient Native Americans knew a thing or two about sustainable agriculture, as evidenced by how they cultivated three of their most important crops: corn, beans, and squash. They called these foods "the three sacred sisters" because the plants protected and nurtured one another as they grew. The corn was planted in a mound of earth and the beans were planted in a circular pattern around the cornstalks. Finally, the squash seeds circled the beans. As the plants grew, the beans climbed up the cornstalks and the squash leaves shaded the tender tendrils put out by the beans. Perfect symbiosis! With this colorful and delicious salad, we pay tribute to the sacred sisters. Be sure to say a blessing to them before eating it. • *serves 4 to 6*

SALAD
2 tablespoons unsalted butter
1 chayote squash, diced
1½ cups fresh or frozen corn kernels,
  blanched and drained
1½ cups cooked Anasazi beans,
  or pinto beans, rinsed
1 green bell pepper, seeded and diced
1 red bell pepper, seeded and diced

SALAD DRESSING:
¼ cup white wine vinegar
Juice of half a lemon
2 tablespoons sugar
1 tablespoon minced fresh tarragon,
  or ½ teaspoon dried tarragon
3 to 5 tablespoons olive oil
Salt and freshly ground pepper, to taste
4 to 6 sprigs fresh cilantro, for garnish
⅓ cup hulled sunflower seeds, lightly toasted,
  for garnish

In a skillet over medium-high heat, melt the butter. Add the diced chayote and sauté for 2 to 3 minutes, until slightly softened and beginning to brown.

In a salad bowl, combine the vinegar, lemon juice, sugar, and tarragon. Gradually whisk in the olive oil. Taste and season with salt and pepper. Add the corn, beans, squash, and bell peppers. Toss the salad, then chill for 1 hour in the refrigerator. Serve garnished with fresh cilantro and toasted sunflower seeds.

VINAIGRETTES AND DRESSINGS

We assemble and dress our salads just before serving at the Fort, which is how they should be made at home, too. While you may opt to wash the greens and cut up many of the ingredients ahead of time, don't mix the salad until you are just about ready to carry it to the table. Drizzle it with the dressing and gently toss it. Hold the ingredients at room temperature before throwing them together; icy cold green salads are not very good. Don't saturate the greens with the salad dressing or you will be in for unappetizing, soggy leaves. Use a light hand but one that ensures all the ingredients are lightly coated and flavored.

We make several dressings and vinaigrettes at the Fort. While vinaigrettes can fall in the category of dressing, I separate them here based on their texture. In my book, dressings are a little creamier and denser than vinaigrettes, which are lighter mixtures primarily of oil and vinegar. We have served all these at various times during our history. For instance, the Bayou Salado Dressing, our version of green goddess salad dressing, was on our original menu in the 1960s. I think we will bring it back for our fiftieth anniversary celebration in a few years. It's named for some lovely marshes of the same name about one hundred miles southwest of the Fort in South Park, Colorado, which have been called the Eden of the West. My dad loved the Damiana Vinaigrette, made with an herb he found in Mexico and always claimed was an aphrodisiac. It takes some advance planning, but once you make it, you'll love it. Our blue cheese dressing, made with irresistibly sharp Maytag blue cheese, is addictive. Maytag is a domestic blue and well worth locating. And yes, in case you were wondering, the same family that made the washing machine also figured out how to make sublime blue cheese.

▼▼▼▼▼▼▼▼▼▼▼▼▼▼▼▼▼▼▼▼▼▼

chipotle honey vinaigrette

Everyone loves this salad dresssing, developed by our former executive chef, Dave Woolley. Its happy notes of hot pepper and sweet honey mingle uproariously with fresh vegetables and the mayonnaise smoothes it out so that it's about as satisfying as any dressing can be. • *makes about 1¼ cups*

1 canned chipotle chile en adobo
1 to 2 tablespoons of the adobo sauce, to taste
¼ cup honey or agave nectar
1 cup mayonnaise
1 to 1½ tablespoons white distilled vinegar, to taste
Salt

In a food processor, puree the chipotle with the adobo sauce. With the machine still running, slowly add the honey. Stop the machine and add the mayonnaise and vinegar. Pulse on and off, until the dressing is smooth. Add the salt to taste.

damiana vinaigrette

• *makes about 2 cups*
½ cup red wine vinegar
1 tablespoon water
¾ teaspoon dried damiana, page 240
1½ cups salad oil
1 tablespoon sugar
Salt and freshly ground white pepper, to taste

Heat the vinegar and water in a nonreactive saucepan to almost boiling, about 190°F. Add the damiana and mix well. Place the vinegar mixture in a sealed glass container, and set aside at room temperature for 2 weeks. Pour through a strainer to remove the leaf. Whisk in the oil, sugar, and salt and white pepper. Taste and adjust the seasonings.

bayou salado dressing

• makes about 1¼ cups
¾ cup mayonnaise

½ cup buttermilk

2 tablespoons tarragon vinegar

1 tablespoon snipped fresh chives or minced green onions

1 tablespoon minced Italian parsley

1 tablespoons minced fresh tarragon leaves or ¼ teaspoon dried

1 small clove garlic, minced

3 to 5 canned flat anchovy fillets, rinsed and chopped

Salt and freshly ground pepper, to taste

In a small mixing bowl, whisk together the mayonnaise, buttermilk, vinegar, chives, parsley, tarragon, garlic, and anchovy fillets. This dressing should be just thick enough to cling to the lettuce, but not heavy. Taste and add a little more vinegar and buttermilk, if needed. Season to taste with the salt and pepper.

chunky maytag blue dressing

• makes about 1¾ cups

1 cup mayonnaise

½ cup full-fat sour cream

¼ cup milk

½ teaspoon Worcestershire sauce

½ teaspoon freshly ground white pepper

1 clove garlic, crushed

¼ teaspoon salt

1½ teaspoons chopped fresh thyme

⅓ cup crumbled blue cheese, with some larger pieces

Place all the ingredients except the blue cheese in a blender or food processor and pulse on and off until smooth. Stir in the blue cheese by hand. Cover the dressing, and refrigerate overnight to allow the flavors to blend. The dressing may be stored for up to 2 weeks in the refrigerator.

jalapeño buttermilk ranch dressing

• *makes about 1½ cups*

1 fresh jalapeño chile

¾ cup mayonnaise

½ cup full-fat sour cream

¼ cup buttermilk

¼ cup diced red bell pepper

2 tablespoons chopped green onion

2 tablespoons chopped Italian parsley

1 tablespoon chopped fresh basil

1 tablespoon chopped fresh cilantro

1½ teaspoons chopped fresh thyme

1 large clove garlic, peeled and minced

⅛ teaspoon dried dill seed (optional)

3 to 6 drops hot sauce, to taste (optional)

3 to 6 drops Worcestershire sauce, to taste

Salt and freshly ground black pepper, to taste

1 tablespoon fresh lime juice

Seed and dice the jalapeño. In a blender or food processor, combine the diced jalapeño, mayonnaise, sour cream, buttermilk, bell pepper, green onion, parsley, basil, cilantro, thyme, garlic, and dill seed, if using. Pulse on and off until the dressing is well blended and almost smooth. Taste and season with the hot sauce, if using, Worcestershire, salt and pepper, and lime juice.

HOW TO ROAST NUTS AND SEEDS

Very simply, I spread the nuts or seeds in a dry frying pan, turn on the flame to medium-low heat, and watch very carefully. I stir the nuts or seeds constantly with a wooden spoon and after 3 to 5 minutes, depending on the pan's contents, they are roasted—or toasted. Seeds cook a little faster and some may only need 30 to 40 seconds to darken slightly and turn fragrant.

I don't use oil; there is enough oil in the nut or seed, but if you're in a hurry, put about a teaspoon of oil in the pan or spray it with flavorless vegetable oil. Heat the oiled pan first and then add the nuts or seeds. As the toasting begins, you will smell a wonderful aroma and watch the nuts or seeds turn golden brown or a shade or two darker than they were. Remove the pan from the heat when their color is still light because they continue to toast a little in the hot pan even off the heat. If desired, sprinkle fine salt over them. I prefer unsalted nuts; they are so good *au natural!*

▼▼▼▼▼▼▼▼▼▼▼▼▼▼▼▼▼▼▼▼▼

the fort's famous black beans

When we opened in the early 1960s, there were very few dishes on the menu that included legumes such as black beans. At the time, most Americans may have been somewhat familiar with pinto or kidney beans but knew very little about any others. In those early days, Luis Bonachea was our manager and being from Cuba, he insisted the black beans, cooked in the Cuban style, were the Rolls Royce of all beans. Our customers agreed with him and since then we have served these black beans, made from a recipe Luis shared with us from his homeland. They are never off the menu and our loyal followers would be decidedly unhappy if we decided to omit them! • *serves 8*

4 cups black beans (sometimes called turtle beans)
6 quarts water
2 yellow onions, finely chopped
4 cloves garlic, crushed
3 ham hocks
4 green bell peppers, seeded and chopped
4 bay leaves
½ teaspoon powdered cloves
½ teaspoon whole black peppercorns
1 cup olive or salad oil
1 cup white vinegar
Salt, to taste

Rinse the beans thoroughly, checking for rocks or gravel. Soak them overnight in enough water to cover them by 4 inches. The next day, drain and rinse the beans; place them in a stockpot and add 6 quarts of water. (Using fresh water helps the beans not be as musical—flatulence producing—as they might be.)

Add the onions, garlic, ham hocks, bell peppers, bay leaves, cloves, and peppercorns. Cover, bring to a boil, then simmer for 3 to 5 hours, until tender. Check on the beans frequently, and if the liquid level has dropped so as to threaten to expose the beans, add more hot water. (Always add hot water, never cold, to beans during cooking; cold water makes them tough.) Keep the heat low and stir occasionally to prevent burning. When the beans soften, remove the ham hocks and separate the meat from the bone. Chop the meat into bite-sized pieces and add to the beans. In the last hour of cooking, add the oil and vinegar. Season to taste with salt just before serving.

heirloom bbq beans

Dave Woolley, who was our executive chef, came up with this recipe for barbecued beans in 2003. Dave and my dad shared a love of beans, and this dish, using heirloom beans, quickly became a great favorite of Dad's. • *serves 8*

16 ounces dried heirloom beans (Anasazi, Zuni Gold, Colorado River,
   or Scarlett Runner beans or a combination of varieties)
1 bottle (19-ounce) Jack Daniels Original Barbecue Sauce
1 bottle (18-ounce) Cattlemen's Golden Honey Barbecue Sauce
½ cup Mae Ploy sweet chili sauce
¼ cup brown sugar
1 large clove garlic, minced
1½ teaspoons ground cumin
1½ teaspoons dried Mexican oregano
1½ teaspoons ground paprika
1½ teaspoons (mild to medium) ground New Mexican red chile
1½ teaspoons kosher salt
1 teaspoon chile caribe (crushed red chiles)
½ teaspoon freshly ground black pepper
3 slices applewood smoked bacon, diced
1 cup chopped yellow onion
½ pound roasted, diced buffalo or beef

Pick over and rinse the beans. Soak them overnight in enough water to cover by 4 inches. If using more than one variety, soak the beans in separate containers. Drain and rinse the beans and place in a heavy-bottomed pot with enough water to cover by 4 inches. If using more than 1 variety, cook the beans separately (different beans have different cooking times). Bring the water to a boil over high heat. Cover and reduce the heat to low. Simmer the beans for 2 to 4 hours, stirring occasionally, until tender. If necessary, add additional hot water so that the beans remain covered.

   Meanwhile in a mixing bowl, combine the barbecue sauces, chili sauce, and brown sugar. Stir in the garlic, cumin, oregano, paprika, ground chile, salt, chile caribe, and black pepper. Set aside.

   In a large skillet, over medium-low heat, cook the bacon until crisp. Add the onion and cook until slightly caramelized. Set aside.

   Drain the cooked beans, reserving the cooking liquid. Place the beans in a large heavy-bottomed pot. Add the sauce mixture, sautéed bacon and onion, and the buffalo roast. Mix together gently. Reheat the barbecued beans over medium to low heat, adding 2 to 6 cups of the reserved hot bean broth if the mixture seems to be getting dry. Serve hot.

bay's georgia green chile grits

My mother, Bay, was a born-and-bred Southerner who developed a great love of the West. She moved back to Georgia after she and my father divorced, but always kept a foot in both places. When I visited her once in 2003, she was working as a historian-interpreter at a living-history farm in Tifton, Georgia, called Agrirama. At the farm, they ground local corn and grits between huge millstones from the 1880s. I asked if they could supply the Fort with the grits and to this day we are fortunate enough to get stone-ground grits from Georgia. The best you'll ever taste! My mom prided herself on her dishes made with grits and this is one of the best. Mom's ashes are now buried next to the big red rock outside the Fort and she lives always through her famous grits. We added a western twist with the addition of Monterey Jack, Colby, or asadero cheese. • *serves 4 to 6*

3 slices applewood smoked bacon, diced
½ cup finely chopped yellow onion
2 roasted, peeled poblano chiles, seeded and diced
1 clove garlic, minced
1 cup heavy whipping cream
3 cups chicken broth
1 cup old-fashioned, long-cooking stone-ground hominy grits, see Note
¾ cup grated mixed cheeses, such as Jack, Colby, or asadero
Salt and freshly ground black pepper, to taste

In a large, deep, sauté pan, over medium-low heat, cook the bacon until crisp, 2 to 3 minutes. Add the onion and sauté until translucent, 2 to 3 minutes. Add the chiles and garlic and cook for 1 minute.

Stir in the cream, broth, and grits. Bring to a simmer over medium heat, stirring frequently. Reduce the heat to low, and cook, stirring frequently, 20 to 30 minutes, until the liquid is absorbed and the grits are thick and creamy. Remove the grits from the heat and stir in the cheeses. Season to taste with salt and pepper. Serve immediately.

Note: If old-fashioned, long-cooking grits are not available in your area, use quick-cooking grits—not instant grits. If you do this, allow the broth and cream to simmer for 10 minutes before adding the grits. Cook the grits for about 5 minutes, until thickened and creamy, and then stir in the cheeses. The texture will not be the same as with long-cooking grits, but will be acceptable in a pinch. Turn to page 240 to find out how to order Agrirama Grits.

carrots or beets with red chile honey

When fall comes to the Rocky Mountains and the aspens shimmer gold in the crisp air, we turn to harvest vegetables for inspiration. Few dishes are better than this, made with the season's best freshly dug carrots and beets. Both turn wonderfully sweet when roasted, and when helped along with red chile honey, they are gloriously sweet, hot, and sour with undertones of fruit. Everyone loves these, from our most discriminating guests to the kids who walk through our doors.

Red chile honey is sold in some supermarkets, but you can easily make it yourself by stirring some pure New Mexico chile powder into mild honey. The chile powder has a lovely sweet-and-hot quality without being overpowering. As an aside, chile honey is an ancient remedy for mouth pain. It doesn't cure a sore but relieves the pain.

This is an easy dish to make because the vegetables can be roasted ahead of time and then cooked for a few minutes to glaze and reheat. • *serves 4 to 6*

2 to 3 cups raw carrots, cut into ¼-inch-thick diagonal slices or 4 to 6 medium-sized fresh beets,
   stems cut to 1 inch and root ends left intact (this helps to keep them from bleeding)
Red chile honey, see Note
Salt and freshly ground black pepper, to taste

Boil the carrots in water until barely tender, about 5 minutes. If you are using beets, boil them, covered, for 30 to 40 minutes or until tender.

When the carrots are done, toss them in the glaze to coat thoroughly, reheating if necessary. If you are using beets, run them under cold water, remove the root and stem ends and pull off the skins. Drain well. Slice, dice, or cut the beets into julienne strips and toss them in the honey to coat thoroughly, reheating if necessary. Adjust the seasoning, adding salt and pepper and more red chile honey to taste.

Note: You can buy chile honey in some supermarkets or make it yourself by stirring a rounded tablespoon of chile powder into a cup or so of honey. I like to use pure New Mexico red chile and think Dixon brand is the best.

zuni succotash
with toasted sunflower seed hearts

Succotash is truly a Native American dish, always made with beans and corn. No one in Europe had heard of it, nor had they heard of the ingredients common in succotash, until Christopher Columbus dropped anchor in the Caribbean in the fifteenth century. Most culinary historians trace the dish's roots to the Narraganset tribe, who lived in the Northeast, where it was a simple dish of corn, lima beans and fish. Further inland, Native Americans made similar dishes with beans, corn, and bear fat. At the Fort, we substitute Anasazi beans for the more familiar lima beans and add sunflower seeds, too. This is to honor the Zunis, whose reservation in northern Arizona is surrounded by the far larger Navajo res. • *serves 4 to 6*

½ cup raw or roasted sunflower seed hearts (hulled sunflower seeds)

2 cups frozen lima beans or 1 cup dried Anasazi beans

2 strips bacon

2 cups fresh sweet corn cut from the cob (about 3 ears) or frozen or canned whole kernel corn

1 medium yellow onion, finely chopped

1 cup canned, chopped mild green chile

1 small red bell pepper, seeded and finely diced

1 small green bell pepper, seeded and finely diced

If using raw sunflower seed hearts, toast them in a small dry skillet over medium-low heat, stirring until lightly browned, about 5 minutes. If you are using frozen lima beans, set them aside to thaw. If using Anasazi beans, soak them overnight in cold water, then drain, rinse, and boil in fresh water for 2 to 3 hours until soft and mealy.

In a large skillet, cook the bacon over medium-low heat until crisp. Remove and drain on paper towels. Sauté the corn and onion in the bacon drippings for about 3 minutes. If you prefer, use vegetable oil instead of the bacon fat. Add the beans, green chile, red and green bell pepper and sunflower seeds, and sauté, over medium heat, until peppers are slightly softened and onion is translucent. Sprinkle crisp crumbled bacon over the hot succotash, and serve.

chayote squash

This ancient squash was first cultivated in Mexico, where it was a great favorite of the Aztecs and Mayans, but now is grown pretty much in most warm regions stretching across our hemisphere. It's even found its way to Europe, where it rates as an exotic vegetable. The French and French Caribbeans called it christophene. Some people call it a vegetable pear because of its size and shape. When chayote is cooked correctly, it has an appealing texture—similar to water chestnuts—and deep, starchy flavor. We cook it simply and it's one of our most popular vegetable dishes. When you buy chayote, refrigerate it and cook it soon after purchase. It's not quite as sturdy as some other squashes.

• *serves 4 to 6*

2 chayote squash
3 tablespoons unsalted butter
²/₃ cup thinly sliced scallions
2 roasted red peppers, cut into small dice
2 tablespoons minced fresh cilantro
Salt and freshly ground pepper, to taste

Cut the chayotes in half lengthwise. Slice the halves lengthwise into ¼-inch-thick slices. Cut the slices lengthwise into thin strips.

Place a large skillet or sauté pan over medium-high heat and add the butter. When the butter melts and the foam begins to subside, add the scallions, roasted peppers, chayote, and cilantro. Sauté about 2 minutes until the squash is tender-crisp. Season with salt and pepper and serve.

spaghetti squash with garden mint

When the mint is fresh in the markets or growing rampant in your backyard, make this amazing side dish. It's one of my favorites and I particularly like it with General Armijo's Grilled Lamb Chops (page 187) or the chilled gazpacho (page 99). • *serves 4 to 6*

1 small spaghetti squash (about 4 pounds)
4 tablespoons (¼ cup) unsalted butter, softened
⅓ cup fresh mint leaves, finely chopped, or 2 to 3 teaspoons dried mint
Salt and freshly ground black pepper, to taste
½ cup grated Parmigiano-Reggiano (Parmesan) cheese (optional)

With a large, heavy chef's knife, cut the squash in half lengthwise. Scrape out the seeds and strings.

To cook in the oven: Preheat the oven to 375°F. Place the squash halves cut side down in a shallow roasting pan. Add enough water to the pan to come up 1 inch from the sides. Cover the pan tightly with aluminum foil. Bake for 40 to 50 minutes, until the squash is tender when pierced with a knife. Set aside for 15 minutes to cool.

Microwave directions: Place the squash halves cut side down, in a microwavable glass dish large enough to accommodate both halves. Add 1 cup of water; cover with microwavable plastic wrap and place in the microwave. Cook on high for 7 minutes. Check to see if the squash flesh is tender. If the flesh is still hard, microwave a few minutes more. Carefully remove the dish from the microwave and let the squash rest for 15 minutes to cool and continue steaming.

With a fork, scrape the strands of squash into a large pasta bowl, or colorful serving dish. Add the butter and chopped mint. Season generously with salt and pepper. Add the grated Parmesan cheese, if using. Toss gently. If the squash has cooled, pop it in the microwave for 2 to 4 minutes before serving.

zucchini and yellow-neck squash with heirloom tomatoes

This is the perfect late-summer side dish to serve alongside grilled meat or chicken. Zucchini is sometimes called green summer squash, and yellow-neck squash is nothing more exotic than yellow summer squash. What you call them depends on where you live. Heirloom tomatoes are sold at many farmers' markets and you may even grow them in your backyard garden, as I do. If you can't find them, never mind. Use any fresh, vine-ripened tomatoes.

• *serves 4 to 6*

¼ cup unsalted butter

2 tablespoons olive oil

1 white or red onion, peeled and chopped

1 clove garlic, peeled and minced

1 zucchini squash, washed and sliced into ¼-inch-thick rounds

1 yellow-neck squash, washed and sliced into ¼-inch-thick rounds

¼ cup dry vermouth

2 to 3 large heirloom tomatoes, blanched, peeled, seeded, and chopped

¼ cup finely chopped fresh herbs (parsley, thyme, and basil)
   or 2 teaspoons dried herbes de Provence

Salt and freshly ground black pepper, to taste

Heat the butter and olive oil in a sauté pan or large skillet until hot. Add the onion, garlic, squashes and sauté over medium-high heat, allowing them to caramelize for 6 to 8 minutes. Add the dry vermouth to deglaze the pan. Add the chopped heirloom tomatoes, herbs, and salt and pepper.

   Cover with a lid and cook for 2 minutes more. Remove from the heat and serve.

FUR TRADE GARDENS IN THE WEST

In the 1960s my mother Bay researched the possibilities of planting a fur trade garden in the Fort's courtyard, reasoning that nineteenth century forts had to have gardens for fresh vegetables and so ours did, too. She was very excited to discover the Museum of the Fur Trade where she could buy heirloom seeds for arikara watermelon, Mandan tobacco, flint and blue corn, hidatsa beans, and much more. As a child, I loved the small round, sweet watermelons that were the size of a softball and just right for a small girl.

Today, the Fort's garden produces squash, chiles, herbs and seasonal vegetables that our chefs use throughout the growing season.

The source for Indian fur trade garden seeds is the Museum of the Fur Trade in Chadron, Nebraska (www.furtrade.org) .

Here's an excerpt from their website on their Indian fur trade garden seeds:

"Because Indian agriculture helped provision the trading posts and transport crews, the museum maintains a botanical exhibit of authentic growing Indian crops. The varieties that we zealously perpetuate for the future are the same ones grown for centuries by Indians of the Missouri Valley and now are all but extinct. Oscar H. Will, pioneer Dakota horticulturist, originally obtained most of the seeds directly from the Indians over 125 years ago. Charles Hanson then acquired the seed stock from Will's son, George."

cha cha murphys

It's not surprising that potatoes were dubbed "murphys" in the nineteenth century, as a nod to the large numbers of Irish immigrants who moved west. They often stayed west of the Mississippi after serving in the army and ended up in Colorado or a neighboring state in search of work. Being in a region also heavily influenced by Mexican cooking, hot salsa cruda was often mixed into potatoes to jazz them up a little. At the Fort, we make a twice-baked potato with salsa. It's been on the menu for years and judging how much our customers like it, it won't be removed anytime soon.

• *serves 6*

4 (8-ounce) russet potatoes
½ to ¾ cup light cream
½ cup salsa cruda
6 ounces Cheddar cheese, grated (1½ cups)
½ cup grated Parmigiano-Reggiano cheese

Peel and quarter the potatoes. Cover with cold water, bring to a simmer, and cook for 20 to 30 minutes, until a knife can easily be inserted. When the potatoes are done, drain the water and return the potatoes to the pan placed over very low heat to evaporate the last of the water. This takes just a minute or two and gives you fluffier potatoes.

Preheat the oven to 350°F.

If you really want to build your arm strength, mash the potatoes with an old-fashioned masher and a colander. I prefer to use a potato ricer, which squeezes the potato through small holes. Bring the cream just to a simmer (don't boil it) and add it to the potatoes. Add the salsa cruda and grated cheese to the mashed potatoes and stir well. Pipe or spoon into individual ramekins or a 9-inch square casserole. You can use the back of a spoon to put the potatoes up into small peaks that will brown nicely. Sprinkle with the grated Parmigiano-Reggiano and bake for 20 minutes. Serve immediately.

san luis fingerling potatoes

If you aren't familiar with fingerling potatoes, here is a good way to try them. They are small, knobby potatoes that tend to be elongated and narrow, hence the name, with a lovely sweetness. While fingerlings are usually white potatoes, they also can be blue. They are small and thin-skinned but are not new (immature) potatoes and so have a more complex flavor. Fingerlings are grown in Colorado's San Luis Valley, which is also known for its quinoa and blue Peruvian potatoes. It's no surprise these crops do well here; we share a lofty altitude with Peru. • *serves 4 to 6*

1 pound fingerling potatoes, washed but not peeled
4 cups chicken broth or water
1 small white or red onion, chopped
1 tablespoon olive oil
Salt and freshly ground black pepper, to taste
¼ cup whipped butter, softened
¼ cup sour cream
1 teaspoon dried dill weed

Boil the fingerlings in the chicken broth for 20 minutes, or until tender when speared with a fork. While the potatoes are cooking, prepare the onion. In a skillet, heat the olive oil and add the onion and sauté over medium heat, until lightly browned and caramelized, 2 to 3 minutes. Sprinkle the onion with salt and pepper and set aside. When the fingerlings are cooked, drain them well.

In a small mixing bowl, whisk together the whipped butter, sour cream, and dill. If the mixture remains lumpy, microwave for 10 seconds, then whisk until smooth and fluffy. Gently fold in the onion. If necessary, warm the potatoes over a low to moderate heat on the stove. Serve topped with the whipped butter/sour cream sauce.

fort-style red potatoes with corn and anasazi beans

Looking for something to serve with a big, juicy, charred buffalo steak? At the Fort we serve all our steaks with this glorious potato-and-corn dish. We get our potatoes from Colorado's fertile San Luis Valley, although I suggest you use the freshest, most locally grown red potatoes you can find. • *serves 6 to 8*

1 cup dried Anasazi beans, soaked for at least 2 hours
1½ pounds small red potatoes, quartered
4 tablespoons unsalted butter
¼ cup canola oil
½ cup finely chopped yellow onion
1 teaspoon seasoned salt
½ cup fresh, frozen, or canned white shoepeg corn, drained
1 fresh green chile, diced (Anaheim chiles are excellent)
½ cup diced red bell pepper
¼ cup chopped Italian parsley
½ teaspoon toasted canola seeds (optional)

Drain the beans and place in a saucepan. Cover with fresh water and boil until soft, about 2 hours. Drain and set aside.

Preheat the oven to 400°F.

Boil the potato quarters in boiling salted water for 20 to 30 minutes, or until easily pierced with a knife, then drain well and bake on an ungreased baking sheet for 15 minutes; the bottoms will brown a bit.

In a large sauté pan, melt the butter with the oil over medium-high heat. When quite hot, add the onion and sauté for about 4 minutes, until lightly browned. Add the seasoned salt, corn, green chile, and red bell pepper. Cook for 2 minutes, then add the potatoes, beans, and parsley. Stir gently until well combined and heated through. Serve with a sprinkle of the canola seeds, if desired.

irish trappers champ

During the last few years of his life, Dad insisted we add this dish to the menu. And so we did, much to the delight of our customers. Dad had researched a potato dish called "champ" that was introduced to the American West in the nineteenth century by Irish immigrants. At the Fort, we serve it as a side dish, although it used to be a main dish, too. It's simple mashed potatoes enriched with lots of butter, cream, and green onions (also known as scallions). In some recipes, each forkful of potato is dipped in melted butter. Talk about rich! Colcannon is a related potato dish made with shredded, cooked cabbage stirred into the potatoes. • *serves 4 to 6*

2 to 2½ pounds red potatoes
½ to ¾ cup half-and-half or light cream
6 tablespoons unsalted butter
1⅓ cups chopped scallions (1 large bunch)
Salt and freshly ground black pepper, to taste

Peel the potatoes and cut into 2-inch pieces. Cook the potatoes in boiling salted water until tender, 12 to 15 minutes. Drain. Meanwhile, in a large deep skillet or sauté pan, combine the half-and-half and 4 tablespoons of butter. Add the scallions and bring to a simmer over medium heat. Reduce the heat to low and cook gently for 2 to 4 minutes.

Add the potatoes to the cream sauce, and season generously with salt and pepper. Stir until the potatoes are heated through and well coated. Spoon the potatoes into a serving bowl and top with the 2 tablespoons remaining butter. Serve at once.

arroz con huevos duros

When she was a nineteen-year-old bride in 1846, Susan Shelby Magoffin and her husband Samuel Magoffin set off down the Santa Fe Trail, which, unlike the Oregon and California trails, was strictly a trade route. Although the couple had honeymooned for six months in Philadelphia and New York, the trip west particularly excited Susan. Her trader husband, who was twenty-seven years her senior, made sure the journey was as luxurious and comfortable as possible for his new wife—for instance, every night a group of workers pitched a special tent and set up an actual bed with a mattress, sheets, blankets, and pillows. Susan, who was born in Kentucky to a wealthy family, was eager to keep a journal of her travels, a diary that was first published in 1926 by Yale University and called *Down the Santa Fe Trail and into Mexico.* In the journal, Susan speaks of stopping at Fort Bent, where the party waited for American soldiers to ensure their safe passage to Santa Fe. Susan was charmed by the Mexicans she met along the way and made an effort to learn to speak Spanish. She was especially impressed with the food, and in the journal she describes a large bowl of rice with hard-cooked eggs. My father researched this dish, among others, and found it was sometimes called *sopa seca,* or dry soup. In this recipe the rice is very moist, almost like a risotto, and could be served as a meatless main course or as a side dish.

When I reviewed Susan' original journal at the Beinecke Library at Yale, I was thrilled to discover more than fifty pages of poetry. No one has published Susan's poetry and so the Tesoro Cultural Center will publish the poetry of Susan Shelby Magoffin in the very near future. • *serves 4 to 6*

2 tablespoons olive or canola oil
1 ripe tomato, finely diced
1½ cups finely diced yellow onion (1 medium)
½ teaspoon dried Mexican leaf oregano
½ teaspoon salt
½ cup chopped green chiles (canned work well)
1 cup long-grain rice
2 cups low-sodium chicken broth
3 to 4 hard-cooked large eggs

OPTIONAL GARNISHES
A sprinkling of New Mexican ground red chile, and fresh cilantro or Italian parsley sprigs

Place the oil in a large deep skillet or sauté pan over medium-high heat. When the oil begins to smoke, add the tomato, onion, oregano, salt, and chiles. Stir quickly over medium-high heat until the onion is translucent and the tomato has browned a little. Add the rice and chicken broth and bring to a boil, stirring.

Reduce the heat to low, cover, and don't peek for 25 minutes. Spoon the rice onto a serving platter, and garnish with the eggs, cut in half lengthwise and placed yolk side up. A little dash of red chile dusted across the top makes for a wonderful presentation, with little sprigs of cilantro or parsley growing from the dish.

rice pilaf

At the Fort, we make rice pilaf with basmati rice from Pakistan, although American-grown basmati is also very good. We make the pilaf with a mixture of rice and quinoa, with the latter providing nuttiness and a chewy texture. We also stir in dried barberries, currants or cranberries. This lightly flavored pilaf is one of the best. • *serves 6 to 8*

1 cup basmati rice, well washed 6 times
8 strands saffron
½ cup dried currants
2 tablespoons barberries, see Note
1 cup quinoa

½ cup pine nuts, lightly toasted
¼ cup finely diced red bell pepper
¼ cup finely diced green bell pepper
½ cup flavorful olive oil
Salt and white pepper, to taste

Rinse the rice in 6 changes of cold water. I use a rice cooker at home to prepare the rice. Simply place the rice in the cooker with 2 cups water, the saffron, currants, and barberries. This marvelous machine will do everything for you and turns itself off when finished cooking. Leave the lid on until ready to use the rice. If you don't have a rice cooker, place the same ingredients in a wide 3-quart (or more) cooking pot with a lid. Bring to a boil, uncovered, and then turn the heat to low and simmer, covered, for about 20 minutes. Keeping the lid on, turn off the heat and let the rice steam for another 10 minutes, then open and fluff with a fork.

For the quinoa: While the rice is cooking, prepare the quinoa. Properly cooked quinoa has a wonderful texture, almost like caviar but without the fish taste. It has a slightly bitter taste, but the commercial milling process usually eliminates most of it. You should rinse the grain with cold water in a chinois or conical sieve, pushing your hand back and forth in it as the water pours through. Any remaining soapy dust will wash away and your quinoa will taste its best.

Cook the rinsed quinoa in 2 parts water to 1 part grain. It will take 12 to 15 minutes, depending on your altitude, far less time than the rice, so begin making it after the rice starts cooking. Don't cook it longer than it takes to soften and swell the little ball-shaped grain. Cooks who leave quinoa unattended will find the grains have gotten too hot and have popped and become flat, not nearly as good to eat.

Empty both the rice and quinoa into a large bowl. Using 2 forks, gently fold in the pine nuts, bell peppers, and olive oil. Because the peppers are finely diced, the heat of the rice will slightly soften them. Add the salt and pepper to taste.

Note: Barberries, which are dried, may be found in Middle Eastern groceries. Dried cranberries or dried sour cherries make interesting and flavorful substitutes, and may be easier to find.

wild mushroom risotto

Risotto is an irresistibly creamy rice dish that really shines when cooked with care. It demands time, standing over the hot stove and stirring, but is well worth it. This one is filled with "wild mushrooms," which are not really wild but are cultivated forest mushrooms with deep, earthy flavors. Try to use Italian Arborio, Carnaroli, or Vialone Nano rice if possible. These medium-grain, imported rices have high starch contents and the starch dissolves as the rice cooks and helps to form the creamy sauce. • *serves 4 to 6*

3 tablespoons unsalted butter

1½ cups chopped yellow onion (1 medium)

2 cups sliced wild mushrooms
(crimini, oyster, shiitake, porcini)

2 cups white Arborio rice

8 cups low-sodium chicken broth

½ cup dry white wine

1½ teaspoons concentrated mushroom bouillon base
(optional)

1 cup grated Parmigiano-Reggiano (Parmesan) cheese

Salt and freshly ground black pepper, to taste

Place the butter in a large, deep sauté pan over medium heat. When the butter melts and turns clear, add the onion and mushrooms. Cook, stirring for about 2 minutes, until the onion turns translucent and the mushrooms are lightly browned. Add the rice and sauté for 2 minutes, until coated with butter. Meanwhile, in a large saucepan, bring the chicken broth to a simmer. Set aside.

Add the wine to the rice mixture, and stir until the rice absorbs it. Stir the mushroom base, if using, into the broth. Slowly, in 1-cup increments, add the hot broth to the rice, stirring over medium-low to low heat, until the rice absorbs the liquid. This should take about 20 minutes. When all of the broth has been absorbed and the rice is creamy and tender, but still slightly firm, stir in the Parmesan cheese. Season with salt and pepper and serve immediately. Risotto may be served as a main course or as a side dish.

THE HISTORY OF RICE IN THE SOUTHWEST

When most people think of western cooking, they may conjure up meals heavy with potatoes, biscuits, and corn, but rice is not something that immediately springs to mind. Of course, when you think of Mexican food, rice is front and center and so it stands to reason it would be a familiar ingredient in the foods of the Southwest.

The Spanish brought rice to the New World in the 1500s and watched the crop flourish. When the conquistadores ventured north from Mexico, they packed rice in their saddlebags because it was easy to carry, easy to cook, and it was always filling. By the 1800s, rice was common in the West. It was served at Fort Bent and many a beaver trapper cooked it over a campfire deep in the Rocky Mountain woodlands.

▼▼▼▼▼▼▼▼▼▼▼▼▼▼▼▼▼▼▼▼▼▼▼▼

breads
from the oven

▾▾▾▾▾▾▾▾▾▾▾▾

indian horno bread

We developed this bread to resemble bread baked in the horno oven. It's not exactly the same, of course, but will give you an idea of how amazing that bread, cooked at a relatively high temperature, tastes. • *makes 2 loaves*

1 tablespoon (1¼-ounce package) active dry yeast

¼ cup lukewarm water

4½ tablespoons melted lard or shortening

4½ cups sifted all-purpose flour

1 teaspoon salt

1 cup water

In the bowl of a standing mixer with a dough hook attachment, dissolve the yeast in the lukewarm water. Let stand until the yeast foams, about 5 minutes. Mix in 2 tablespoons of the melted shortening, blending thoroughly. Sift together the flour and salt, then add the flour and water alternately, mixing until a smooth dough forms. Place the dough in an oiled bowl, turning once so that the top is oiled. Cover with a damp cloth and let rise until double in size, about 1 hour. Two fingers stuck into the dough will leave impressions.

Preheat the oven to 400°F.

When the dough has doubled, punch it down and knead vigorously on a lightly floured board for at least 5 minutes. Shape into 2 balls and place on a greased baking sheet. Brush the loaves with the remaining 2½ tablespoons melted shortening and let them rise in a warm place for 15 minutes. Bake for 50 minutes or until the loaves are lightly browned.

High/Low Altitude Baking Guide

Our recipes are designed to be baked in the Fort's kitchens, which are at 6,000 feet. If you live at a different elevation, you will have to make adjustments. Adjustments for sea level baking are included with those recipes that are affected. We also provide this guide, which works with our recipes.

Baking powder and baking soda:
At sea level, increase each teaspoon by ¼
At 3,000 feet, increase each teaspoon by about ⅛
At 7,000 feet, decrease each teaspoon by about ½
At 10,000 feet, decrease each teaspoon by about ⅔

Flour:
At sea level, decrease each cup by 2 tablespoons
At 3,000 feet, decrease each cup by 1 tablespoon
At 7,000 feet, increase each cup by 3 to 4 tablespoons
At 10,000 feet, increase each cup by 2 to 4 tablespoons

Sugar:
At sea level, increase amount by 2 tablespoons
At 3,000 feet, increase each cup by 1 tablespoon
At 7,000 feet, decrease each cup by 2 to 4 tablespoons
At 10,000 feet, decrease each cup by 3 to 4 tablespoons

Liquid:
At sea level, decrease each cup by 2 to 3 tablespoons
At 3,000 feet, decrease each cup by 2 tablespoons
At 7,000 feet, increase each cup by 3 to 4 tablespoons
At 10,000 feet, increase each cup by 3 to 4 tablespoons

Baking temperatures and baking times:
At sea level, decrease the oven temperature by 25 degrees if it is higher than 350°F.
At sea level, add 5 to 8 minutes of baking time for every 30 minutes of baking.

OUR HORNO OVEN

In the courtyard of the Fort is a beautiful adobe oven called a horno and very similar to those you find on the Pueblo reservations in Arizona and New Mexico. While baking in one of these ovens is a centuries-old tradition, it's not as ancient as you might think. Horno ovens were introduced to the Southwest by the Spanish, many of whom were of Moorish descent (the Moors, who were part of the Islamic Empire, ruled Spain for nearly seven hundred years). The ovens are similar to those used in North Africa, which is not surprising when you know the history of Spain and the settling of Mexico and the Southwest United States.

The Spanish, with their Moorish heritage, introduced technologies beyond the horno oven that were quickly embraced by the people living in the New World. These included adobe bricks and the craft of making mosaic tiles so that today, exquisite, colorful Mexican tiles are admired around the world. The Spanish brought domesticated farm animals with them, too, and soon Navajos were weaving their now-famous rugs from the wool of churro sheep.

Our horno oven is used primarily for demonstrations; we don't bake bread in it for the restaurant. The bread we pull from the oven during these demonstrations is earthy and full flavored and with each bite reconnects you to a way of life that has, for most of us, become a dim memory.

The oven has an arched opening and a tiny smoke hole near the top of the structure. We light the wood and let it cook for at least three hours. To ensure that the oven reaches a high temperature, the burlap used to cover the opening is soaked in water and then put in place. We build the fire with hardwood, which burns for a long time, although we have been known to use aspen and pine as well. Once the wood has burned down to coals, it's raked from the oven and the bread, which has had ample time to rise, is immediately put in the oven. By this time, the interior of the oven is about 450°F, although we don't use a thermometer to gauge the heat. We hold our hand just inside the oven's opening and if we can't keep it there for longer than three seconds, the oven is ready for the bread.

Once the bread is put in the oven, the door and smoke hole are sealed, the former with the burlap flap and the latter with a stick wrapped in burlap. After about 20 minutes, the bread is checked. If it's golden brown and sounds hollow when thumped, it's done.

▼▼▼▼▼▼▼▼▼▼▼▼▼▼▼▼▼▼▼▼

herb bread

A bread seasoned with no fewer than five different herbs and garlic is sure to get your senses going. We served this at the Fort throughout the 1990s with soups and salads and it still finds its way onto our menu from time to time.

• *serves 8 to 10; makes 2 loaves*

1 tablespoon (1 package) active dry yeast

1 tablespoon sugar

1 cup lukewarm water

2 tablespoons vegetable oil

3 to 3½ cups all-purpose flour

1 teaspoon salt

1 teaspoon garlic powder

1 teaspoon ground oregano

1 teaspoon dried leaf oregano

1 teaspoon dried thyme

1 teaspoon dried rosemary

1 tablespoon dried dill weed

2 tablespoons dried parsley

A sprinkling of cornmeal

In a large mixing bowl, dissolve the yeast and sugar in the water and set aside for about 10 minutes so that it bubbles and foams. Add the oil. In a separate bowl, stir together the flour, salt, and herbs. Add to the yeast mixture and mix thoroughly to form a soft dough. Place it in an oiled bowl, turning the dough once so that the top is oiled. Cover with a wet cloth and let rise in a warm place until double in size, about 1 hour.

Punch the dough down and let it rise again for about 1 hour. This helps develop the flavor of the yeast. Turn out onto a floured board. Shape into two 12-inch French loaves and place them on a greased cookie sheet that has been sprinkled with cornmeal. Slash the tops diagonally. Cover and let rise again for about 1 hour or until doubled.

Preheat the oven to 375°F (350°F at sea level). Bake for 25 to 30 minutes until golden. Let the bread cool on a wire rack. Serve warm or cooled to room temperature.

ranch-style pan bread

This quick bread is easy to make and has a light, cakey texture. When folks traveled west on wagon trains, they did not have ovens to bake bread, and so they devised ways to make bread in deep pots and skillets. The Germans, many of whom were from Pennsylvania and were called the Pennsylvania Dutch, are responsible for the term "Dutch oven" as a pot for baking. • *serves 4 to 6*

2 cups sifted all-purpose flour (decrease flour by 2 tablespoons at sea level)
3 teaspoons baking powder (3¾ teaspoons at sea level)
1 teaspoon salt
6 tablespoons vegetable shortening
1¼ cups milk (1 cup + 2 tablespoons at sea level)

Preheat the oven to 450°F (425°F at sea level).

Combine the flour, baking powder, salt and shortening in a food processor, and pulse on and off until the mixture has the texture of coarse meal. Add the milk and pulse on and off until the dough comes together, being careful not to overmix. The dough will be quite sticky.

Scrape the dough into a greased, 9-inch, heavy iron skillet, smooth the top, and bake for 25 to 30 minutes (30 to 35 minutes at sea level) or until deep golden brown. Trust your eyes to tell you when this bread is done, not the clock.

For crustier bread, spread the dough more thinly in a 10-inch greased iron skillet and bake until deep golden brown.

bannock bread with dried western fruit

Bannock bread is another easy quick bread. It was developed to be cooked in whatever pan was handy and often on top of the stove or over a campfire, although in this recipe, it's baked in the oven. It's thought of as a western bread since the pioneers made it on the trail and also when they homesteaded. Because of this history, it's also called bush bread or trail bread. Bannock was one of the first homemade breads we served at the Fort in 1963 when we opened and, although I was a child, I have fond memories of waiting for it to be pulled, piping hot, from the oven. I loved to break a piece off the loaf and smell the aroma of warm dried fruits and yummy bread. • *serves 6*

⅓ cup melted unsalted butter

2 cups all-purpose flour

2 teaspoons baking powder (reduce to 1½ teaspoons
   or 1 teaspoon at high altitudes)

½ teaspoon salt

2½ teaspoons sugar

⅓ cup sweetened dried cranberries

⅓ cup dried blueberries or currants

¾ cup milk

Preheat the oven to 350°F. Brush the bottom and sides of a heavy, 9-inch iron skillet or 8- to 9-inch shallow baking pan with butter. Reserve remaining butter.

Sift the flour, baking powder, and salt into a medium mixing bowl. Stir in the sugar and dried fruit. Add the milk and the remaining butter, and stir with a wooden spatula to form a moist, but not sticky dough. Gently press the dough into the buttered skillet. Bake on the middle rack of the oven for about 30 minutes, until the loaf is golden brown. Serve bannock warm with sweet butter.

INDIAN FRY BREAD, DESCRIBED BY SAM'L ARNOLD

It's not known exactly when or how fry bread came to the Plains Indians. It was certainly not until they had metal kettles for frying and that was after trade began with whites. There is no indication that frying in pottery or on a hot rock was part of the pre-Columbian culture, and so it stands to reason that the cooking method was probably introduced to the Indians in the form of the German or Dutch settlers' doughnuts called "oily cakes."

This recipe was first prepared for me in 1969 by a woman from the Brule tribe, a branch of Sioux Indians in South Dakota. I was visiting the Rosebud Sioux Indian Reservation to film traditional American Indian dishes for my PBS series, *Frying Pans West.*

The woman prepared the dough by hand, mixing dry ingredients in a bowl and then beating in small amounts of water with a long wooden spoon until a moist but firm dough had formed. After kneading it well, she rolled out a grapefruit-sized ball of dough with a piece of broom handle to about ½-inch thick and cut it into pieces measuring about 4 by 5 inches. Pueblo Indians, on the other hand, traditionally make disks with ¾-inch holes punched through their centers. The hole serves two purposes: It allows the hot fat to flow through and cook the top surface of the bread and it allows for easy removal when the bread is done.

In South Dakota, the baker dropped the dough pieces into an iron kettle filled with very hot, nearly smoking melted pork lard and immediately began spooning hot fat over the dough. The resulting steam inside the dough caused it to puff up beautifully. We ate the fry bread with honey and sprinkled with cinnamon sugar, both traditional toppings.

▼▼▼▼▼▼▼▼▼▼▼▼▼▼▼▼▼▼▼▼▼

lakota indian fry bread

We serve Indian fry bread at the Tesoro Cultural Center's annual Indian Market Powwow held in mid-May, following a recipe very similar to this one. It's for basic bread dough leavened with baking powder. The dough is formed into flat rectangles or disks and cooked in hot lard. The process is quick and uncomplicated and the crispy light bread makes a marvelous treat. • *serves 4 to 6; makes about 20 pieces of bread*

1 quart tallow, lard, or canola oil for deep-frying

1 3/4 cups all-purpose flour (decrease by 2 1/2 tablespoons at sea level), plus more for rolling out

1 1/2 teaspoons baking powder (1 3/4 teaspoons at sea level)

3/4 teaspoon salt

Honey or cinnamon sugar, for serving

Heat the oil in a deep pot to 380°F. The best flavor comes from either beef tallow (rendered beef fat) or lard, but with today's food fashion, health-conscious people use canola oil.

The easiest way to make fry bread is with a dough hook attachment on an electric mixer. In the mixer bowl, thoroughly combine the flour, baking powder, and salt. Add 3/4 cup water and mix until a supple, uniform dough forms. Add more water if needed to achieve a dough that is not too sticky but not too dry.

Divide the dough into 4 to 6 equal portions, and form each portion into 3 or 4 rounds. Roll out the rounds on a floured surface to a thickness of between 1/2 and 1/4 inch.

If you'd like to try Pueblo-style fry bread, use your finger to make a 3/4-inch hole in the center of each piece of dough. If you don't have a thermometer to check the heat of your oil, carefully lower a small piece of dough into the hot oil. It should blister and puff up instantly. In the first few seconds of frying, use a spoon to pour fat over the bread to make sure all surfaces fry immediately. Remove and drain on a paper towel. Allow a full minute between batches to bring the oil back up to temperature.

Many people dip fry bread in honey or bite a hole in the side and squeeze honey into the center. Others sprinkle cinnamon sugar on it. Whatever your pleasure, the most important thing about fry bread is that it must be eaten hot immediately after it's cooked.

jalapeño cornbread

This bread is one of the most requested dishes at the Fort, and for good reason. We spike it with jalapeños and enrich it with coconut milk, admittedly not a common ingredient in the Old West! Indigenous people across the continent introduced settlers from Europe to corn and all its uses, and so today, cornbread is as commonplace in New England as New Mexico. I love this with a hearty soup or stew. • *serves 6*

1 tablespoon plus 1½ teaspoons vegetable oil

1 cup yellow or white cornmeal

1 cup all-purpose flour

¼ cup sugar

2½ teaspoons baking powder (1 tablespoon at sea level)

1 teaspoon salt

2 large eggs

2 cups coconut milk

⅓ cup minced fresh jalapeños, seeds and ribs removed

½ cup well-drained, canned, golden corn kernels

Preheat the oven to 425°F. Grease a 9-inch heavy cast-iron skillet or square baking pan with 1½ teaspoons vegetable oil.

In a large mixing bowl, stir together the cornmeal, flour, sugar, baking powder, and salt. In a separate bowl, whisk together the eggs, coconut milk, jalapeños, corn, and the remaining 1 tablespoon of oil. With a wooden spatula, mix the wet ingredients into the dry ingredients until just combined.

Pour the batter into the prepared skillet and place on the middle rack of the oven. Immediately reduce the oven temperature to 350°F. Bake for 35 to 45 minutes, until the bread is a pale golden brown. Do not overbake. Serve cornbread warm with sweet butter.

bay's southern spoon bread

My mother Bay may have adopted Colorado as her home for many years, but she was a Southerner, born and bred in Georgia and part of a family with roots dating back to the eighteenth century. This recipe was first written in the 1700s and passed down through the generations until it landed in my mother's childhood kitchen. In a lovely ostrich leather-bound notebook, Mom wrote down this and many other recipes in her clear, beautiful handwriting. It goes without saying that I treasure this small book. Most of the recipes are accompanied with a few lines of family history and this one is meant to be served on Sunday evenings "with a silver spoon, of course." I adore the spoon bread's pure cornmeal flavor and custard-like texture. My husband prefers it flavored with cheese or spices; I like it best with cane syrup, molasses, or raw honey. • *serves 4 to 6*

1 ½ tablespoons unsalted butter
2 cups half-and-half or whole milk (1 ¾ cups at sea level)
1 cup white or yellow cornmeal (preferably stone ground)
3 large eggs, separated
1 teaspoon baking powder (1 ¼ teaspoons at sea level)
1 teaspoon salt
Cane syrup, molasses, or honey, for serving

Preheat the oven to 350°F. Generously butter a shallow, 8-inch baking dish that can be brought to the table. Reserve the remaining 1 tablespoon butter.

In a large saucepan over medium heat, bring the half-and-half almost to a simmer. Gradually stir in the cornmeal, whisking constantly until the mixture thickens, 2 to 3 minutes. Off the heat, whisk in the egg yolks, one at a time, the baking powder, salt, and the remaining 1 tablespoon butter. In the clean bowl of an electric mixer, beat the egg whites until they stand in stiff peaks. Fold the beaten whites into the cornmeal mixture.

Spoon the batter into the prepared baking dish and smooth the surface. Bake for 35 to 45 minutes or until the spoon bread has set and is beginning to turn golden. Serve as soon as possible, with a silver spoon, of course! Drizzle with cane syrup, molasses, or honey.

Variation: *Cheddar and Ham Spoon Bread:* To the recipe above, add ¼ teaspoon freshly ground black pepper, ¼ teaspoon freshly grated nutmeg, ⅛ teaspoon cayenne pepper, 1 tablespoon butter, 1 cup shredded sharp Cheddar cheese, and ¾ cup chopped ham.

Prepare the corn batter as described in the master recipe, and add the pepper, nutmeg, and cayenne to the seasonings. Fold the cheese and ham into the warm cornmeal mixture. Fold in the stiffly beaten egg whites and bake as described above. Serve this savory spoon bread as a light main course, accompanied by a green salad.

quinoa muffins

Quinoa contains more usable protein than any other grain, and it is said that a man can easily work a twelve-hour day on one cup of it. So far this claim has gone unproven at the Fort; with so much great food around, who can stop after a single cup of quinoa? We have an accommodating and faithful staff, but none of them has volunteered to test it. Nevertheless, these healthful muffins are divine—nutty, a little crunchy and with undertones of orange and just a tiny bit sweet. • *makes about 1 dozen muffins*

2 large eggs
½ cup canola oil
½ cup brown sugar (½ cup + 2 tablespoons at sea level)
⅓ cup honey
1 teaspoon baking soda (1¼ teaspoons at sea level)
½ teaspoon orange oil or 1½ teaspoons finely grated orange peel
¾ cup quinoa flour
½ cup all-purpose flour
¼ cup wheat germ
2 tablespoons yellow cornmeal
¾ teaspoon baking powder (1 teaspoon at sea level)
½ teaspoon salt
¼ cup canola seeds (poppy seeds may be substituted)
½ cup coarsely chopped walnuts, toasted
¼ to ½ cup milk, plus more if needed

Preheat the oven to 375°F (350°F at sea level). Grease a 3-inch muffin pan or fill it with paper liners.

In a mixing bowl, combine the eggs, oil, brown sugar, honey, baking soda, and orange oil, blending thoroughly. Add both flours and the wheat germ, cornmeal, baking powder, salt, canola seeds, and walnuts. Mix well and add ¼ cup milk. If the batter seems too dry, add a little more milk. The batter should be thick but not stiff.

Fill greased or paper-lined 3-inch muffin tins to three-quarters full and bake for about 20 to 25 minutes until golden brown. Cool the muffins in the pan for a few minutes and then remove from the pan and serve warm or cooled to room temperature.

pumpkin-walnut muffins

A 1975 Fort menu reads: "The pumpkin-nut muffins are a closely guarded secret; the recipe is asked for nightly but never revealed." Finally, the secret is out! Turns out, it's not much of a secret at all but is all about the pumpkin. These muffins contain nearly twice as much as other recipes. Because of this, they're cooked for a relatively long time at a moderate temperature and turn out especially dense, moist, and flavorful.

• *makes about 3 dozen mini muffins or 12 to 16 large muffins*

1 ⅓ cups all purpose flour (1 cup + 3 tablespoons at sea level)
½ cup brown sugar (½ cup + 2 tablespoons at sea level)
⅓ cup granulated sugar (⅓ cup + 2 tablespoons at sea level)
1 tablespoon baking powder (1 tablespoon + ¾ teaspoon at sea level)
1 ½ teaspoons ground cinnamon
¼ teaspoon salt
½ cup chopped lightly toasted walnuts
½ cup golden raisins
1 large egg
⅓ cup plus 1 tablespoon canola oil
⅓ cup plus 1 tablespoon 2% milk (⅓ cup at sea level)
1 can (15-ounces) pumpkin (not pie filling)

Preheat the oven to 350 F. Grease 2 mini muffin tins or 1 large muffin tin or line with paper baking cups.

In a large mixing bowl, combine the flour, sugars, baking powder, cinnamon, and salt. Stir in the walnuts and raisins until all the ingredeints are well mixed

In a separate bowl, whisk the egg, canola oil, milk and pumpkin until well combined.

Gradually stir the pumpkin mixture into the dry ingredients just until well mixed. The batter should be easy to scoop. If it is too thick, add a little more milk.

Fill the muffin tins three-quarters full and bake 25 to 30 minutes for mini muffins and 45 to 50 minutes for larger muffins, or until a toothpick inserted in the center of a muffin comes out clean. Rotate the muffin tins once halfway through baking to insure even baking.

Let muffins cool for about 10 minutes before removing them from the tins. Let them cool completely on wire racks before removing the paper baking cups. Because they are so moist, these reheat beautifully.

MY DAD TALKS ABOUT PUMPKINS IN THE WEST

The bright orange pumpkins dotting the fields throughout Colorado played a great role in the state's history. The first domesticated pumpkin was grown in 7000 BC in Mexico's northeastern Tamaulipas region. Seeds were traded to other tribes, and by 3000 BC, pumpkins had traveled to Puebla, Mexico. Within another five hundred years, pumpkins had journeyed as far as Peru.

Pumpkins traveled north, too. The basket makers in Colorado's Durango and Mesa Verde areas grew them before AD 400. The Indian diet consisted of corn, beans, and various squashes, including our common pumpkin. When the fur trappers arrived in the region in the early 1800s, pumpkin became a major part of their diets. Mountain men such as Kit Carson, Uncle Dick Wootten and others who frequented the original Bent's Fort were familiar with pumpkin.

On an 1842 visit to Colorado's Fort Lancaster (later Fort Lupton), Rufus Sage tells of a trading party of Mexicans from Taos who brought with them pack horses and mules laden with corn, bread, beans, onions, and dried pumpkin to barter for the buffalo robes, furs, guns, and tobacco sold at the Fort. Today thousands of pumpkins are grown near Fort Lupton.

▼▼▼▼▼▼▼▼▼▼▼▼▼▼▼▼▼▼▼▼▼▼

meats of the
great plains

world's best beef or buffalo prime rib roast

We've been serving juicy prime rib buffalo since the 1960s and our customers have always loved it. We roast it surrounded by onion skins and the outer layers of the onion, which impart amazing flavor to the meat as it smokes and chars in the oven. When I was a little girl, the aroma of roasting buffalo and caramelizing onion literally made my mouth water. When the roast comes to the table, you might be tempted to shout "Hip, hip, huzzah!"—and for good reason! • *serves 8 to 10*

1 (5- to 6-pound) beef or buffalo prime standing rib roast
   or 1 (4- to 5-pound) boneless prime rib roast
½ cup beef base concentrate (available at meat markets or in specialty stores)
¼ cup freshly pureed garlic (about 2 heads)
½ cup dried rosemary
Coarsely ground black pepper
¼ cup vegetable oil
Outer peels of 4 large onions

Rub the roast with the beef base concentrate and then the garlic. Sprinkle the rosemary and pepper over all, letting it stick to the beef base. Wipe the oil on your hands and gently rub the herbs into the roast.

Let stand 1 hour at room temperature.

Preheat the oven to 500°F. Place the roast on a foil-covered roasting pan. Arrange the onion peels around the base of the roast and place in the oven. Roast for 8 minutes, so that the onion peels burn and the smoke lightly penetrates the meat, then lower the heat to 250°F. Roast for 18 minutes per pound, or until a meat thermometer read 125°F for rare or 138°F for medium rare. The low temperature will keep the roast tender. Don't cook buffalo any longer; because of its leanness, it will be tough if cooked more than medium rare.

Remove the roast from the oven and allow it to rest for 15 to 20 minutes before carving. The temperature will rise about 10 degrees while resting, bringing the meat to the correct serving temperature.

william bent's buffalo tenderloin filet mignon

In my opinion, this is the best meat in the house. Clearly a lot of others feel the same way, as we sell more than seventy thousand buffalo entrées every year, and 70 percent of those are tenderloin. Recently, a guest approached me and announced he was from Paris, France. "All my life I have thought that Chateaubriand was the *ne plus ultra* of cuts, but now I must return to France and tell my friends that Chateaubriand is garbage. The best meat in the world is buffalo tenderloin." Need I say more?

Make sure your butcher cuts away the tough, sinewy strap running along the tenderloin. This makes the cut look almost square. It should be 1- to 1½-inches thick. You don't need more than eight ounces, unless you are very hungry!

• *serves 1*

½ teaspoon fine sea salt

⅛ teaspoon lemon crystals (citric acid or sour salt)

¾ teaspoon freshly ground black pepper

1 (8-ounce) buffalo or beef tenderloin steak

Canola oil

1 teaspoon minced Italian parsley (optional)

2 teaspoons Herb Butter, recipe follows, or plain unsalted butter

Preheat the broiler or heat a grill to high. Combine the sea salt, lemon crystals, and pepper. Dust each steak with the mixture, coating liberally on both sides, then brush lightly with the oil. (The order is important here—no oiling before seasoning.)

Place the steaks about 6 inches from a medium-hot fire. Cook for 11 to18 minutes (depending on thickness), or until the meat is medium rare. Turn every 4 minutes. Because bison is so lean, it tends to be tough when cooked more than medium rare, so it's important not to overcook.

Sprinkle with the parsley, if using. A disk of herb butter gives this steak even greater magnificence. This is not precisely what the doctor ordered, but if your weight and cholesterol are fine, go for it every blue moon. It's worth a lot of penance. The smell of the butter melting on a hot steak is intoxicating.

Note: This recipe works beautifully with beef T-bone steaks, too. Splurge and buy the best beef you can, which means USDA prime meat, or a high-grade of USDA choice, such as Angus. A thick T-bone—1- to 1½-inches thick—will probably result in leftovers, but since the meat makes great sandwiches, this is rarely a problem. If you cook thinner steaks, watch them very carefully so that they don't overcook. Porterhouse steak, which is similar to a T-bone, just with a bigger eye or tenderloin, works well for 2 servings. Cut the meat away from the bone before serving so that you can cut the tenderloin into 2 portions. Slice the strip side crosswise into an even number of pieces and then divide the meat.

herb butter

- *makes about 1 pound*

2 tablespoons chopped shallot (1 medium)
2 tablespoons chopped Italian parsley
2 tablespoons chopped fresh basil leaves
1 tablespoon snipped fresh chives
1 tablespoon chopped fresh cilantro leaves
1½ teaspoons minced garlic (1 clove)
1½ teaspoons fresh thyme or ¼ teaspoon dried leaf thyme
1½ teaspoons fresh rosemary leaves
1½ teaspoons fresh lemon juice
1 teaspoon kosher salt
1 pound unsalted butter, at room temperature
1 to 2 tablespoons white wine
1 teaspoon Worcestershire sauce

Place the shallot, parsley, basil, chives, cilantro, garlic, thyme, and rosemary in a food processor. Pulse on and off until pureed. Add the lemon juice and salt. Put the butter and herb puree in an electric mixer and beat with the paddle attachment. Add the wine and Worcestershire and beat until all the ingredients are fully incorporated.

Wrap the butter in plastic wrap, forming it into 2 logs, about 2 inches in diameter. Store in the refrigerator or freezer until firm. With a sharp knife dipped in cold water, cut off a ½-inch-thick slice of herb butter to top a sizzling hot steak. Herb butter may be stored in the refrigerator for several days and in the freezer for up to 2 months.

BISON NUTRITION INFORMATION

	Mg/100 grams			
	Protein	Fat	Calories	Cholesterol
Bison rib-eye	22.2	2.2	148	61
Beef choice rib-eye	22.0	6.5	180	72
Skinless chicken breast	23.6	0.7	167	62
Pork rib-eye	22.3	4.9	165	71

toothless charlie's ground buffalo or beef steak

Ground buffalo or ground sirloin make delicious burgers and this one is about as good as it gets. We named it after our friend Chief Big Cloud, also known as Charlie Randall, whose poor teeth prevented him from chewing steak, but he happily can eat this. We add the vanilla and ice as "secret ingredients" to provide the desirable moisture.

• *serves 6*

6 (8-ounce) beef or buffalo tenderloins, chopped into ¼-inch pieces
½ cup finely minced white onion or Bermuda onion
2 tablespoons Worcestershire sauce
1½ to 2 teaspoons seasoned salt
1 teaspoon pure vanilla extract
1½ cups finely crushed ice
Salt and freshly ground black pepper
Toasted walnut halves for topping (optional)
1 large bunch whole Italian parsley leaves, for serving

Heat a skillet or charcoal grill to high heat. Combine the meat, onion, Worcestershire, seasoned salt, vanilla, and ice in a mixing bowl. Divide the mixture into 6 equal portions and form patties approximately 1-inch thick. Be careful not to compress the meat too much. I prefer these medium rare with a well-done outer crust. You can ensure this by waiting until your grill or skillet is really hot before the meat goes on. Season with salt and pepper while grilling and try to turn only once.

If Uncle Charlie is indeed toothless, then don't add nuts. But I enjoy these steaks best topped with toasted walnut halves or "eagles" and placed on a bed of parsley.

Note: If using buffalo, be sure to watch it carefully on the grill. The meat's leanness makes it very easy to overcook, and overcooking buffalo is a travesty.

A SHORT HISTORY OF A BIG ANIMAL, BY SAM'L ARNOLD

Early writers tell us that Boston's crooked streets leading down to the Charles River originally were buffalo trails. The last bison east of the Appalachians was killed in about 1830, although by that time the great herds of the plains had hardly been touched by the relatively few Native Americans living there. Colorado, for example, was believed to be home to fewer than eight thousand Indians, and these were small bands of Cheyenne, Sioux, Arapaho, Lakota, and Ute, just a few people in a territory the size of New Zealand and far fewer than go to a shopping mall on a Saturday afternoon. The bison were far from endangered, and the Native Americans took only what they needed.

The Indian used every part of the carcass. Tongues, hearts, livers, kidneys, and testicles were removed for choice eating and the rest of the meat was sliced along the grain into thin sheets for drying to make jerky. Drying racks in Indian camps were always filled with meat, so necessary for winter stews made with dried squashes, cattails, prairie potatoes, wild onions and garlic, and dried maize. This stew was called washtunkala by the Sioux and is still eaten today. It's pretty good!

When the "white eyes," as the Indians called the white mountain men, went west, they learned Indian ways of cooking. Pieces of buffalo meat skewered on wood sticks were called buffalo en appolas and were broiled over open fires. Jerked buffalo meat was commonplace, too. Pounded with chokecherries and mixed with melted kidney fat, it formed a pasty mixture called pemmican and was the sustainable ration of both Native Americans and mountain men.

The ultimate delicacy was the buffalo tongue, which has a fine, smooth grain and delicate flavor. It was served by the train-car full at the finest restaurants in the nation. I've looked high and low for a nineteenth century cookbook with recipes for buffalo or bison but can find none, although many letters and journals make references to eating it.

As trains crisscrossed the nation, train companies ran advertisements promising to "clean and dress the buffalo" if one of their passengers "bagged one." The train engineer would drive the locomotives into the middle of buffalo herds crossing the tracks and passengers could shoot them from the train windows. Not quite the same sport as riding bareback into the center of a herd with bow and arrow, pumping hunting arrows into fat young cows surrounded by mean old bulls! Low-paid buffalo skinners dressed the kills on the spot, salting the hides to preserve them until the mighty train hunter returned to St. Louis, where it was transformed into a buffalo robe for winter sleigh-riding comfort.

It is little wonder that by 1910 reports indicated that only 254 buffalo existed worldwide—and this count included a bison in a zoo in Calcutta, India. By the time James Fraser designed the Indian head buffalo nickel, minted from 1913 until 1938, the white men had effectively wiped out the animals. In so doing, they stripped Native Americans of food, clothing, and shelter, efficiently destroying their way of life and forcing them to join the white man's world.

By the first half of the twentieth century, bison became largely mythical creatures not only of the American West but of the past. Small herds were seen by lucky travelers to national parks such as Yellowstone in Wyoming.

I knew little about these animals in 1963 when I opened the Fort, but when I set out to learn all I could about the original Bent's Fort, I found that Kit Carson had had a contract with the Best St. Vrain Company to bring in one thousand pounds of meat a day, and most of it was buffalo. I looked into serving buffalo and found several ranches in the western states. Instead of being extinct, I discovered that the herds were steadily increasing.

When we began offering buffalo, we had a hard time getting people to try it. "I'm not a tourist, I'm from around here and I've tasted buffalo," they'd say. "I'll stick to beef!" The attitude was understandable because quality was spotty and sometimes just plain bad. Once in a while we'd get meat so tough it had to have come from an old cow. I quickly got to know my purveyors and since then we at the Fort have been insistent on getting nothing but the best meat from young bulls that are between eighteen and twenty-six months old.

Today we serve buffalo tenderloin steaks, New York-style strip steaks, sirloin on a skewer, and roast prime rib. Appetizer plates include broiled split buffalo marrow bones, tongue, homemade sausage called "boudies," and testicles, also known as Rocky Mountain oysters.

By the dawn of the twenty-first century, buffalo numbered well over 350,000 in this country and herds are increasing quickly in size and number. Buffalo ranches exist in all fifty states, including Rhode Island. Countries such as Germany and Switzerland boast a few herds, too. The renaissance of the American bison is an important trend in food history. It's an essential part of our New World American heritage, truly a food of the Old West.

gonzales steak

Our customers love this steak, which has been on the menu since 1964—although its presence was made possible only after a good-natured squabble between my dad and Elidio Gonzales, the renowned wood carver from Taos, New Mexico, who was so important to the Fort in its early days (see page 81). Here is how my father described the sequence of events that led to the creation of this full-flavored steak dish.

"On April 1, 1964, Elidio Gonzales, the gifted Taos *madero* (wood craftsman) came to Denver to give wood-carving demonstrations at the Fort. When he called me from town for help, hopelessly lost among Denver's one-way streets, I was tempted to repeat to him what he'd told me in late October after a heavy snowfall. At that time, I had harangued him for being three months late finishing the Fort's doors. "People in Hell always want ice water!" Elidio had said.

The old adage about wanting what you couldn't have had taken the wind out of my sails and I had waited patiently for another month before the doors arrived. Elidio now needed my help. As I drove to town and led him back to the Fort, I pondered how I could teach him an April Fool's Day lesson. The solution came to me when he asked for a steak with chiles.

"This is no Mexican restaurant!" I thundered. "We don't have any chile here," I fibbed.

"Oh, you damned gringos, you don't know what's good," he replied. "All you eat is meat and potatoes!"

I then went back to the kitchen, cut a pocket into a thick sirloin, stuffed it with chopped green chiles, and grilled the steak. I placed it in front of a grumbling Elidio and watched him take a bite. "April Fools, Elidio!" I shouted.

"April Fools to you, too!" he replied without missing a beat. "You're the bigger fool for not having this on your menu!"

He was right, of course. The Gonzales steak has happily and proudly been on the menu since. Elidio passed away years ago, but his furniture and his steak live on. • *serves 1*

3 green Anaheim chiles, roasted and peeled (canned will do, but fresh are best)
Salt
1 clove garlic, chopped
Pinch of dried Mexican oregano
1 (10- to 12-ounce) thick cut, New York strip, top sirloin, or tenderloin, buffalo, or beef steak
1 to 2 teaspoons canola oil
Freshly ground black pepper
1 teaspoon unsalted butter (optional)

Slit the chiles to remove the seeds, and chop 2 chiles into fine dice and mix with the salt, garlic, and oregano. (New Mexicans traditionally like to leave a few of the seeds in the dish. "The seeds give it life," they say.) Reserve the remaining whole chile.

With a very sharp knife, cut a horizontal pocket into the steak. Stuff the chopped chiles into the pocket. Brush the meat and the remaining chile with oil. Grill the steak on both sides to the desired doneness. If using buffalo, watch carefully so as not to overcook! Because it contains less fat than chicken, bison cooks much faster than beef and is best medium rare.

Salt and pepper the meat. Grill the remaining whole-roasted chile to get a nice patterning of grid burn on it. Lay it across the steak as a garnish. A teaspoon of brown butter drizzled over the steak as a special treat is heaven, if desired. To make brown butter, simply place the butter in a sauté pan over medium-high heat and allow it to melt and turn golden brown.

HOW TO COOK A BUFFALO

Hardly any other cut of meat compares to a good "buff tender," which is what we call tenderloins. The texture of buffalo is similar to beef except that it is less fatty. Its taste is slightly sweeter than beef, and has been likened to beef injected with extra beef flavoring.

Since the best meat comes from young bulls between eighteen and twenty-six months old, the body weight of a dressed carcass runs between 550 and 650 pounds, most of it bone and lesser cuts. This is easy to understand if you picture the buffalo on the Indian head buffalo nickel. The head and shoulders are large, but the hind end is small and scrawny. Since the steaks come from the small end, this translates into 11 to 12 pounds of tenderloin from a single 550-pound carcass. This explains why it is costly to produce.

Cooking buffalo is much like cooking beef, except that since it is extremely low in fat, when it's grilled it should be kept rare or medium rare to avoid toughening. Slow oven roasting is best for prime ribs because the low temperatures will not drive off all the juices and fat. If you marinate or braise the meat, use an acidic liquid such as wine, beer, vinegar, yogurt, or citrus juices, which tenderize the meat by softening the collagens in the cells.

▼▼▼▼▼▼▼▼▼▼▼▼▼▼▼▼▼▼▼▼

uncle dick's "incorrect" buffalo or beef steak

My dad named this steak, first focusing on the incorrect part, because while he deemed this meal as glorious as "a first kiss," it includes egg and cheese, two foodstuffs that should not be eaten with beef if you care about your cholesterol or your diet in general. But where's the fun in that? Every now and again, nothing is better! We like to honor historic figures at the Fort who we imagine would like our food. We named this for Uncle Dick Wootten, a mountain man of yore who is perhaps best known for establishing the first toll road in Colorado along the Santa Fe Trail. When you travel south today on I-25 near Raton you still cross over Wootten's Pass, but the toll is gone. A steak as decadent as this one perhaps needs a toll! Serve this with a side of Fort-Style Red Potatoes with Corn and Anasazi Beans (page 127). • *serves 1*

1 (8- to 12-ounce) beef sirloin steak, cut 2 inches thick
Canola oil
Sprinkling of commercial dry rub for beef, such as Char Crust,
    or salt and freshly ground black pepper
1 large egg
¼ cup shredded sharp white Cheddar cheese
¼ cup Red Chile Sauce, page 77

Lightly coat the steak with canola oil and generously season with the dry rub.

Cook the steak over high heat on a charcoal grill (with mesquite) or a gas grill for 6 to 8 minutes per side for medium rare.

While the steak is grilling, cook the egg sunny-side up on a griddle or in an egg pan. When the steak is ready, top it with the cheese, Red Chile Sauce and the egg.

smokehouse buffalo bbq ribs

When Bobby Flay visited the Fort to film his television show, we featured these ribs, which Chef Flay declared were the best he had eaten all year! High praise indeed, but no surprise as they are great favorites with us, too. Our very creative Chef Dave Woolley came up with the recipe, which relies on a lip-smacking barbecue sauce made with Jack Daniels whiskey. Buffalo ribs are larger than beef ribs and harder to find. Don't forgo this because you can't find buffalo ribs; substitute beef or baby back pork ribs instead. • *serves 4 to 6*

1 cup Jack Daniels or another bourbon
1 cup molasses
½ cup orange juice concentrate
¼ cup whole cloves garlic, peeled and crushed with the flat side of a chef's knife
¼ cup fresh thyme sprigs or 1 teaspoon dried leaf thyme
2 bay leaves
1½ teaspoons salt
3 cups water
5 pounds buffalo (or beef) back ribs
Hickory wood smoking chips, or 2 to 3 hickory aluminum foil smoker bags, page 240
Jack Daniels BBQ Sauce, recipe follows

In a large nonreactive saucepan, combine the Jack Daniels, molasses, orange juice concentrate, garlic, thyme, bay leaves, salt, and water. Bring to a boil over medium-high heat, stirring often. Reduce the heat to low and simmer gently, stirring occasionally, for 20 minutes.

Place the ribs in a large shallow braising pan and pour the braising liquid over them. Cover the pan tightly with aluminum foil. Braise in a 200°F oven for 6 to 8 hours, until very tender.

Remove the ribs from the liquid and allow to cool. Pour the liquid through a strainer into a saucepan. Discard the bay leaves and other solids left in the strainer. Cook the liquid over medium-low heat, stirring often, for 8 to 10 minutes, or until the liquid is reduced to about 1 cup. Reserve this liquid to add to the BBQ sauce.

Smoke the ribs over hickory chips on a grill, or in hickory aluminum foil smoker bag on the bottom rack of a preheated 450°F oven for 1 hour. On the grill, baste with Jack Daniels BBQ Sauce during the last 15 to 20 minutes. If using smoker bags, baste with the sauce after smoking is complete.

jack daniels bbq sauce

• makes about 2 cups (3 cups with the added braising liquid)

1 cup Jack Daniels or another bourbon

1 cup molasses

¾ cup chilli sauce

¾ cup orange juice concentrate

½ cup A-1 Sauce

¼ cup Worcestershire sauce

½ cup water

In a large nonreactive saucepan combine Jack Daniels, molasses, chilli sauce, orange juice concentrate, A-1 Sauce, Worcestershire, and water. Bring to a boil over medium-high heat, stirring. Simmer gently, over low heat, stirring occasionally, for 20 to 30 minutes until sauce begins to thicken and is reduced to about 2 cups. If desired, when preparing Smokehouse Buffalo Ribs, add the flavorful reduced rib braising liquid to the sauce.

BEE-NANAS

Back in the early days of the Fort, we put a grilled banana on just about every plate as a side dish, particularly with steak. We called these "bee-nanas" because before grilling them, still in their skins, we injected the fruit with honey. When the skin turned black, it was pulled back to reveal soft, honey-colored and lightly steaming fruit. When we ran out of honey, we cooked the bananas without it and the heat of the grill caramelized the fruit's natural sugar so that they were nearly as sweet as bee-nanas.

Luis Bonachea, our first manager who was from Cuba, suggested serving these alongside Cuban black beans and rice with salsa cruda and we also found them popular with steak and pork. And they make a quick, simple, and yummy dessert with a scoop of ice cream.

▼▼▼▼▼▼▼▼▼▼▼▼▼▼▼▼▼▼▼▼▼▼▼

elk chops st. vrain

Our famous game plate, a very popular dish at the Fort, includes these chops. It also boasts William Bent's Teriyaki Quail (page172) and buffalo tenderloin (page 151). Ceran St. Vrain, a French nobleman, founded Bent's St. Vrain Trading Company in the 1830s and his family were original settlers in St. Louis. • *serves 4*

1 (2- to 3-pound) cervena (elk) rack, cut into 8 bone-in chops
Canola oil
4 tablespoons Char Crust Original Hickory Grilled Dry Rub, optional
Salt and freshly ground black pepper, to taste
1 cup huckleberry preserves, page 241

Lightly coat the chops with the canola oil and season both sides with the Char Crust and salt and pepper.

Grill over high heat, 3 to 5 minutes per side for medium rare.

Serve 2 chops per person with 2 to 3 tablespoons of warm huckleberry preserves.

MOST POPULAR ENTREE AT THE FORT: THE GAME PLATE

Guests sometimes ask what to order and when we suggest the Fort's game plate, they are never sorry. It's our version of a sample plate and includes four ounces of each type of game meat we serve and for which we are so well known. These are buffalo filet mignon (page 151), the Elk Chops St. Vrain on this page, and the grilled quail (page 172).

At the Fort, we serve more than 70,000 buffalo entrees a year, and very often these are part of the game plate. We augment its appeal with Fort-style potatoes (page 127) and a vegetable side dish, very often the chayote squash (page 120). After eating the game plate, our guests want to sit back and shout out a hearty "WAUGH!", as a true mountain man or woman!

▼▼▼▼▼▼▼▼▼▼▼▼▼▼▼▼▼▼▼▼▼▼▼▼▼▼

buffalo blue corn tamale pie

Chances are you are familiar with blue corn chips and blue corn tortillas, but if you haven't tried blue cornmeal in a tamale pie such as this one, you don't know what you are missing. Many Indians and other southwesterners still use the meal ground from dark-colored corn into cornmeal called maiz azul. • *serves 6*

1 to 2 tablespoons olive or canola oil
1 pound coarsely ground beef or buffalo chuck
1½ cups chopped yellow onion (1 large)
2 cloves garlic, peeled and minced
1½ teaspoons dried Mexican oregano
½ teaspoon fennel seed, crushed
Salt, to taste
2 cups pine nuts or coarsely chopped walnuts
⅓ cup Red Chile Puree, page 78
2 quarts chicken broth
2 cups blue cornmeal
½ cup cold water
1 cup medium whole pitted ripe olives
2 cups grated sharp Cheddar cheese
½ cup each red and green bell pepper strips cut attractively, for garnish (optional)
Avocado, sliced, for garnish (optional)
¼ cup toasted pine nuts or whole walnut halves, for garnish (optional)
Several sprigs of parsley or cilantro, for garnish

Wipe a large skillet with oil and brown the meat in small batches over high heat, removing to a bowl as each batch is cooked. Cooking too much meat at once will steam it rather than brown it.

In the same pan, over medium heat, cook the onion, garlic, oregano, fennel, ¼ teaspoon salt, and the nuts for 3 to 5 minutes, stirring often, until the onion is softened and lightly browned. Add this mixture to the meat, and stir in the Red Chile Puree.

Bring the chicken broth to a boil in a large stockpot. (The cornmeal will bubble and splash if the pot isn't deep enough.) While the broth is heating, combine the blue cornmeal and cold water and whisk well. This will keep it from clumping when it's added to the hot broth. When the broth reaches a boil, stir in the cornmeal mixture. If you are using a salty chicken base, don't add more salt. Otherwise, add ¾ teaspoon. Lower the heat and simmer, stirring often for 20 to 30 minutes, until the cornmeal mush is smooth and very thick. (A spoon should almost be able to stand upright in it.) Be sure to scrape the bottom as you stir to prevent scorching.

Preheat the oven to 375°F. Lightly oil or spray a 4-quart cazuela or other ovenproof casserole with a nonstick cooking spray. Pour half the mush into the cazuela, and then alternately layer the meat mixture and the olives. When both are used up, top with half of the grated cheese and then the remaining cornmeal mush. Bake for approximately 1½ hours. Do not underbake, or the mush will not cook through. (It'll still taste great, but it won't look very good.)

Remove from the oven and top with the remaining 1 cup cheese. You may garnish the pie with wheel designs made of strips of red and green peppers, avocado slices, and toasted pine nuts or walnuts, if desired. These will sink into the cheese as the cheese melts. Return to the oven for 15 minutes more, allowing the cheese to brown a bit. Sprinkle with parsley or cilantro.

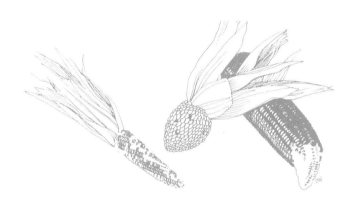

GREEN RIVER KNIVES

Green River skinning knives make great steak knives, which is why we sell them at the Fort in the Trade Lodge. The knives have been made by the Russell Harrington Cutlery Company in Massachusetts since 1834, when they were mostly used by trappers and hunters. Kit Carson carried a Green River knife—and that's good enough recommendation for us. When we first opened, customers bought a steak knife, which we kept for them until they returned and needed to use it. Today, our guests can purchase the knives and take them home.

▼▼▼▼▼▼▼▼▼▼▼▼▼▼▼▼▼▼▼

THE SUMMIT AT THE FORT

You can imagine how thrilled my dad and I were when we got the call that the Clintons had selected the Fort to host the official dinner for the global leaders attending the 1997 Summit of Eight. Bill Clinton's advance team set up shop on our second floor about two months before the event, installed 50 extra phone lines, and got to work making sure everything would run like clockwork.

We developed a menu with Larry DiPasquale of Epicurean Catering, the food supplier selected by the government for the week the world leaders were in the country, and ran it by the White House executive chef, Walter Scheib. Because the government's budget did not include food for the press, we planned a shadow menu for the 150 journalists who were chosen to be part of the entourage. This featured Fort specialties such as Rocky Mountain oysters and buffalo tongue. The press corps, and especially the Italians, loved these unfamiliar delicacies.

We had planned to shoot one of the cannons mounted outside the Fort during dinner. President Clinton was not sure about doing so but when Italy's prime minister Romano Prodi teased him by asking, "What's wrong with you Americans? You have cannons but they don't fire," Bill gave the executive order. "Fire the cannons!" he said—much to the glee of our cannoneers who were at the ready.

As evening drew near, a spectacular double rainbow straddled the valley, which someone commented bode well for world peace. With a giant summer moon hanging in the sky, it was a breathtaking end to a true Shinin' Time at the Fort.

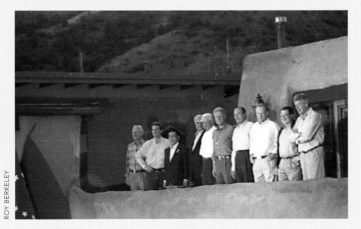

ROY BERKELEY

*The President and Mrs. Clinton welcome you to
Dinner At The Fort
on the occasion of the Denver Summit of the Eight
Saturday, June 21, 1997*

*Tequila and Lime Smoked Salmon
with American Sturgeon Caviar on Blue Corn Blinis*

*Masa Tempura-Fried Squash Blossoms
filled with Wild Mushrooms and Rattlesnake*

~~

*Seared Medallions of American Buffalo
with Whisky Tortilla Sauce*

Mesquite Grilled Quail with Prickly Pear Glaze

Coriander-Cured Clear Creek Trout

Cinnamon Smoked Colorado Lamb with Cider Adobo Sauce

~~

Escabeche of Sweet Peppers, Tomatillos and Wild Garlic

*Wood-Grilled Vegetable Salad with Balsamic Syrup
and Crumpled Goat's Cheese*

Roasted Beets and Watercress with Spicy Walnuts

Molasses Grilled Squab with Mango and Arugula

Three Tomato Salad

Cowboy "Roll Ups" of Black Beans, Chipotle and Avocado

Salad of Jicama, Chayote and Grapefruit with Sweet Basil

Fingerling Potato Salad with Grain Mustard and Rosemary

~~

Apple and Gooseberry Cobbler

Vanilla Bean Ice Cream

Blackberry Sauce

~~

Fisher Whitney's Chardonnay 1994

Edmunds St. John Grand Heritage 1993

washtunkala cast-iron kettle stew

As I write about on page 154, *washtunkala* is the Sioux word for a stew made with dried meat and cornmeal. Our version at the Fort uses fresh meat and corn and we enrich the broth with a buffalo demiglace to ensure a rich-tasting gravy. Outstanding—particularly with the Fort-Style Red Potatoes (page 127). • *serves 4 to 6*

1½ to 2 pounds buffalo or beef tenderloin tips, cut into 1½-inch cubes
3 to 4 tablespoons olive oil
Salt and freshly ground black pepper, to taste
¼ cup fresh thyme sprigs
One 12-ounce package frozen pearl onions
One 12-ounce package frozen corn
1½ cups chopped mild green chiles (one 7-ounce can, plus one 4-ounce can)
4 cups rich buffalo stock or beef broth
½ cup roasted sunflower seed hearts (hulled seeds)

Pat the buffalo cubes dry with paper towels.

In a large sauté pan, over high heat, brown the buffalo in oil, making sure not to crowd the pan. Sprinkle the browned meat with salt and pepper and add the thyme. Add the onions, corn, and chiles. Sauté for 1 minute. Add the buffalo stock and sunflower seeds. Reduce the heat to low and simmer for 8 to 10 minutes until the broth is slightly thickened.

GRADING BEEF

The USDA grades the beef everyone buys. To qualify as prime beef, the meat has to have a significantly high ratio of fat to meat—the result of feedlot fattening. Less than 2 percent of the beef sold in the U.S. is prime, which makes it pretty hard to find. Below prime is choice, which is also very good beef, although the top levels of choice beef are better than the lower ones. Most shoppers end up with choice beef, which is never a bad thing. Below choice is select, a lesser grade, and below that are industrial cuts rarely, if ever, seen by consumers.

Angus is a top-grade choice, as are some others. The best bet when buying meat is to find a butcher you can trust and stick with him or her. You may not have a butcher shop in your city or town, but talk to the guys behind the meat counter at the local supermarket. They usually are only too glad to help you choose the best meat for your needs.

▼▼▼▼▼▼▼▼▼▼▼▼▼▼▼▼▼▼▼▼▼

from the yard

charbroiled quail with red chile honey

My dad told me how honeybees were imported to our continent by European settlers and quickly adapted to every climate and region. Early settlers relied on honey to sweeten just about everything because cane sugar from the Caribbean was expensive and in short supply. Native Americans viewed the insects as harbingers of encroaching change: When they saw bees, they knew white men were about fifty miles away. On the other hand, quail are indigenous to North America and were commonly hunted, along with grouse and prairie chickens, by trappers, settlers, soldiers, and Indians. When red meat was scarce, upland game was a good substitute. • *serves 4*

1 rounded tablespoon pure ground New Mexico red chile (Dixon is best)
1 cup honey
8 partially boned quail, see Note
Canola oil

Simmer the chile in the honey for 10 minutes to combine their flavors.

Brush the quail with the oil and charbroil them over a slow part of the grill for 3 to 5 minutes per side. Brush both sides of the birds with glaze when they are nearly cooked. If you glaze them too soon, the honey will burn and you will end up with charred quail. After placing the quail on the plate, brush them once more with glaze.

Note: If you use quail that are not partially boned, allow 6 to 8 minutes additional cooking time.

william bent's teriyaki quail

Since much of the West was built by Asians, many of whom were from Japan, it's not surprising that teriyaki sauce would find its way into the cooking pretty early in the game. John Jacob Astor hired Hawaiians to work as Northwest trappers, and these folks took to teriyaki as well. We serve more than one thousand quails a week at the Fort so I figure we must be doing something right! We partially bone the little birds by removing the rib cages and serve them with the legs, thighs, and wings attached to the breast meat. Two or three quails make a fantastic dish. • *serves 4*

TERIYAKI MARINADE
1 cup soy sauce
1 cup orange juice
1 cup water
½ cup Mirin rice wine or dry sherry
¼ cup sugar
¼ cup finely chopped orange peel
2 tablespoons minced fresh ginger
3 cloves garlic, finely minced or smashed
2 whole star anise

8 (2½- to 3½-ounce) partially boned quail
4 orange slices, for garnish

In a saucepan, combine the soy sauce, orange juice, water, rice wine, sugar, orange peel, ginger, garlic, and star anise and bring to a boil over high heat. Lower the heat and simmer for 5 minutes. Let cool.

Place the quail in a single layer in a pan, pour the marinade over, and let the quail marinate in the refrigerator for 2 to 4 hours. Do not leave the birds in the marinade for longer than 8 hours because they will become unpalatably salty.

When ready to cook the quail, heat the grill to medium or preheat the broiler. Cook the quail for 3 to 5 minutes on each side or until cooked through. Garnish each bird with an orange twist.

SISSY BEAR: THE FORT'S BEST AMBASSADOR

During the early years of the Fort it took about an hour to drive from Denver to Morrison, where we're located. We were pretty well known fairly quickly, but were not yet a destination restaurant and so we turned to anything we could think of to attract customers.

One of our most successful ploys was to lead Sissy Bear, our tame Canadian black bear, to the state road and stand there until a passing car slowed down to get a better look. Hearing that Sissy was attached to the nearby magnificent adobe building and that there was a restaurant in the building, very often the driver and his passengers were eager to follow us down the driveway to the restaurant, Pied Piper style.

Sissy was always a big hit at the Fort. She was my pet and most of the time I made sure she stayed clear of the hubbub, but every now and then she was allowed to come to the bar for a soda pop. We trained her to drain a bottle of the sugary liquid in minutes, and she also could take a cherry from someone's mouth while standing upright. We called this "kissing" and some of our more eminent guests were kissed by Sissy: historian Arnold J. Toynbee, the prince of Uganda, author James Michener, and tea magnate Sam Twining.

Holly's brother, Keith Arnold

Sissy Bear, napping on the picnic table

quail en quinoa

My father became enamored with quinoa when he first traveled to Peru. It's cultivated high in the Andes and does well in our Rocky Mountains, too. A mild-tasting grain packed with nutrition, when it is paired with quail, its nuttiness and soft texture absorb the birds' juices for a delectable dish. This is essentially a one-dish meal, and it is also a great addition to a buffet, hot or cold. • *serves 4 to 6*

3 tablespoons unsalted butter
3 tablespoons olive or canola oil
4 to 6 partially boned quail
2 cups quinoa
4 to 6 Portuguese linguiça sausages
1½ cups chopped yellow onion (1 large)
2 cups chopped mild green chiles (two 7-ounce cans)
½ cup pitted ripe olives
6 cups chicken broth
½ cup lightly toasted walnut halves

Preheat the oven to 325°F. Place the butter and oil in a large sauté pan or skillet over medium-high heat. When the butter begins to turn clear, add the quail, in small batches, and brown on both sides, 6 to 8 minutes. Remove the quail to a cutting board and cut into quarters.

Butter a 3- to 4-quart baking dish or casserole.

In a sieve, carefully rinse the quinoa in cold or lukewarm running water to remove any bitter residue. Place half of the quinoa in the prepared baking dish, spreading it into an even layer.

Cut the linguiça sausages into bite-sized pieces and arrange them on top of the quinoa. Add the quail pieces, onion, green chiles, and olives. Cover with the remaining 1 cup quinoa and add the chicken broth. Cover tightly with aluminum foil, and bake for 60 to 80 minutes, until the quinoa is fluffy and most of the liquid has been absorbed. Garnish the casserole with walnuts just before serving.

applewood smoked duck breast

Our former executive chef, Dave Woolley, developed this recipe when my dad and I craved crispy *magret de canard*, reminiscent of the duck we had tasted in France. The duck has a layer of fat on top of the breast that is broiled until crispy and the breast meat tastes delicately smoky. I think this is best served on a bed of sautéed spinach with a side of Cha Cha Murphys (page 125). • *serves 2 to 4*

3 tablespoons hot water
1 tablespoon brown sugar
1 tablespoon kosher salt
2 (6-ounce) boneless duck breast fillets
1 applewood or hickory aluminium foil smoking bag, page 240

Mix the water, brown sugar, and salt until the salt and sugar are dissolved to make a brine. Place the duck in a shallow pan and add the brine and enough cold water to cover the duck. Let sit covered overnight in the refrigerator.

Preheat the oven to 250°F.

Remove the fillets from the brine and place in the smoking bag. Fold the end of the bag to seal. Place bag on the middle rack of the oven and smoke 35 minutes for rare, 40 minutes for medium, and 45 minutes for well done. Let the duck rest in the bag for 5 to 10 minutes. Open the bag carefully to avoid being burned by the hot steam. Remove the skin from the fillets and discard. Slice the breasts and serve.

cha cha chicken

Our first restaurant manager, Luis Bonachea, joined us when we opened in 1963 and brought with him culinary influences from his native Cuba. This chicken is typical of the sort of dishes cooked in that Caribbean nation, with a sweet fruitiness that caramelizes on the meat during cooking to give it a superb agridulce or sweet-and-sour flavor. If you want to use small chicken legs (called "drumettes") or wings, prepare them in advance and serve them as party appetizers. Delicious! • *serves 4 to 6*

MARINADE
2 cups orange juice without pulp
¼ cup soy sauce
5 tablespoons honey
4 tablespoons fresh lime juice
3 tablespoons butter, melted
2 tablespoons chopped Italian parsley
2 tablespoons chopped fresh cilantro
2 tablespoons dry mustard
2 tablespoons finely minced fresh peeled ginger
½ teaspoon cayenne pepper
2 cloves garlic, peeled and minced

CHICKEN
4 to 6 bone-in split chicken breasts,
    or 4 to 6 whole chicken legs (drumsticks and thighs)
    or 2 to 3 Cornish hens, cut in half
1 orange, thinly sliced
1 lime, thinly sliced
1 tablespoon canola oil
Dash of salt
Cayenne

Fresh mint sprigs, for garnish
1 recipe Rice Pilaf, page 130

In a food processor or blender, combine the orange juice, soy sauce, honey, lime juice, melted butter, parsley, cilantro, mustard, ginger, cayenne, and garlic. Pulse on and off until well blended.

Place the chicken in a glass bowl and cover with the marinade and the orange and lime slices. The chicken needs only a few hours to marinate; however, longer is better and overnight is dandy.

When you're ready to cook the chicken, preheat the oven to 325°F. Remove the chicken from the marinade and place it on a shallow baking pan completely lined with aluminum foil that has been coated with oil. Parchment paper also works - cut it large enough to extend all the way up the sides of the pan to prevent the syrup from leaking beneath it. Sprinkle with salt and cayenne and bake for 35 minutes, then raise the heat to broil and cook another 10 minutes, until the skin is nice and crispy.

Garnish with the mint sprigs. Serve chicken on a bed of pilaf.

baked stuffed pumpkin

This recipe, which was served at the Fort in the early 1960s, is one of my personal favorites and because it's served in a pumpkin, it's a natural for Halloween. When we decided to write this book, I invited my editorial team to dinner on a cool fall evening and served the stew. We dug in and got even more excited about the book! Native Americans prepare something very similar, which makes sense as pumpkin is a squash, and one of the three sacred sisters. They also use a lot of toasted sunflower meal, which gives this a distinctive flavor. Bring out your favorite hot sauce as a condiment to serve with this comforting autumn dish. • *serves 6 to 8*

1 (4- to 5-pound) sugar pumpkin

2 tablespoons unsalted butter, melted

Fine sea salt, to taste

Coarsely ground black pepper, to taste

2 tablespoons olive oil

2 cups chopped white onion (1 large)

1 pound ground buffalo or lean ground beef

2 cups fresh corn kernels or 1 can (11 ounces)
   white shoepeg corn, drained

2 cups fresh green beans

1 cup chopped green bell pepper

1 cup diced, cooked chicken

1 cup hulled sunflower seeds

4 cups chicken broth

2 fresh peaches, peeled, pitted, and sliced

Hot pepper sauce (optional)

Preheat the oven to 350°F.

   With a large, sharp knife, cut the top off the pumpkin, jack-o'-lantern style. With a large spoon, scrape out the seeds and strings (save the seeds to salt and bake for a snack). Rub the inside of the pumpkin generously with melted butter, and season with salt and pepper. Place the pumpkin in a roasting pan. Bake, with the top off, for about 45 minutes, or until the pumpkin is tender, but still holds its shape. Check after 30 minutes for liquid buildup. Using a long handled ladle, remove any juice, and discard. The pumpkin may collapse while baking if you don't remove the liquid.

   Meanwhile, in a Dutch oven or heavy-bottomed sauté pan, heat the olive oil. Add the onion and cook over medium heat until translucent, about 5 minutes. Add the buffalo and sauté until browned, 6 to 8 minutes. Stir in the corn, green beans, bell pepper, diced chicken, sunflower seeds, chicken broth, and peaches. When the liquid comes to a boil, reduce the heat to low and simmer the stew gently for about 40 minutes to blend the flavors.

   Carefully lift the baked pumpkin onto a round, serving platter. Ladle the stew into the pumpkin and top with the lid. As you serve, be sure to scrape the inside of the pumpkin to mix some of its delicious flesh into the stew.

baked chicken adobe

This is one of our most popular entrées, conceived by our sous chef, Juan Zepeda. Juan told me he came up with the idea to tempt his children and divert their attraction from fast food. He relied on his Mexican heritage to make the chicken taste as it does—and it's a winner! • *serves 4*

4 (8- to 10-ounce) whole, boneless, skinless chicken breasts
6 ounces Monterey Jack cheese, cut into 4 sticks, approximately 1½ inches by ½ inch
4 (¼-inch-thick) slices ham
1½ cups finely ground tortilla chips
½ cup bread crumbs
¾ cup all-purpose flour
Salt and freshly ground black pepper, to taste
1 to 1½ cups milk
Canola oil, enough to fill a medium skillet ½ inch deep

Lightly pound the chicken breasts between sheets of plastic wrap to flatten. If one is particularly thick, you may want to butterfly it. Wrap each cheese stick in a slice of ham. Place a ham and cheese bundle on the rougher textured cut side of each chicken breast, folding the short ends of the chicken up over the ham. Fold in the long sides of the breast to completely enclose the bundle. Place the breasts seam side down in a pan with the smooth side up, and freeze.

Preheat the oven to 350°F.

Combine the ground tortilla chips and bread crumbs on a plate. This should be enough breading, but if you are using very large chicken breasts, you may need more. On a separate plate, combine the flour, and salt and pepper. Place the milk in a widemouthed shallow bowl.

Dip the frozen chicken breasts first in flour, and then in milk. Dredge the chicken in crumbs, pressing firmly so that the breading adheres.

Place the skillet of oil over high heat. Fry the chicken breasts, one at a time, in hot oil, turning with tongs to brown on all sides. Place the browned chicken first on paper towels to drain the excess oil, then arrange on a baking sheet. Bake for 20 to 30 minutes until cooked through. This technique allows the chicken to cook evenly and thoroughly with minimal frying.

country captain chicken

When my mother and father opened the Fort in 1963, I was still a girl but eagerly tucked into the food served in the restaurant. This was one of my favorites back then and it still holds up all these years later. I attribute its place on our menu to my mom, who was from the South where the mild chicken curry dish originated. The story goes that curry was introduced to the lowlands of South Carolina, where rice was a significant crop, by a sea captain who had sailed to India sometime in the 1700s. We adapted this recipe from one in the *American Heritage Cookbook,* and while it has a long list of ingredients, don't let that scare you. It's quick and simple to put together and oh-so-good!

• *serves 4 to 6*

½ cup all-purpose flour

1 teaspoon salt

¼ teaspoon freshly ground black pepper

3 pounds skinless, bone-in chicken parts

4 to 6 tablespoons unsalted butter

½ cup finely chopped yellow onion

½ cup finely chopped green bell pepper

1 large clove garlic, peeled and minced

1½ to 2 teaspoons curry powder

2 to 3 curry bush leaves (optional), see Note

½ teaspoon dried thyme

1 can (14.5-ounce) stewed tomatoes

3 tablespoons dried currants

4 cups cooked white rice

½ cup blanched sliced almonds, lightly toasted

Mango chutney, for serving

Combine the flour, salt, and pepper on a plate.

Pat the chicken pieces dry with paper towels and coat with the seasoned flour.

Place 4 tablespoons of the butter in a large sauté pan or skillet over medium heat. When the butter turns clear, add the chicken. Reduce the heat to medium-low, and cook for 10 to 12 minutes, until well browned on both sides. If all the fat is absorbed before the chicken browns, add the remaining butter. Remove the chicken and set aside.

Add the onion, green bell pepper, garlic, curry powder, curry bush leaves, if using, and thyme to the skillet and cook for a few minutes over low heat, stirring in all the brown particles. Add the tomatoes and chicken, cover and simmer for 20 to 30 minutes, until tender.

Just before serving, stir in the currants. Serve the chicken over hot, fluffy, white rice. Garnish with toasted almonds and serve the chutney on the side.

Note: Curry bush leaves are sold in Asian markets. You can also order them from the Internet. See page 240.

thanksgiving turkey with piñon-nut stuffing

We started making this stuffing for the Fort's Thanksgiving turkeys in the 1960s, at which time we smoked whole birds outside in a large smokehouse. The aroma of smoking poultry wafted over the valley and attracted bears to our property. Try as they may, they could not get into the smokehouse, which was securely locked. I used to joke that these large marauders were suitors for my pet bear, Sissy, but I knew even then that they were more interested in the turkeys than in Sissy. When we ventured from the Fort's walls, we had to bang metal pans together to scare away the bears! My son, Oren, makes this stuffing for his family every Thanksgiving. • *serves 6 to 8*

STUFFING

½ pound chestnuts, either fresh roasted, peeled and chopped, or dry-roasted from a jar

8 tablespoons (1 stick) unsalted butter

1 clove garlic, peeled and minced

2 cups stale bread cubes

⅔ cup chicken broth

2 tablespoons dry sherry

½ cup heavy cream

½ cup chopped green chiles, canned or fresh

2 shallots, peeled and minced

2 stalks celery, diced

½ cup chopped Italian parsley

¼ cup whole cilantro leaves

2 to 3 teaspoons freshly ground black pepper, to taste

1 teaspoon chopped fresh rosemary

1 teaspoon salt

2 pinches fresh thyme leaves or 1 pinch dry

½ cup toasted pine nuts

TURKEY

½ pound (2 sticks) unsalted butter

Salt

Freshly ground black pepper

1 (15-pound) turkey

1 cup dry white wine

3 tablespoons fresh or 1 tablespoon dry rosemary

To roast the chestnuts, cut an "X" on the flat side of each nut. Place the nuts in a dry cast-iron skillet and toast over medium-high heat, shaking the pan often, until the shells start browning and the edges of the "X" begin to pull away from the nut. Parts of them will be quite dark, and they will smell wonderful! Chestnuts peel more easily when they're warm. Use a sharp paring knife to peel back both the outer shell and the inner membrane. The inner membrane can be quite stubborn, but the result justifies the effort.

For the stuffing: Melt the butter in a sauté pan over medium-low heat and cook the garlic until golden. Add the bread cubes and stir constantly over medium heat, until golden. Remove the bread with a slotted spoon, and set aside. In the same pan, combine the chicken broth, sherry, cream, chiles, shallots, celery, parsley, cilantro, pepper, rosemary, salt, and thyme. Simmer for 2 minutes, over medium heat, to release the flavors. Add the bread cube mixture, chestnuts, and pine nuts. Mix well, cover, and bring to room temperature before using to stuff the bird.

To prepare the turkey: Melt the butter and stir in the salt and pepper. Rub the turkey with the butter mixture inside and out. Use the remaining butter to make the basting sauce. Combine the butter with the wine and ⅓ of the rosemary in a small saucepan. Boil for 2 minutes on high heat, then remove from the heat and use to baste the turkey every 15 minutes, while roasting.

Preheat the oven to 375°F.

Fill both cavities of the bird with the stuffing. Sew up with a trussing cord and bind the wings and drumsticks tight alongside the bird's body. Cover the wings and drumsticks with aluminum foil for the first hour to prevent overcooking. Sprinkle the remaining rosemary over the bird.

Reduce the oven temperature to 325°F.

Place the turkey on a rack in a shallow roasting pan. Do not add water. Cover the turkey with a loose tent of aluminum foil and roast for 15 minutes per pound plus 1 hour for the stuffing.

Remove the foil 30 minutes before roasting is done. Test for doneness with a reliable meat thermometer; this is the only way to be sure it is done. The final temperature for safety and doneness is 180°F in the thigh and at least 165°F in the breast and stuffing. The juices should run clear, not pink. Test the temperature early and often. An overcooked turkey is dry, tough, and pasty in texture.

Variation: *Hickory Smoky Turkey:* You can also use a covered barbecue or smoke roaster to cook the turkey over indirect heat and use damp hickory chips on the fire for a smoke flavor. Don't overdo the amount or length of smoke—15 minutes of smoke is enough. Roast the bird until a meat thermometer registers 180°F in the thigh and at least 165°F in the breast and stuffing, usually about 4 hours. A pan of water in the cooker under the bird helps to keep it moist.

Note: You may make the stuffing a day ahead of time and refrigerate it overnight, but warm it slightly before you stuff the bird. Bringing the stuffing to room temperature before filling the bird is necessary to allow the stuffing to cook all the way through. Be sure to remove all the stuffing from the carcass after dining and store in a separate bowl.

ROCKY MOUNTAIN PINE NUTS

Pine nuts from New Mexico and Colorado are called piñones (peen-YO-nays) or piñons. In Italy they are called *pignoli* or *pignolia*. The seeds from pine trees, the small, elongated nuts are found nestled in the large cones. For centuries, they have been gathered in the wintertime in our neck of the woods, first by Native Americans and then by settlers in our mountains. After the first snowfall, it's easy to follow the tracks of ground squirrels to their burrows, where several gallons of nuts can be dug up and toted away. Most folks leave enough for the squirrels so that they don't starve—and live to lead us to their burrows next year.

Everyone roasts the nuts to accentuate their sweet flavor. I love them in salads, stuffings, and sauces. The Indians still crack them between their teeth and skillfully extract the meat with their tongues. Today, it's common in Santa Fe movie theaters to find a carpet of empty pine nut shells on the floor after the lights go up.

dixon and ancho chile rub pork tenderloin

Pork tenderloin is a great choice for a dinner party or family gathering. It takes on the flavors of a rub or marinade as readily as does chicken and cooks in a short time without losing any of its natural moisture. Our executive chef Geoffrey Groditski came up with this dry chile rub for pork, made with Dixon red chile powder and dried ancho chiles, which have a degree of sweetness. We like to serve it with Rice Pilaf (page 130) and Zuni Succotash with Toasted Sunflower Seed Hearts (page 119). • *serves 4 to 6*

CHILE RUB

½ yellow onion

¼ cup roasted, peeled cloves garlic

1 tablespoon Dixon
  or other New Mexican ground red chile

1 teaspoon ground ancho chile

1 teaspoon ground cumin

¼ cup canola oil

¼ cup sweet Thai red chili sauce

2 tablespoons cider vinegar

Salt and freshly ground black pepper, to taste

PORK TENDERLOIN

2 to 3 (1-pound) pork tenderloins, trimmed

2 to 3 tablespoons olive or canola oil

VEGETABLES

2 tablespoons unsalted butter

1 cup fire-roasted corn

1 cup chopped mild green chiles, fresh or canned

1 small red onion, peeled and thinly sliced

1 cup diced zucchini

Salt and freshly ground black pepper, to taste

CHIPOTLE SAUCE

2 chipotle chiles en adobo (canned), minced

2 teaspoons olive or canola oil

1 cup heavy cream

2 tablespoons white wine

Salt and freshly ground black pepper, to taste

2 to 3 cups hot, cooked wild rice

In a food processor, combine the onion, garlic, ground Dixon and ancho chiles, cumin, oil, sweet chili sauce, and vinegar. Pulse on and off until almost pureed. Taste and season with salt and pepper.

Rub the tenderloins with the seasoning mixture. Cover and marinate, refrigerated, overnight.

Preheat the oven to 400°F.

Place the oil in a large sauté pan or skillet over medium-high heat. Sear the tenderloins, turning with tongs to brown them on all sides. Remove the seared tenderloins to a shallow roasting pan. Roast on the middle rack of the oven for 15 to 20 minutes, until the pork is medium to medium well. Allow the tenderloins to rest for 5 minutes, then slice on the bias.

In a sauté pan over medium heat, melt the butter. Add the corn, green chiles, onion, and zucchini and sauté for 3 to 5 minutes until tender-crisp. Season to taste with salt and pepper.

Sauté the chipotle in the olive oil over medium-high heat for 1 minute. Add the cream and wine and cook, stirring until the sauce is reduced to about ¾ cup. Season with salt and pepper.

Serve the sliced tenderloins with wild rice and sautéed vegetables. Drizzle each serving with the chipotle sauce.

santa fe pork adobada

In Santa Fe more pork is eaten during the winter holidays than any other meat or poultry. The tradition harkens back to the very early days of the city, which was established by the Spanish in 1610. The Europeans had claimed the region as the Kingdom of New Mexico in 1540 and had set up the capital in San Juan Pueblo in 1548, about twenty-five miles north of Santa Fe. Don Pedro de Peralta moved the capital to Santa Fe in 1610, where it remains to this day. As well as organizing their own style of government, the Spaniards introduced domesticated animals to the area: pigs, sheep, cattle, chickens, and horses. For economic reasons, the locals ate more pork, poultry, and mutton than they did beef, and during Christmas, residents still prepare pork posole, pork-filled tamales, barbecued pork ribs, and deep-fried crispy pork pieces called carnitas. Pork Adobada is a popular dish as well, with warm, deep flavors that pop from the chile marinade. We served it at the Fort in the 1960s—and still love it today. • *serves 4 to 6*

MARINADE
1 cup chicken broth
½ cup medium red chile caribe (coarsely ground chile)
½ teaspoon dried Mexican oregano
½ teaspoon salt

4 to 6 (7-ounce) thickly cut, lean, pork rib chops
4 cups cooked white rice or mashed potatoes

In a shallow baking dish, large enough to hold the chops, combine the chicken broth, chile, oregano, and salt. Dredge the chops in the marinade to coat well. Place the chops in the marinade, cover, and refrigerate for at least 4 hours. They are even better when marinated, refrigerated, for 8 hours!

Preheat the oven to 350°F.

Transfer the chops and marinade to a foil-lined pan and bake, covered tightly with aluminum foil for 35 minutes. Remove the foil, baste with pan juices, and continue to bake for 10 minutes. If the juices evaporate, and the chile threatens to burn, replace the foil for the last few minutes. Serve the chops over hot fluffy rice or mashed potatoes.

crispy southwestern pork shanks

My dad, who was born in Pennsylvania and influenced by German cooking during his childhood, was so fond of *schweine haux* (swine hocks) that we put our version on the menu in 1999. Our customers were delighted with these deep-fried shanks (in place of hocks). One evening my husband Jeremy was drafted to help out in the restaurant kitchen, and after submerging one pork shank after another in sizzling fat and seeing the skin crisp on the meat and nearly fall off the bone, he dreamed of nothing else but eating them. We dined at the Fort the next night expressly to satisfy Jeremy's hunger! You will probably have to ask the butcher to order pork shanks. Allow 1 shank per serving and expect each one to weigh from 16 to 18 ounces. • *serves 4 to 6*

4 to 6 pork shanks
1 large onion, quartered
4 carrots, peeled and quartered
4 sticks celery, cut into 2- to 3-inch lengths
4 to 6 cloves garlic, crushed
1 teaspoon salt
½ teaspoon freshly ground black pepper
Canola oil, for deep frying
2 to 3 tablespoons unsalted butter
16 ounces fresh baby spinach
½ cup caramelized onions
1 cup buffalo or veal stock or reduced-sodium beef or chicken broth
1 recipe Bay's Georgia Green Chile Grits, page 117
1 cup Chipotle BBQ Sauce, recipe follows

In a large Dutch oven, put the shanks, onion, carrots, and celery and add enough water or chicken stock to cover. Toss in the garlic and season with the salt and pepper. Cover the pot and bring to a boil over high heat. When the liquid boils, reduce the heat to low and braise for about 1½ hours, checking occasionally. The pork should be tender when done, but not quite falling off the bone. Remove the shanks and let them cool before going on to the next step.

Preheat the oven to 400°F. Pour the oil into a deep-fat fryer and heat to 325°F. Carefully lower the pork shanks, one at a time, into the hot oil and cook for about 5 minutes. Drain the shanks on paper towels, then transfer them to a baking sheet. Roast in the oven for about 10 minutes to ensure that the shanks heat all the way through.

Meanwhile, in a large sauté pan over medium heat melt the butter. Add the spinach and onions and sauté for 2 to 3 minutes, until slightly wilted. Add the stock and cook over medium-high heat, stirring, until the liquid is reduced by half. Place the grits and spinach in each individual serving bowl and place a cooked shank on top. Drizzle with Chipotle BBQ Sauce.

chipotle bbq sauce

• *makes about 2 quarts*

¼ cup diced onion

2 tablespoons roasted garlic

1 tablespoon canola oil

1 quart chicken broth

1 (14.5-ounce) can fire-roasted diced tomatoes

1½ cups tomato paste

½ cup honey

¼ cup molasses

¼ cup apple cider vinegar

3 ounces canned chipotle peppers in adobo sauce

1 jalapeño chile, seeded

1 tablespoon ground New Mexican red chile (preferably Dixon)

1 tablespoon minced Italian parsley

1½ teaspoons dried Mexican oregano

1 teaspoon ground cumin

1½ teaspoons salt

Juice of ½ lime and ½ orange

In a Dutch oven over medium-low heat, sweat the onion and garlic in the oil until translucent, 3 to 4 minutes. Stir in the chicken broth, tomatoes, tomato paste, honey, molasses, vinegar, chipotles, jalapeño, ground chile, parsley, oregano, cumin, salt, and lime and orange juices.

Bring the sauce to a simmer over medium-high heat. Puree with an immersion blender, then continue to simmer for 20 to 30 minutes over low heat, stirring often, until hot and well blended.

antonio archuleta's
red chile-blue corn enchiladas

Antonio, who now makes the Fort's very special furniture, shared his family's very special enchilada recipe with me—and believe me, it's amazing. His children and grandchildren beg him to make this all the time. I am honored to know how to re-create it, and to share it with my readers. • *serves 6*

PORK

1 (2½-pound) boneless pork roast

1 onion, peeled and quartered

5 to 6 cloves garlic, peeled,
   and crushed with the flat side of a chef's knife

2 teaspoons salt

2 teaspoons dried Mexican oregano

RED CHILE SAUCE

3 tablespoons canola oil

3 tablespoons all-purpose flour

3 tablespoons medium to hot
   ground red New Mexican chile

1 clove garlic, peeled and minced

FOR SERVING

3 to 5 tablespoons canola oil

12 blue, yellow, or white corn tortillas

4 cups (about 1 pound) shredded Cheddar cheese
   (preferably Long Horn sharp Cheddar)

1 small yellow onion, peeled, finely chopped

2 to 3 ripe plum tomatoes, diced

2 to 3 cups shredded iceberg lettuce

Cut the pork roast into 2-inch pieces and place in a Dutch oven with enough water to cover by 2 inches. Add the onion, garlic, salt, and oregano. Bring to a boil over medium–high heat. Skim off and discard the foam that rises to the top. Reduce the heat to low and simmer gently for about 1 hour, until very tender. Remove the pork with a slotted spoon and set aside. Boil down the meat broth to about 5 cups and reserve for the chile sauce. When cool enough to handle, shred the pork into small pieces, and remove and discard any excess fat. Strain the broth and discard the onion and garlic. Reserve the broth for the sauce.

To make the chile sauce: In a large deep sauté pan or skillet, combine the oil and flour. Cook, stirring, over medium heat for 2 to 3 minutes, until the flour turns golden brown. Remove from the heat, and stir in the ground red chile. Mix well, then add the pork broth. Mix well again, and add the minced garlic. Simmer the chile over low heat for 20 minutes, stirring often, until the sauce begins to thicken and is reduced to about 4 cups.

To assemble the enchiladas: Preheat the oven to 375°F. Lightly oil a large ovenproof platter or large, shallow baking dish. In a saucepan, combine the shredded pork and 1½ cups of the chile sauce. Heat, stirring, until the mixture comes to a simmer, then set aside. In a separate skillet, heat the oil. With tongs, dip a tortilla in the hot oil to soften, then dip it in the chile sauce. Arrange 6 dipped tortillas on a platter, overlapping slightly. Sprinkle about ⅓ of the cheese over the tortillas, then sprinkle with ½ of the chopped onion. Top with half of the shredded pork and a little extra chile sauce. Add another layer of tortillas, cheese, onion, pork, and chile sauce. Top with the remaining cheese. Bake the enchiladas for 10 minutes, until hot and bubbling. Remove and garnish with diced tomatoes and shredded lettuce.

general armijo's grilled lamb chops

As my dad explained it, General Manuel Armijo was the last governor of New Mexico while it was still under Mexican rule, and it's no coincidence that he governed at the end of an era. He was not well liked, and when it became apparent that Mexico had no money to wage war against General Stephen W. Kearny's army during the Mexican-American War, he took a bribe and skedaddled. Detractors claimed that he'd also been a sheep thief, stealing sheep and then selling them back to the original owners. Our lamb chops are named for this notorious scoundrel. Serve them with Red Chile Sauce or mango chutney. • *serves 6*

4½ teaspoons medium ground black pepper
3 teaspoons fine sea salt
¾ teaspoon lemon crystals (citric acid or sour salt)
6 (¾- to 1-pound) double rib or loin lamb chops, trimmed of fat
Canola oil
1 recipe Sweet Red Chile Sauce, page 75

Preheat the oven to broil or heat a grill to high. Combine the pepper, sea salt, and lemon crystals and rub each chop with the mixture, then brush with the oil. Place the chops about 6 inches from the heat source.

The grilling time will depend on the thickness of the chops. For a chop that's a nice juicy, pink, medium rare on the inside and wonderfully charred on the outside, about 7 minutes per side will do. Before turning, swab the tops with oil. Serve with Red Chile Sauce on the side.

Note: While you can find a lot of New Zealand lamb, it's usually too young to have much taste. I prefer hoggit or yearling lamb because the meat is much more flavorful. If you cannot find a butcher to cut double chops, buy the thickest rib or loin chops you can find. If you are preparing this dish for a large number of people, butterflied leg of lamb works very nicely and is a little less expensive. Because the meat is not of uniform thickness, there will be parts that range from medium-rare to well-done to satisfy the palates of your guests.

herbed lamb chops

Double lamb chops are tender and sweet and so good, they are always an indulgence. These are cut from racks of lamb and therefore are sometimes called rib chops. Cut through the racks so that each chop has two long bones, with the meat scraped away to make them "frenched." These are divine rubbed gently with garlic and fresh herbs.

• *serves 4 to 6*

6 to 8 cloves garlic, peeled
½ cup Italian parsley
½ cup fresh mint leaves
4 sprigs fresh rosemary
Salt and freshly ground pepper to taste
2 racks of lamb, frenched, and cut into double chops (2 bones each)
Rice Pilaf, page 130

In a food processor, combine the garlic, parsley, mint, rosemary, and salt and pepper. Pulse on and off until finely chopped. Rub the lamb with the herb seasonings.

Preheat the oven to 400°F.

Place a large sauté pan or skillet over medium-high heat. Place the lamb chops fat side down in the hot pan. With tongs, turn the chops to brown evenly on all sides. Remove the lamb from sauté pan to a sheet pan and roast in a 400°F oven for 10 to 12 minutes for medium rare to medium. Serve with the rice pilaf.

quick vegetarian posole

I was so taken by a vegetarian posole made during a cooking demonstration at the Fort, I had to come up with my own version. The original was absolutely delicious and was cooked in a micaceous clay pot by Charlie and Debbie Carillo from Santa Fe. He is an artist from that New Mexico city and a *santero*, or "carver of saints." To enhance this a little, serve it with sour cream or shredded Monterey Jack cheese. • *serves 6*

1½ cups chopped onion (1 medium)
1 cup chopped red bell pepper (1 large)
2 to 3 teaspoons minced fresh garlic (2 to 3 cloves)
1 to 2 tablespoons canola or olive oil
1 tablespoon New Mexican ground red chile (preferably Dixon)
4 cups vegetable broth
1 can (29-ounce) Mexican-style hominy, drained and rinsed
1 can (14.5-ounce) fire-roasted diced tomatoes with medium green chiles
Salt and freshly ground black pepper, to taste
Fresh cilantro sprigs, for garnish (optional)

In a large sauté pan or skillet over medium-high heat, sauté the onion, red bell pepper, and garlic in the oil until the onion is translucent. Reduce the heat to medium-low, add the ground chile and cook, stirring, for 2 minutes. Stir in the vegetable broth. Add the hominy (posole) and tomatoes and bring to a boil. Reduce the heat to low and simmer for 20 minutes. Season with salt and pepper.

Ladle the hot posole into bowls and garnish with cilantro, if desired.

WHAT'S A TAMALE?

Tamales are nearly always individual servings made from a base of cornmeal (masa harina) and wrapped in leaves that are discarded before eating. The leaves most often are cornhusks, but can be banana leaves or something similar. Tamales usually are steamed, although they also may be baked. The cornmeal base is mixed with any number of ingredients, from squash, beans, chiles, and mushrooms to shredded meat or poultry. The mixture generally is highly seasoned, although not necessarily spicy. Mexican tamales tend to be a little lighter in texture than Tex-Mex tamales and preferences for one or the other are purely personal. These are rarely small bites but substantial servings that are lovingly handcrafted and meant to be enjoyed with **gusto.**

▼▼▼▼▼▼▼▼▼▼▼▼▼▼▼▼▼▼▼▼▼▼▼

vegetarian nacatamales

When I was at the International Fancy Food Show about ten years ago I discovered a company from Oaxaca, Mexico, that exported vegetarian tamales wrapped in banana leaves. We imported them for the Fort until 2001, when the company stopped exporting them, but because our customers were wild about them, we developed our own recipe. They are our top-selling vegetarian entrée and also are popular served alongside buffalo or quail.

• *serves 4 to 6; makes 12 tamales*

MASA

3 cups masa harina de maiz (corn tortilla mix)

1½ tablespoons baking powder

1 teaspoon salt

½ cup vegetable shortening

2½ to 3 cups warm vegetable broth or water

ANCHO CHILE SAUCE

3 dried ancho chiles

1 clove garlic, peeled

½ teaspoon dried Mexican oregano

Salt, to taste

2 whole cloves

2 whole peppercorns

1 tablespoon olive oil

CALABACITAS (MEXICAN SQUASH) FILLING

3 tablespoons olive oil

1½ cups chopped carrots

¾ cup chopped red onion

3 large cloves garlic, peeled and minced

3 to 4 small calabacitas (or yellow squash and/or zucchini), chopped (about 2 cups)

3 plum tomatoes, cored and chopped

1 small bunch of spinach (about 20 leaves), rinsed and chopped

Salt, to taste

1 pound fresh or frozen banana leaves

12 ounces Monterey Jack cheese, cut into 3¾ by ½-inch strips

EQUIPMENT NEEDED

Kitchen twine

Large steamer or a stockpot with a steamer rack

Prepare the masa: Combine the masa harina, baking powder, and salt in a mixing bowl. With an electric mixer, beat the shortening until fluffy. Add 1 cup of the masa harina mixture and 1 cup of warm broth to the shortening and beat until well combined. Continue adding the dry ingredients and broth, until all are mixed together and the dough has a smooth consistency.

Prepare the sauce: Rinse the chiles under warm water, and use a paring knife to slit them down one side. Open the chiles and remove the seeds and veins. Add the seeds to the mix if you want more heat!

Place a griddle or large skillet over medium heat. Flatten out the dried chiles, and place on the griddle. Press down on the open chiles and leave for a few seconds. Turn the chiles over and repeat. Do not toast or burn the chiles, just heat them until the rinsing water evaporates.

Place the chiles in a small saucepan and add enough water to cover. Bring to a boil. Remove from the heat and let sit for 10 minutes, until the chiles have softened and plumped up. *continued*

Reserving the soaking water, remove the chiles from the pan and place in a blender. Add the garlic, oregano, ½ teaspoon salt, cloves, peppercorns, and 1½ cups of the soaking liquid. Blend until the sauce is completely smooth. Taste the sauce and adjust the seasoning. If you want more heat, add a few of the seeds or veins and blend some more. Taste, and add salt if needed.

Press the sauce through a sieve into a skillet. Add a tablespoon of olive oil to the sauce. Bring to a simmer and reduce the heat to maintain the simmer. Cook for 10 minutes, stirring occasionally. Skim off the foam that rises to the top. Remove the sauce from the heat and reserve.

Prepare the calabacitas filling: Coat the bottom of a sauté pan with olive oil and place over medium heat. Add the carrots, onion, and garlic to the hot skillet. Sauté for 2 to 3 minutes, until the onion begins to soften, then add the squash and tomatoes and cook for 1 minute. Add the spinach and cook, stirring, until just wilted. Remove from the heat. Stir ½ cup of the red chile sauce into the sautéed vegetables and season to taste with salt.

Prepare the banana leaves: If you are using frozen banana leaves (available at many Asian and Mexican markets), rinse them under warm water to defrost. Cut away the thick edges of the leaves. If you are using fresh banana leaves, also cut away the thick edges (and central stem if you are using freshly cut leaves). If using fresh leaves, rinse them under warm water. Banana leaves may be brittle and tear when you try to fold them. One way I've heard of to soften them is to soak them in warm, salted water for about an hour. Another way, which I have found effective, is to hold them over a gas burner or place them on a hot griddle for a few seconds until they turn color (brighter green) and soften. If you heat them too long, they will toast and become brittle again. Cut the banana leaves into 8- by 10-inch rectangles, and pat them dry with paper towels.

Assemble the tamales: Banana leaves have two sides. One side, the top of the leaf, is deep green and has somewhat thick ridges. The other side, the bottom of the leaf, is lighter green and is smoother. You will want to place the masa on the lighter green, smoother side of the leaf.

Lay out the rectangle of banana leaf, light side up. Place ¼ to ⅓ cup of the masa in the center of the banana leaf. Press down on it with the palm of your hand to spread it out a bit.

Spread 1 teaspoon of the red chile sauce over the masa. Place a strip of Monterey Jack cheese on top. Place about ¼ cup of the vegetable mixture on top of the cheese.

Bring together the two long sides of the banana leaf and fold over, tucking one edge over the other. Fold the two remaining sides under the tamale. Secure with kitchen string or a strip of banana leaf. Or, you can skip the tying step all together and just fold them well.

Steam the tamales: Add enough water to the steamer to come almost up to the level of the rack. Place extra banana leaves in the bottom of the steamer basket.

Carefully arrange the tamales in layers on the bottom of the pan. When you have added all of the tamales, add another layer of banana leaves. Cover the pot.

Bring to a boil, then reduce the heat to a simmer. Steam the tamales for approximately 1 hour.

three sacred sisters tamale pie

Because I was a strict vegetarian in the 1970s and 1980s—almost vegan—I know how tough it is to find a really good vegetarian entrée in a restaurant celebrated for its meat. This tamale pie gives the most succulent buffalo tenderloin a run for its money! It's an aromatic, complete protein dish and when it's carried to the table, meat lovers crane their necks to get a better view. The pie includes the corn, beans, and squash that are representative of the Indian diet and that for generations has been referred to as the three sacred sisters. • *serves 4 to 6*

VEGETABLES

2 tablespoons olive or canola oil

1 cup chopped yellow onion (1 small)

2 teaspoons minced garlic (2 cloves)

2 teaspoons mild to medium
  ground New Mexican red chile

1½ teaspoons ground cumin

1 teaspoon dried Mexican oregano

2 cups fresh or frozen corn kernels

1 cup fresh or canned chopped,
  mild green chiles

1½ cups vegetable broth

½ cup fire-roasted tomato puree

2 cups cooked Anasazi beans or pinto beans
  (a 15-ounce can, rinsed and drained)

2 cups finely diced zucchini (2 to 3 small zucchini)

Salt and freshly ground black pepper

MASA CRUST

1½ cups masa harina de maiz (corn tortilla mix)

1½ teaspoons baking powder

½ teaspoon salt

¼ cup vegetable shortening

1 to 1¼ cups warm vegetable broth or water

1½ cups shredded Monterey Jack and Colby cheese

Place the oil in a large sauté pan or skillet over medium heat. Add the onion and garlic and cook, stirring, over medium-low heat, for 3 to 5 minutes, until the onion is softened and translucent. Stir in the ground chile, cumin, and oregano. Add the corn and green chiles and stir in the vegetable broth and tomato puree. Add the beans and zucchini, and simmer over medium heat for about 5 minutes until the zucchini is slightly tender (al dente). Taste and season with salt and pepper.

In a mixing bowl, combine the masa harina, baking powder, and salt. In a food processor, with a steel knife blade, beat the shortening until fluffy. Add the masa mixture and pulse on and off a few times. Add the warm broth and pulse on and off until the dough comes together.

Divide the vegetable mixture among 4 to 6 ovensafe serving dishes and top with masa dough. Bake for 10 to 15 minutes until lightly browned. Top with the shredded cheese and bake another 3 to 5 minutes until the cheese is golden.

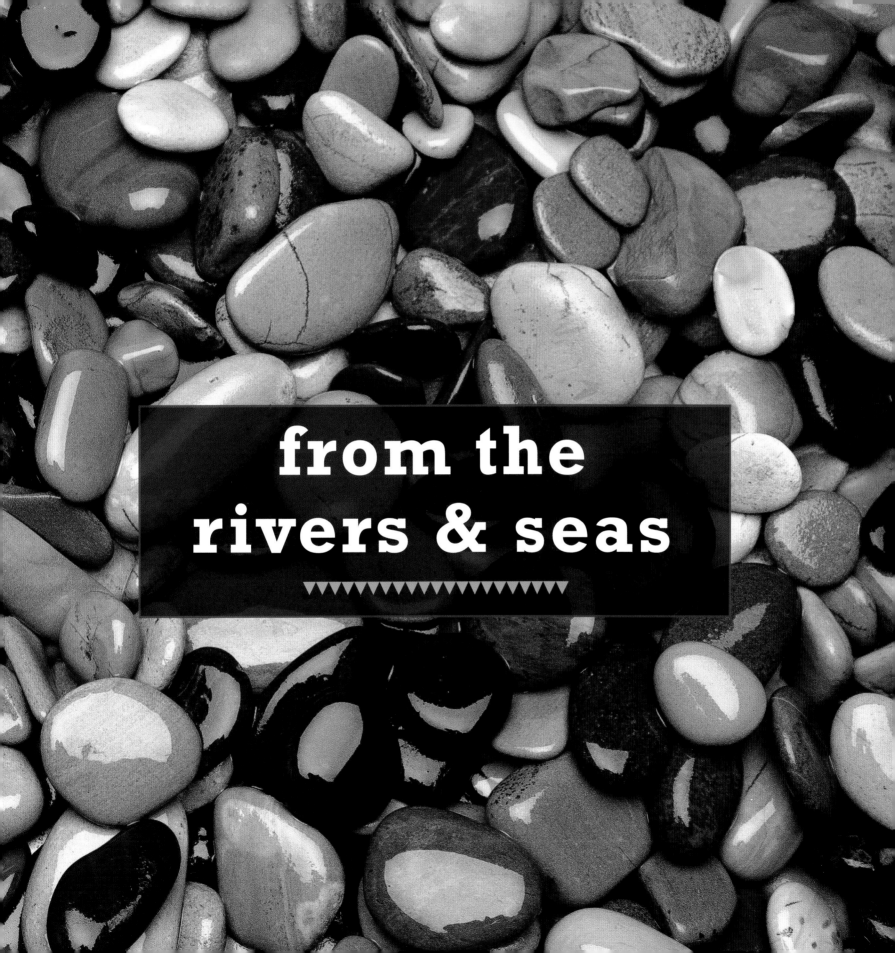

from the
rivers & seas

taos indian-style trout

When my father wrote about this traditional Native American recipe, he explained that he had gotten the recipe from his friend Mary Schlosser, a full-blooded Taos Indian married to Carl Schlosser. The couple ran Carl's Trading Post for many years in Taos, New Mexico. "It sounds a bit odd, but it is excellent," Dad said of the dish. "The bacon with the mint leaves imparts a delicious herbal taste."

This was on our menu for many years but was removed in 1976 when we sold the Fort. My family bought the restaurant back again in 1986, and although Dad wanted it back on the menu immediately, our chefs were not sure our patrons would embrace a dish that featured a trout with head and tail intact. Shortly after my father died, we honored his request and put the trout on the menu. Dad was right. Our guests love it! You will, too. • *serves 1*

1 (12- to 16-ounce) boneless, butterflied trout with head and tail attached
6 sprigs fresh mint
Salt
2 tablespoons olive oil
Freshly ground black pepper
2 strips bacon
Fresh lemon slices

Rinse the trout and pat dry with a paper towel.

Combine the short mint sprigs with the salt and olive oil and mash well. Fill the cavity of the trout with the mint mixture and sprinkle with pepper. Then, using a toothpick, pin one end of a bacon strip near the tail of the fish and wind it around the fish toward the head. Pin it there with another toothpick. Repeat the process with the second strip of bacon, starting on the other side of the fish. The trout may now be covered and refrigerated for several hours until ready to broil.

Preheat the oven to broil for about 20 minutes. Place the fish on a broiling pan and broil 5 inches from the heat for 5 to 7 minutes on each side, until the bacon is well crisped and the fish flakes. Remove and discard the toothpicks. Serve the trout with lemon slices.

owl woman's smoked trout

I found a description of this trout dish on a typed menu from 1963, which was stapled to a colorfully woven Mexican mat and evidently is named for William Bent's Cheyenne wife. Back in the '60s, the smoked fillets were prepared for us by Toklat in Ashcroft, Colorado. Sometimes large and sometimes small, the trout are boned, gently steamed to bring out the smoked flavor, and served with butter, chervil, and lemon sauce. Serve with wild rice or quinoa. • *serves 4 to 6*

4 to 6 smoked trout fillets
4 to 6 tablespoons unsalted butter
Juice of ½ lemon (about 2 tablespoons)
1 tablespoon minced fresh chervil or 1 teaspoon dried

In a steamer basket, over boiling water, gently steam the trout fillets for 3 to 4 minutes, or until warm.
   Meanwhile, in a small saucepan over low heat, melt the butter. Stir in the lemon juice and chervil.
   Spoon the sauce over the warm fillets and serve.

trout stuffed with corn, piñones, and green chiles

Trout is in good supply in Colorado, where mountain streams and rivers offer them happy homes. We serve a lot of the freshwater fish at the Fort, and this is one of our favorite recipes for special occasions. I first tasted this at the home of Priscilla Hoback, a renowned sculptor from Galisteo, New Mexico, and the daughter of my father's dear friend, Rosalea Murphy. Priscilla is a marvelously creative cook and although we had to adapt the recipe for the restaurant, it was inspired by her talent. • *serves 4 to 6*

1 cup fresh kernel corn (or canned or frozen)
¾ cup chopped fresh, frozen, or canned medium-hot or mild green chiles
½ cup dried bread crumbs
¼ cup toasted piñones (pine nuts)
1 large egg
2 teaspoons chopped fresh dill or ½ teaspoon dried dill weed
½ teaspoon dried leaf thyme
Salt and freshly ground black pepper
4 to 6 (12-inch) rainbow or cutthroat trout, deboned and butterflied
2 to 3 tablespoons canola oil

Preheat the oven to 350°F.

In a mixing bowl, combine the corn, green chiles, bread crumbs, and piñones. In a separate bowl, beat the egg with the dill, thyme, and salt and pepper. Add the egg to the corn mixture and stir to combine. Stuff the cavities of the trout with the corn mixture. Brush the stuffed trout with oil and place them in a shallow baking pan. Tent loosely with foil. Bake the trout on the middle rack of the oven for 20 minutes. Remove the foil and bake an additional 15 minutes, until cooked through.

cedar plank achiote salmon

Native Americans from the Pacific Northwest have cooked salmon on planks of cedar for generations, a technique that has become popular with the rest of the country during the past few decades. According to our purveyors, we sell more salmon than any other restaurant in the Rockies, which leads me to believe we must be doing something right! • *serves 4 to 6*

2 cedar or alder wood cooking planks
2 ounces achiote (annatto seed) paste, page 240
5 to 6 tablespoons canola oil
4 to 6 (6-ounce) salmon fillet portions, with skin on
Sea salt and freshly ground black pepper, to taste
4 to 6 lime wedges

Soak the planks in water, to cover, for at least 1 hour before cooking the fish. Preheat the oven to 400°F. Place the soaked planks on the middle rack of the oven.

In a food processor, blend the achiote paste and 4 tablespoons of the oil to make a smooth paste. Coat the salmon fillets with this seasoning paste, and sprinkle with salt and pepper.

Coat a large nonstick skillet with 1 to 2 tablespoons of oil and place it over medium–high heat. Arrange the fillets flesh side down in the hot skillet and sear for 2 minutes, turn, and cook the skin side for 30 seconds. Place the fillets flesh side up on the hot planks and cook in the oven for 8 to 10 minutes, until cooked to taste. Garnish with lime wedges.

SALMON: FRESH OR FROZEN?

In the late 1980s, my dad discovered the benefits of flash-frozen fish. At the same time, I owned a public relations company and had a new client from New Zealand called Skeggs that promoted flash-frozen orange roughy for sale in supermarkets. Together we learned a lot about the process and how it results in a very good product. Dad wrote about it:

"I had always stressed the value of 'fresh only' for the fin fish served at the Fort," my father said. "Thus, at the Aspen Food and Wine Festival years ago, I was vexed and disbelieving when a salmon salesman from Norway announced that the Fort was serving the fish he sold. I did not know that my chef had been using whole frozen Norwegian salmon. Noting my horror, the sales rep promised to prove to me that what we were serving was as good or better than fresh. We ran some cooking and taste tests and the proof was clearly in our mouths. The so-called fresh salmon didn't taste as fresh as the frozen salmon from Norway. The texture of both was identical.

"I came to learn that the Sekkingstad family in Bergen, Norway, had been licensed by the Japanese company that had developed a remarkable new freezing technique." At that time, my father wrote, they were the only company in Norway to have the proper equipment.

He went on to explain that my stepmother Carrie and he traveled to Norway to look into the method. The salmon were farmed in fjords that are sometimes three thousand feet deep and filled with cold, clean water. The fish were harvested when they were three feet long and processed at water's edge where they went through the freezing process within moments of coming out of the water.

"The result is that in Denver, Colorado, in our walk-in cooler, the thawed fish starts out with a very low bacteria count (less than 3 percent), whereas fresh fish arrive with bacteria counts of more than 30 percent," Dad continued. "The frozen Norwegian salmon have a longer shelf life, which begins only when the fish are thawed in the cooler, instead of the two days that is the case of the fresh fish sent from Alaska, Canada, or Chile.

"Today at the Fort we pride ourselves on serving the freshest tasting salmon available. It's easy to determine when fish are fresh if you buy them from a reputable market: First, look at the eye for clarity. If they are sunken and dull, the fish is old. Next, open the gills with your fingers and make sure they are bright red. Finally, push against the meat of the fish's body with your finger. If the indentation springs back, you have a fresh fish. If the indentation remains in the flesh, look for another fish. And if there is an odor other than a faint smell of the sea, move on."

▼▼▼▼▼▼▼▼▼▼▼▼▼▼▼▼▼▼▼▼▼▼▼▼

astrid's broiled salmon with scandinavian dill sauce

The Gustermans were close friends of my parents who lived in Georgetown, a small mining hamlet high in the Rockies. My mother had always loved the flavors of fresh dill sauce served with salmon and so asked Astrid for her authentic Swedish recipe, which she put on our menu in the 1960s. This dish is a tribute to Astrid, both for her outstanding cooking and her loyal friendship. • *serves 4*

CUCUMBER DILL SAUCE

1 cup sour cream

1 tablespoon peeled, deseeded,
  and finely diced cucumber

1 teaspoon chopped fresh dill

5 drops Worcestershire sauce

Dash of salt

SALMON

4 (6- to 8-ounce) salmon fillets, with skin on

Canola or vegetable oil

Paprika or cayenne (optional)

Juice of ½ lemon

2 to 3 tablespoons unsalted butter, melted

1 tablespoon chopped fresh dill
  or 1 teaspoon dried dill weed

2 lemons, halved

At least 8 hours in advance, combine the sour cream, cucumber, dill, Worcestershire, and salt and refrigerate, covered, until serving time.

Preheat the oven to broil or heat your grill to high.

If you purchase a whole salmon instead of 8 ounce fillets, use a boning knife to cut along the backbone on either side and remove the fillets. Check for small bones near the dorsal fin and any leftover bones you may have missed when filleting. A pair of long-nosed tweezers is used by most fish butchers to pull hidden bones. Feel with your fingers and then tweeze them out.

Brush the steaks with oil to keep them from sticking to the grill. Dust the flesh side with paprika, if using. Broil 3 to 4 minutes per side, skin side down first, over low to medium heat. Watch carefully and don't overcook. The skin can be removed from the fillet before serving, but it serves to hold the fish nicely together while it's on the grill. Brush it with lemon juice and butter and sprinkle it lightly with dill. Serve with lemon halves and cucumber dill sauce on the side.

Note: These days many people like their fish nearly raw. It is fashionable to sear the outside and leave the inside barely warm. If that's what you like, cut down the cooking time and put it closer to the heat. The fish needs to be extremely fresh if you are going to cook it this way.

fort edmonton canadian white fish

When my dad and I visited historic Fort Edmonton near Edmonton, Canada, we learned that the Hudson Bay Trading Company, which ran the fort, hired cooks to prepare wonderful meals for traders and soldiers. At Christmastime in 1834, these cooks reportedly served Canadian white fish sautéed in buffalo bone marrow. Upon hearing this, both Dad and I whipped around and grinned at each other. We could do this! When we returned to Denver, we began importing fresh Canadian white fish from a First Nations Tribe of Canada. It's no longer possible to buy imported Canadian white fish, but any white fish, such as arctic char, does very nicely. If you can't find buffalo bones for the marrow, try beef or veal bone marrow. This is well worth trying—it's surprisingly delicious!

• *serves 4 to 6*

4 to 6 (6-ounce) fillets of Canadian white fish or Arctic char
½ cup cornmeal
½ cup all-purpose flour
½ teaspoon cayenne pepper
Sea salt and freshly ground black pepper, to taste
2 large eggs, beaten with 2 tablespoons water
2 to 4 tablespoons olive oil
4 to 6 (½-inch-thick) slices of Herbed Prairie Butter, recipe follows
2 small lemons, thinly sliced
Italian parsley sprigs, for garnish

Rinse the fish fillets under cold water and pat dry with paper towels. Sift the cornmeal, flour, cayenne, and salt and pepper onto a plate. Place the egg wash in a widemouthed shallow bowl. Dip the fillets in the egg, then dredge in the cornmeal mixture.

Place 2 tablespoons of olive oil in a large skillet over medium-high heat. Arrange the fillets in the hot pan flesh side down. Do not crowd the pan; work in batches, if necessary, adding more oil as needed. Reduce the heat to medium, cover and cook for 3 to 4 minutes, until the crust is golden brown. Turn the fillets, cover, and continue to cook for 2 to 4 minutes, until cooked to taste.

Serve the fish with hot fluffy wild rice. Garnish each fillet with a disk of Herbed Prairie Butter, lemon slices, and parsley sprigs.

herbed prairie butter

• *makes ¹/₄ pound*

1 buffalo femur bone, split or 2 pounds beef or veal marrow bones, split

¹/₄ pound Herb Butter, page 152

Preheat the oven to 500°F. Arrange the bones in a shallow roasting pan and roast 15 to 20 minutes. Allow the bones to cool slightly, then scoop out the marrow and chop it roughly.

Put the butter and marrow in an electric mixer, and whip on medium speed until the marrow is incorporated into the butter.

Remove the butter from the mixer and place on cooking parchment to roll into cylinders. Refrigerate or freeze the cylinders for later use.

THE SCOOP ON SHRIMP

We serve shrimp at the Fort, not because they are caught anywhere nearby but because they are so loved by many of our customers and lend themselves to so many remarkable preparations. They are sized according to how many headless, raw shrimp there are in a pound. For instance, U15 shrimp means there are 15 or fewer shrimp in the pound weight. When it comes to commercial names, for jumbo shrimp expect from 9 to 11 of the crustaceans in a pound; large shrimp, 15 to 20; and medium shrimp, 25 to 31.

When my father wrote about shrimp, he explained that they come in three varieties, generally indicated by the color of the uncooked product. White shrimp, sometimes known as Gulf shrimp, are the most expensive and generally come from the Gulf of Mexico. Pinks are less expensive, and brown shrimp are the least expensive. Freshwater farmed "tiger" shrimp from Thailand and the Philippines can be very good, but be sure to choose firm, clean-smelling specimens. At times, we have been able to acquire giant shrimp from Cadiz, Spain, which weigh about 4 ounces each, almost like a small lobster.

My father recommended buying shrimp whole. It may be easier to buy peeled, deveined shrimp but they tend to lack flavor. If you possibly can, peel it yourself. You will spend less money and end up with a better dish.

Shrimp are delicate. When they are frozen (and most are), thaw them in the refrigerator overnight and then use them very soon. If you can't cook them the day they thaw, cover them with water, squeeze some lemon juice over them, and refrigerate for no longer than two days. If you buy a large quantity of frozen shrimp in a block, run the block under cold water, separate the amount you need, and then rewrap and refreeze the others.

▼▼▼▼▼▼▼▼▼▼▼▼▼▼▼▼▼▼▼▼▼▼▼

gulf shrimp en globo

My dad observed that when shrimp are broiled over a hot grill, they lose so much moisture that they shrink into unappetizing specimens, and so he came up with a dish he dubbed Gulf Shrimp en Globo. Five or six shrimp, dabbed with a little herb butter, are encased in an aluminum foil packet, which balloons during cooking and renders the shrimp moist and tender. Besides its glorious flavor, I love that this can be prepared in advance. After cleaning the shrimp, making the herb butter, and then sealing the shrimp in foil, the packets can be refrigerated until it is time to cook them. • *serves 4*

6 fresh basil leaves
8 sprigs Italian parsley
2 cloves garlic, crushed
Juice of ½ lemon (about 2 tablespoons)
4 to 6 tablespoons unsalted butter
16 squares aluminum foil, approximately 10 inches square
2 pounds Gulf white shrimp as large as you can find, peeled and deveined
4 cups cooked white rice (optional)

Using a mortar and pestle or food processor, blend the basil, parsley, garlic, lemon juice, and butter. Set aside. For each serving, lay 2 squares of aluminum foil on top of each other and fold their edges so that they are securely attached. Double layering prevents spillage and breaking. Divide the shrimp and herb butter among the 4 foil packets. Cover each packet with 2 additional sheets of foil, fold over the edges, and seal well. Store in the refrigerator for a few hours until ready to use or freeze for later use.

When ready to cook, preheat the grill. Turn the heat to medium and place the foil packets over the fire for about 5 minutes, until they puff up, then remove from the fire. If the shrimp are frozen, they will have to cook for another 3 minutes until done.

The shrimp may be removed easily from the packets by snipping with scissors. They're delicious over a bed of rice, if desired. Or serve in the closed packets and allow your guests to open them at the table.

chipotle skewered shrimp
or shrimp en appolas

The smokiness of the chipotle blends beautifully with grilled shrimp so that these become a simply irresistible appetizer or main course. The shrimp are a popular request for private parties at the Fort, where we pass them as appetizers. • *serves 4*

4 bamboo or metal skewers

½ cup olive oil

1 clove garlic, peeled and minced

Juice of 1 lemon (about 3 tablespoons)

3 dashes of chipotle sauce or ½ teaspoon mashed chipotle peppers in adobo sauce

1 teaspoon honey or sugar (optional)

20 jumbo shrimp with tail on, peeled and deveined

Rice Pilaf, page 130

Fresh cilantro or Italian parsley sprigs, for garnish

If you are using bamboo skewers, let them soak in water while you prepare the sauce so they won't burn on the grill.

About 1 hour before cooking, whisk together the olive oil, garlic, lemon juice, and chipotle sauce. Adding a teaspoon of honey or sugar to the sauce will give the shrimp a slight caramelized glaze, if you wish.

Add the shrimp to the sauce and allow to marinate for 1 hour.

Preheat a charcoal grill to medium. Thread the heads and tails of each shrimp onto a bamboo skewer, 5 per skewer, and grill for 2 minutes, brushing with the sauce while they cook. Serve on a bed of pilaf. A sprig or two of cilantro or parsley makes a nice garnish.

three-legged lobster with lemon butter

As my dad once said: "One of the joys of lobster, scallops, and crab is that when they're grilled, the slightly burned taste much improves their overall flavor." This recipe calls for browning and then arranging the lobster for a presentation your guests will not soon forget. It works best for lobster tails that weigh at least 8 ounces. • *serves 4 to 6*

4 to 6 lobster tails, 8 ounces or larger
8 tablespoons unsalted butter, melted
Juice of ½ lemon (about 2 tablespoons)
Paprika
2 lemons or limes, halved, and wrapped in cheesecloth

Preheat the grill to medium.

Place the lobster tails on the counter so that they rest on the shell. Using kitchen scissors, cut along the lower edge of the shell to remove the bottom cover skin. Reach between the meat and the shell to gently loosen the entire tail, leaving the extreme back end attached. With a sharp knife, slit the meat lengthwise up the middle, making two "legs" of the meat. Meanwhile, combine the butter and lemon juice. Brush the lobster with some of the lemon butter and sprinkle lightly with paprika. Place the lobster tails on the grill and cook over low to medium heat. When they've browned a bit, turn them over and brown the other side.

When the meat is opaque and cooked through, remove the tails to a serving plate. Stand each of them up to form a tripod of shell and both "legs" of meat. Place a small cup of melted butter combined with lemon juice in front of the lobster tail beside half of a lemon or lime wrapped in a square of cheesecloth twisted at the top and tied with a piece of string.

lobster and shrimp enchilada suiza

During the 1960s, my father's famous Chicken Enchilada Suiza was on the menu, and I loved it. When I was about ten years old, I remember asking the chef to make it for me and pack it up so that I could take it to the top of the ninety-foot red rock next to the restaurant and eat it while watching a spectacular Rocky Mountain sunset. Years later, my son Oren made it and called it Orenchilada and the *Denver Post* wrote a feature story about it. I have altered the recipe so that now it's made with lobster and shrimp—and it is richer and more seductive than ever.

I make this with rock lobster, also called *langouste,* and not to be confused with Maine lobsters, which have big claws. The langouste grow in both warm and cold waters but the best are found in the chilly waters off the coasts of Australia and New Zealand. • *serves 6*

4 tablespoons unsalted butter
2 tablespoons all-purpose flour
2 cups (1 pint) light cream or half-and-half
1 clove garlic, crushed
1½ teaspoons dried Mexican oregano
½ teaspoon salt
1 cup full-fat sour cream
12 corn tortillas
½ pound uncooked shrimp,
    peeled, cleaned, and deveined

½ pound raw lobster meat
1 yellow onion, finely chopped
1½ cups chopped mild green chiles (fresh or canned)
½ cup chopped walnuts, lightly toasted
½ cup sliced ripe olives
2 cups grated Monterey Jack cheese
2 cups grated sharp Cheddar cheese
Avocado wedges, strips of red pimiento,
    black and green olives, or toasted walnuts
    or pine nuts, for garnish (optional)

Preheat the oven to 350°F.

In a large saucepan, melt the butter over medium heat. Add the flour and cook, stirring for 1 minute. Gradually whisk in the cream, and add the garlic, oregano, and salt. Cook, stirring, for about 1 minute, until the sauce begins to thicken. Remove from the heat and whisk in the sour cream.

Line a 9- to 10-inch, shallow buttered casserole with half of the corn tortillas. Overlap them to cover the bottom and sides completely. Scatter half of the shrimp and half of the lobster over the tortillas, then half of the onion, chiles, walnuts, and olives. Pour over 1 cup of the warm sauce. Combine the grated cheeses and sprinkle half over the casserole.

Repeat the process with the remaining ingredients, beginning with the corn tortillas and finishing with the cheeses.

Bake for about 1½ hours, until well heated. When the cheese bubbles and becomes golden brown, the enchilada is ready to eat. If your casserole is deeper than it is wide, the enchilada may take longer to cook all the way through. In this case, when the cheeses have browned, cover the dish with aluminum foil and continue to bake. Garnish as you like with avocado, pimiento, olives, or toasted nuts.

TORTILLAS

In Spain, a tortilla is an omelet. In Mexico, tortillas are pliable flatbreads, just as most Americans think of them. Because I live in the Southwest and not Spain, I am only interested in the latter. These flatbreads are amazingly versatile and at the Fort we rely on them for myriad dishes.

There are two kinds of tortillas, defined by their ingredients. Wheat tortillas, most popular in northern Mexico and southern New Mexico and Arizona where wheat is grown, usually measure between 6 and 12 inches in diameter and may be as thick as half an inch when leavened with yeast or baking powder. They are mild tasting and pale in color.

Corn tortillas generally are smaller than wheat, rarely measuring larger than 6 inches across and often less. They are made from cornmeal ground from corn kernels first cooked in slaked lime (calcium hydroxide), which removes the tough outer skin of the corn. Their flavor is immediately recognizable as coming from corn and blends deliciously with any number of southwestern ingredients.

Both kinds of tortillas are baked on a flat griddle or grill. The most authentic device for cooking them is a *comal,* a flat pan used throughout Mexico that resembles a skillet or a flat griddle and is used for tortillas as well as to toast spices. In much of South America, the same pan is called a *budare.* If you don't have a comal, you can bake tortillas in skillets, iron griddles, or even on a sheet of steel set over a source of heat.

If you like to make yeast bread, you can make flour tortillas. Make your favorite dough, form some into a ball about the size of a small apple, and then using a rolling pin, roll the dough into a flat, thin round about 8 inches in diameter. Heat a skillet or comal over medium heat, sprinkle the hot surface with about ½ a teaspoon of salt to prevent sticking, and then pan-fry the tortilla until lightly browned and still flexible. Turn and fry the other side.

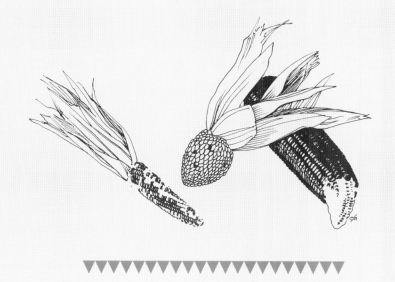

hangtown oyster fry

The story goes that the dish originated in a California Gold Rush town called Hangtown, which had gotten its name thanks to an overzealous judge who was not afraid to mete out the ultimate punishment. Today, Hangtown is a peaceful place called Placerville, but back in 1849, it was a rough-and-tumble settlement. A prospector arrived in town after ten hard months in the mountains, ready to celebrate with his newfound gold. He asked the owner of a tent restaurant to fix him up with the richest dish he could and ended up with this, which he named Hangtown Fry. • *serves 2*

5 large eggs
2 tablespoons beer or water
½ cup all-purpose flour
½ teaspoon cracked black pepper
½ teaspoon salt

10 select fresh oysters, shucked
4 tablespoons unsalted butter
4 tablespoons coarsely chopped Italian parsley leaves
4 slices hot buttered toast

In a mixing bowl, beat or whisk the eggs with the beer until frothy. In another bowl, combine the flour, pepper, and salt. Dry the oysters on a paper towel, then roll in the flour mixture.

Heat the butter in a large skillet, rotating the skillet to coat the bottom and partway up the sides. Place the floured oysters evenly around the skillet and sauté for 3 minutes, turning with a spatula, until browned.

Pour the egg mixture over the oysters. Lower the heat under the skillet and cook for about 4 minutes, swirling the pan and poking holes in the cooking eggs so that all the egg is cooked. Use a spatula to gently loosen the eggs from the walls of the pan. Gradually, when the bottom is firm enough and lightly browned and the center is very moist but not runny, fold the omelet in half. Slide it onto a serving platter and garnish with parsley. Serve with hot buttered toast.

OYSTERS IN SANTA FE

Susan Shelby Magoffin was one of the first Anglo women to come across the Santa Fe Trail in 1846, traveling with her trader husband, Samuel Magoffin. She kept a diary that the Yale Press still publishes today, in which she describes eating oysters on the half shell and drinking the finest French Champagne at a party in Santa Fe. Where did they get fresh oysters in landlocked Santa Fe? They pulled them from the Chesapeake Bay, of course! The shippers layered the live oysters in large oak casks, their "mouths" facing upward, and then covered them with shaved ice and cornmeal. As the wagon train traveled from one town to the next, the drivers replenished the ice and cornmeal to keep the oysters alive and well fed. Week by week, month by month, town by town, eventually the wagon train arrived in Santa Fe with plump, living oysters ready to be shucked and eaten with chilled Champagne.

▼▼▼▼▼▼▼▼▼▼▼▼▼▼▼▼▼▼▼▼▼▼

holly's sweet cupboard & icehouse

cider-cooked trappers' fruit

It comes as no surprise that both the early trappers and soldiers, as well as the Native Americans, relied heavily on dried fruits to get them through the winter. The fruits were accompanied by other dried foods such as buffalo jerky and fat, and gathered nuts, all survival foods. Indians often subsisted on a mixture of fat, dried meat, nuts, and fruits called pemmican, and while it may not appeal to our modern palates, it was a nutritious substitute for a substantial meal; traders, trappers, and the army often turned to pemmican, too. We don't serve pemmican at the Fort but instead we make this dried fruit compote to spoon over ice cream, or occasionally to accompany meat. As the dried apples, spices, hazelnuts, and rum cook, the compote just turns more syrupy, mellow, dark, and delicious. • *serves 8*

4 quarts apple cider

2 pounds dried apples

2 cups applesauce

½ cup fresh lemon juice (juice of 2 or 3 lemons)

½ cup golden raisins

3 tablespoons brown sugar or honey

1 tablespoon coriander seeds

1 tablespoon pure vanilla extract

½ teaspoon ground cinnamon

½ teaspoon ground cloves

½ teaspoon grated nutmeg

½ cup lightly toasted, coarsely chopped hazelnuts

1 cup dark rum

In a large pot, combine the apple cider, dried apples, applesauce, lemon juice, raisins, brown sugar, coriander seeds, vanilla, cinnamon, cloves, and nutmeg. Bring to a boil over high heat. Lower the heat and simmer for at least 1 hour to reduce the liquid.

Trappers' Fruit will be ready to eat whenever you're ready to eat it. At the Fort we like to cook it, covered, for several hours, stirring frequently to prevent burning. Just before serving, stir in the toasted hazelnuts and add the rum.

vera's caramel canola brownies

Our guests love these brownies and without doubt, you will, too—if you like fudgy treats! My dad wrote about these brownies, recalling a telephone call he got out of the blue in 1998 from a woman named Vera Dahlquist. Would he consider hiring a baker who was eighty years old? she asked. "You bet I would!" Dad said. "She probably knows more about baking than the rest of us put together." Vera, who had emigrated from Finland as a child, was a gifted baker and we all enjoyed her banana cream pies and fragrant dinner rolls, but our very favorite were these brownies. They have a chewiness that makes them both a brownie and a candy. To achieve this glorious texture, hand mix the batter rather than relying on an electric mixer so that you don't beat too much air into it. • *makes 15 large brownies*

2 ½ cups all-purpose flour (2 ¼ cups at sea level)
3 cups brown sugar (3 cups + 2 tablespoons at sea level)
3 teaspoons baking powder (3 ¾ teaspoons at sea level)
¼ teaspoon salt
4 large eggs
1 ¼ cup (2 ½ sticks) butter or margarine, melted
1 teaspoon vanilla extract
1 cup chopped walnuts or pecans
¼ cup canola or poppy seeds

Preheat the oven to 350°F. Grease and line the bottom of a 9- by 13-inch baking pan with parchment paper.

In a large bowl, blend together the flour, brown sugar, baking powder, and salt.

In a small bowl, beat the eggs slightly. Stir in the butter and vanilla. Add the egg mixture to the dry ingredients and blend well.

Stir in the nuts and seeds.

Spread the batter in the prepared pan. Bake for 25 to 30 minutes, (30 to 35 minutes at sea level), or until the center can be touched without leaving an indentation. Do not overbake!

Note: Do not use an electric mixer for this recipe; you don't want too much air beaten into the batter. Hand stirring will yield a chewier brownie.

biscochitos (new mexico shortbread cookies)

These delicate, anise-flavored cookies are indulgently rich, yet still light. Plus, they are easy to make. The cookie was brought to the Southwest by the Spanish in the early 1600s, and like most traditional recipes, there are nearly as many versions as families who claim them as their own. It's so popular that New Mexico declared the biscochito its official state cookie in 1989. I have been eating the cookies all my life partly because they are so common in this part of the world and also because my father had a special fondness for them, which I share. In 1948, Dad attended a prayer ceremony and midnight mass at a pueblo near Santa Fe called San Felipe, where he tried his first biscochito. Clearly it left a significant impression. • *makes 3 to 4 dozen cookies*

½ cup lard or vegetable shortening
1 cup sugar
3 large eggs
1 tablespoon anise seeds
2 to 2¼ cups sifted all-purpose flour
Rum or bourbon
Ground cinnamon
Pinch of ground New Mexican red chile (optional)

Preheat the oven to 350°F.

With an electric mixer, beat together the lard and sugar until light and fluffy.

Add the eggs and anise seeds and beat until well combined and pale yellow in color. Gradually mix in the flour until a stiff, smooth, dough forms.

Gather the dough into a ball. Cover and chill for 1 hour.

Roll out the dough on a floured board until it is very thin, no thicker than ¼ inch. Cut it into your favorite cookie shapes. Brush the tops of the cookies with rum or bourbon, and sprinkle with cinnamon mixed with a pinch of chile, if desired.

Bake for 3 to 5 minutes, or until barely brown. These are perfect with hot cider, steaming coffee, or cocoa.

bay's brandied pumpkin pie

My mother thought this was the best pumpkin pie she had ever eaten—and I have to say I agree. Since we first made it in the 1960s, it's been one of my favorites and I can't let a Thanksgiving go by without it, nor can I make a pumpkin pie without brandy. It's an old Pennsylvania Dutch recipe from my father's grandmother, Gunny, who lived in Pennsylvania.

• *serves 4 to 6*

One 9-inch pie shell

1 can (15-ounce) pumpkin

1 cup heavy cream or evaporated milk

1 cup sugar

3 large eggs, slightly beaten

2 to 3 tablespoons brandy or Cognac

¾ teaspoon nutmeg

¾ teaspoon ground cinnamon

½ teaspoon ground ginger

½ teaspoon salt

¼ teaspoon ground mace

Place a baking sheet on the middle rack of the oven. Preheat the oven to 375°F.

Line the pie shell with a round of baking parchment and fill with pie weights or dried beans. Set the shell on the hot baking sheet, and blind-bake for 10 minutes.

Meanwhile, in a mixing bowl, whisk together the pumpkin, cream, sugar, eggs, brandy, nutmeg, cinnamon, ginger, salt, and mace.

Remove the pie shell from the oven; set aside the parchment and weights. Fill the shell with pumpkin filling.

Reduce the oven temperature to 350°F. Bake the pie for 45 to 55 minutes, until the crust is golden brown and the filling doesn't shake.

CHRISTMAS FAROLITOS

Santa Fe, New Mexico, celebrates Christmas brilliantly, and one of my favorite customs is that the narrow, ancient streets are illuminated with thousands of farolitos, little paper bag lanterns filled with sand and lit with a candle. The cool winter nights glow with their soft light and the crisp air is perfumed with the smoke from cedar and pine nut fires. Walking through the old city is nothing short of magical.

At the Fort, we celebrate the winter holidays in November when we light farolitos in our courtyard. On Christmas Eve, the Tesoro Cultural Center celebrates in much the same way. At both events, we serve biscochito cookies and hot mulled apple cider.

chile-chocolate bourbon cake

While this cake started as the Fort's house cake for birthday and anniversary celebrations, customer demand convinced us to put it on the menu as an everyday offering. We still serve a complimentary slice to anyone marking a special occasion at the Fort—and set a ceremonial headdress on their head, too, as the staff shouts, "Hip, hip, huzzah!" We don't do anything halfway at our restaurant!

We make the cake with some red chile to honor the ancient Aztec tradition of spiking their drinking chocolate with a little heat. This makes sense when you remember that it wasn't until the Europeans took chocolate back to the Old World that anyone thought to sweeten it. Before then, it was made into a bitter but much appreciated ceremonial brew. You'll feel a slight burn at the back of the throat when you eat this, but that will quickly turn into a warm glow. The bourbon-flavored frosting adds its own kick. This cake is best when made 1 to 2 days before serving as it gives the flavors time to blend. • *serves 12*

CAKE

1 to 2 tablespoons New Mexico medium ground
   red chile powder (Dixon is the best), to taste

2 cups water (³⁄₄ cup at sea level)

1 tablespoon pure vanilla extract

1 cup plus 2 tablespoons all-purpose flour

1 cup plus 2 tablespoons cake flour (not self-rising)

½ cup unsweetened, nonalkalized cocoa powder,
   such as Hershey, Nestlé, or Ghirardelli
   (do not use Dutch processed)

1 teaspoon baking soda (2 teaspoons at sea level)

½ teaspoon salt

1 cup (2 sticks) unsalted butter,
   cut into pieces and softened

2 cups sugar

2 large eggs, at room temperature

½ cup buttermilk

FROSTING

¾ cup unsweetened nonalkalized cocoa powder
   (do not use Dutch processed)

¼ cup plus 2 tablespoons buttermilk

4 to 5 cups confectioners' sugar

2 to 3 tablespoons bourbon

1 tablespoon pure vanilla extract

1½ cups chopped walnuts, lightly toasted
   (optional)

For the cake, preheat the oven to 350°F, and place a rack in the center of the oven.

Butter two 9-inch round cake pans. Lightly dust the sides of the pans with flour, tapping out the excess, and line the bottom with circles of parchment or waxed paper. Butter and flour the paper circles as well.

In a small saucepan, heat the chile powder in the water over medium heat until simmering. Remove the pan from the heat, stir in the vanilla, and set aside.

continued

In a large bowl, mix together the flours, cocoa powder, baking soda and salt. With a wire whisk, whisk 7 or 8 times to blend well.

Using an electric mixer with the paddle attachment, beat the butter until creamy, 2 to 3 minutes. Add the sugar and beat for 3 to 4 minutes longer or until smooth and creamy. Add the eggs, 1 at a time, and beat after each addition.

Reduce the speed to low and slowly beat in the dry ingredients, alternating with the buttermilk and chile powder and water mixture. Be sure to scrape the bottom of the pan to remove all the chile powder. Beat the batter just until smooth and combined.

Divide the batter evenly between the pans and smooth the batter in the pan so that the surfaces are level. Bake for 35 to 40 minutes, or until a toothpick inserted in the center of each layer comes out clean.

To cool, set the pans on a wire rack for 15 minutes. Turn the cakes out onto the rack, remove the paper from the bottom, and immediately invert so that the risen tops don't flatten. Let the layers cool completely before frosting.

For the frosting, combine the butter and cocoa in a large saucepan and melt over medium heat. Stir in the buttermilk. Add the confectioners' sugar, a little at a time, stirring with a wire whisk between additions. Stir in the bourbon and vanilla and continue to whisk until the frosting is smooth and glossy. The frosting should stiffen as it cools. (In warm weather you may need to refrigerate it.) When it is still warm, but has reached a spreadable consistency, you can assemble the cake.

If necessary, trim the tops of the cakes so that they are level. Place one of the cake layers on a 9-inch round cardboard cake circle. Spread 1 cup of the frosting over the layer. Sprinkle 1 cup of the chopped walnuts, if using, evenly over the frosting. Place the second layer of cake on the frosted base. Use the remaining frosting to cover the top and sides of the cake. Finish the top of the cake by holding the spatula at a slight angle and making several strokes to smooth the top. To decorate the cake, press the remaining walnuts onto the lower half of the sides and on top of the cake.

Variation: *"Red Hot" Chile-Chocolate Bourbon Cupcakes:* Preheat the oven to 350°F. Mix the cake batter and frosting following the instructions in the master recipe. Place cupcake papers in regular or mini muffin pans. Divide the batter evenly among the cups filling the paper liners to 1/4-inch from the top. You can pour the batter from a pitcher or use a ladle. Bake on the middle rack of the oven, 20 to 25 minutes for regular cupcakes and 10 to 15 minutes for minis. When done, the cupcake tops should be slightly firm to the touch and a toothpick inserted in the center should come out clean. Cool the cupcakes in their pan for 5 minutes and transfer them still in their paper liners to a wire rack to cool completely. Frost the cooled cupcakes and decorate them with red cinnamon candies.

• *Makes 24 regular cupcakes or 48 mini cupcakes*

bobbie's cheesecake

Our family friend Bobbie Chaim introduced us to this delectable cheesecake—the creamiest, lightest, moistest slice of heaven you will ever put in your mouth! Bobbie used to bring one of these every Christmas as a gift for my father, and I couldn't keep out of the refrigerator where the leftovers were stored, slicing a sliver for a sinful late-night snack. The crust contains vanilla sugar, which Bobbie claims is the secret of Viennese baking. The tablespoon sprinkled over the cake before baking makes all the difference in the world. And using Philadelphia cream cheese is critical: Other packaged cream cheeses are too salty and fresh cream cheese does not contain the necessary stabilizers.

A quick note on the baking: The time and temperature for this recipe work perfectly at Denver's mile-high altitude. At sea level, bake for 22 minutes at 350°F and 4 minutes at 500°F. • *serves 12*

GERMAN MURBTEIG CRUST

1½ cups all-purpose flour

¾ teaspoon baking powder

⅓ cup sugar

Pinch of salt

1 tablespoon vanilla sugar, see Note

1 large egg

8 tablespoons (1 stick) butter or margarine, softened

FILLING

4 large egg whites, at room temperature

1 cup sugar

¼ teaspoon pure vanilla extract

24 ounces Kraft Philadelphia brand cream cheese

TOPPING

1 pint full-fat sour cream

2 tablespoons sugar

½ teaspoon pure vanilla extract

Preheat the oven to 350°F.

For the crust: In a mixing bowl, combine the flour, baking powder, sugar, salt, and vanilla sugar. Add the egg and softened butter and mix until the dough forms a ball. This is easiest to do in a standing mixer with a dough hook attachment. Pat the dough in an 8-inch springform pan, lining the bottom and sides all the way to the top. Try to achieve a uniform thickness.

For the filling: Beat the egg whites until fairly stiff but not dry. Add the sugar slowly and then add the vanilla. Slowly, in small amounts, add the cream cheese. Mix to smooth the major lumps, but be careful not to overbeat. Pour into the crust-lined pan and bake on the middle rack of the oven for 25 minutes. Remove from the oven and set aside.

Raise the oven temperature to 500°F. While the oven is heating, prepare the topping. Combine the sour cream, sugar, and vanilla. Spread very gently on the top of the cheesecake and bake for 5 minutes. Let cool at room temperature and then refrigerate. Remove the springform pan and keep tightly covered with plastic wrap. Serve well chilled.

Note: To make vanilla sugar, place several vanilla beans in a tall jar. Pour the sugar over the beans to nearly fill the jar. Shake it up a bit, then put the jar in your spice cabinet. After a week, you'll have lovely vanilla sugar. Simply replace the sugar with fresh sugar as you use it.

bananas flambé with hudson's bay rum

Bananas flambé may not seem like a typical Western dessert, but we put it on our menu when we first opened in 1963. It's so tasty and universally loved, why not? We used to flambé it with Hudson Bay Company 151-proof rum, which had such a high level of alcohol, the pan fired quickly and burned off the alcohol to leave behind the dark, luscious rum flavor—after a spectacular tableside show. In 1987, the HBC sold its distilling operations to Seagram's and so while you can't find its rum any longer, you can use Bacardi's 151-proof rum instead for a delicious outcome.

The Hudson Bay Company was once the largest land holder in North America, with most of its property in Canada. It was founded in 1620 and for many years prospered so successfully that by the early days of the nineteenth century it was a multimillion-dollar empire. In 1833, the Bent St. Vrain Company in southern Colorado and the North American Fur Trade Company owned by John Jacob Astor were in head-to-head competition with HBC. • *serves 4*

4 bananas (not overly ripe)
4 tablespoons unsalted butter
2 tablespoons dark honey
Juice of 1 small lime
Dash of ground cinnamon
¼ cup (151-proof) dark rum
Vanilla ice cream

Cut the bananas in half lengthwise, then in half crosswise, yielding 4 pieces per banana.

In a chafing dish over a high flame, combine the butter, honey, lime juice, and cinnamon and bring to a boil. Gently place the bananas in the chafing dish, flat side down. Lower the heat and simmer for 1 minute, then add the rum. Light a long fireplace match and carefully flame the dish. Coat the banana pieces well with sauce and arrange 4 pieces of banana around a scoop of ice cream on each dessert plate.

colorado peaches flambé

Peach flambé can be set alight with rum, but at the Fort we have always used Scotch whiskey and no one has complained! It's a lovely summertime dessert when the peaches are ripe, juicy, and sweet. Even better if you have homemade vanilla ice cream. It's a dessert with history, too, since the story goes that Thomas Jefferson learned of it on one of his trips to France and introduced it to this country. • *serves 4*

4 tablespoons unsalted butter
½ cup sugar
Pinch of cinnamon
4 ripe peaches, peeled, halved, and pitted
¼ cup high-proof Scotch whiskey
Vanilla ice cream

In a skillet or sauté pan, combine the butter, sugar, and cinnamon. Place over low heat just until the butter melts and the sugar dissolves.

Add the peach halves cut side down and bring the heat up to medium-low. Cover and let simmer for 4 to 5 minutes until tender when pierced with a knife. Turn the peaches over and continue to simmer uncovered for another 2 to 3 minutes.

Add the Scotch to the pan and let warm for 10 seconds. Carefully ignite the whiskey and let the flames die out naturally.

To serve: Place 2 peach halves in each bowl on top of a scoop of vanilla ice cream and drizzle with the remaining syrup. Serve immediately.

HOW TO FLAMBÉ

Pay attention to the bananas, cherries, peaches, or anything else you set afire by dousing it with alcohol—the flames can get quite high! This is dramatic to be sure, but the flames might lick over anything flammable in the vicinity and cause some trouble, so don't wear floppy sleeves and pull back long hair. When the initial flame subsides, a small blue flame will continue to burn for several seconds. This is when you should rotate the pan to expose the fruit to any more alcohol that might ignite and burn off. The goal is to keep the blue flame alive for as long as possible to caramelize the sugars in the alcohol, reduce any raw alcohol flavor, and entertain your guests.

▼▼▼▼▼▼▼▼▼▼▼▼▼▼▼▼▼▼▼▼▼▼▼

colorado cherries jamboree

Clearly we liked flambéed desserts in the early days of the Fort, both because they taste good and because they are impressive to prepare at the table. Cherries from Colorado's Western Slope make a delicious cherry jamboree, which is also known as cherries jubilee. • *serves 4 to 6*

½ cup sugar

2 tablespoons cornstarch

¼ cup water

¼ cup orange juice

1 pound Bing or other dark, sweet cherries, rinsed and pitted,
  or use 1 package (16-ounce) frozen pitted cherries

½ teaspoon finely grated orange zest

Vanilla ice cream

1 tablespoon cherry brandy or liqueur or ¼ teaspoon cherry extract

¼ cup Cognac or brandy

Whisk together the sugar and cornstarch in a skillet or sauté pan. Stir in the water and orange juice; bring to a boil over medium-high heat, whisking until thickened. Stir in the cherries and orange zest, return to a boil, then reduce the heat, and simmer for 6 to 8 minutes for fresh cherries, or 2 to 3 minutes for frozen cherries.

While the cherries are cooking, spoon the ice cream into serving bowls.

Remove the cherries from the heat, and stir in the cherry brandy. Carefully ignite it using a long fireplace match. Gently shake the pan until the blue flame has extinguished itself. Spoon the cherries over the bowls of ice cream.

holly's adobe brick sundae

We serve a lot of ice cream sundaes at the Fort, including one I "invented" when I was ten years old. I named it Holly's Adobe Brick Sundae. In those days, you could get a small brick of vanilla ice cream, which I put on a salad plate, sprinkled generously with a mixture of Nestlé's hot cocoa mix, sugar, and cinnamon, and grabbed a spoon. As the ice cream melted, I stirred the dry mixture into the creamy liquid to create a sauce. My parents thought it was so innovative for a kid, they put it on the menu, where it has remained in one form or another to this day! If you want to try it, my formula is 1 cup of cocoa mix with 1 teaspoon of sugar and 1 teaspoon of ground cinnamon for 4 servings.

• *serves 6 to 8*

1 ½ quarts vanilla ice cream

1 cup Nesquik or another sweetened chocolate milk mix

2 tablespoons raw sugar or granulated sugar

1 teaspoon ground cinnamon

GARNISH

Lightly sweetened whipped cream, flavored with vanilla

6 to 8 sprigs fresh mint

Fill a small loaf pan (4½ by 9 inches) with slightly softened vanilla ice cream. Return to the freezer for several hours, until the ice cream has hardened.

In a small bowl, combine the chocolate mix, sugar, and cinnamon and set aside.

To serve: Run a thin-bladed kitchen knife around the inside edges of the loaf pan, and invert the pan onto a cutting board. If the ice cream loaf doesn't unmold easily, place a clean dish towel soaked in cold water, and rung out, over the loaf pan to loosen the bottom, then lift off the pan. Dip the blade of the knife in cold water and cut 1½- to 2-inch-thick slices (bricks) off of the loaf.

Sprinkle the chocolate mixture over the ice cream. Garnish each serving with a dollop of whipped cream and a sprig of mint. Serve immediately.

homemade butterscotch sundaes

My husband Jeremy loves homemade butterscotch, and this is one of his favorites. Spoon it over any flavor of ice cream you like. • *serves 4 to 6*

1 tablespoon corn syrup
About 2 tablespoons water
   (just enough so the bottom of the saucepan is covered)
1 ½ teaspoons fresh lime juice
1 ½ cups sugar
Cream of tartar
1 cup heavy cream
3 tablespoons unsalted butter
Ice bath for the pot
1 quart vanilla bean ice cream
¼ cup lightly toasted pine nuts
Whipped cream

In a medium saucepan, combine the corn syrup, water, and lime juice. Then, over medium heat, add the sugar and dust the cream of tartar lightly over the top of it. Do not stir! Just jiggle the pan once in a while. When the sugar is melted and a dark caramel color is achieved, 1 to 2 minutes, turn off the heat.

Slowly whisk in the cream. When the cream is thoroughly mixed in, begin to add the butter. Stir until the butter is melted. Return the sauce to the heat. Stirring constantly, bring it to a simmer. Once the simmer point is achieved, cook, stirring, for 60 seconds exactly. Remove from the heat and set the saucepan in an ice bath. Serve warm or at room temperature. The sauce may be made in advance, covered, and refrigerated for up to 1 week before serving.

Place 2 scoops of ice cream in each sundae dish. Top with warm butterscotch sauce, a sprinkling of pine nuts, and a dollop of whipped cream. Serve immediately!

THE NEVER-ENDING APPEAL OF ICE CREAM

During the first snowfall of the winter, my mother always sent us outside to fill a bowl with fresh, clean snow so that we could make snow ice cream. We rapidly mixed the snow with cream, sugar, vanilla, chocolate syrup, or cinnamon and happily spooned the mixture from the bowl. This was so exciting for my brother and me—the first taste of winter's snow.

I have read that as early as AD 65, Roman Emperor Nero sent his slaves to the mountains to collect snow so that he could mix it with fruit and honey. Centuries later, Marco Polo allegedly brought a recipe for snow mixed with yak milk for an early version of ice milk home to Italy from China, and a few centuries later, Catherine de Medici introduced ice milk to France. Although Catherine was from Florence, she became queen of France in 1533, and the French, not content with the Italian version, reportedly added chocolate and strawberries to the icy dessert. Charles I of England is said to have taken ice cream to his country, and from there it was not long before it became popular in the New World. In America, both Thomas Jefferson and Dolley Madison were known for serving ice cream, the former at Monticello and the latter at her husband's Inaugural Ball in 1813. While some historians refute this information, I appreciate its charm and bigger message that throughout history people have been drawn to sweet, cold desserts.

The evolution of ice cream as we know it today follows the trajectory of the invention of refrigeration. Today, we think of ice cream as an all-American treat. Ice cream shops and supermarkets offer a staggering number of different flavors, one more tempting than the next. If you are an ice cream lover, it's a magnificent time to be alive!

One of my favorite ice cream desserts is a prickly pear sundae. It's not really a recipe, since you pour prickly pear syrup over vanilla ice cream and have at it, but I could not write this book without mentioning it. If you want to try it, you can buy prickly pear syrup in some specialty stores or order it through the Internet. Turn to page 241 for a source.

green chile ice cream

When I was experimenting with different flavors of ice cream, I discovered that if I rinsed canned green chiles and added them to the mixture, they tasted almost like pineapple when they were processed in the ice cream machine. I started with the avocado ice cream my dad had made for an old television show called *Frying Pans West*, so I guess you could say this ice cream is a joint venture between Dad and me. • *serves 4 to 6*

2 ripe avocados
Juice of 1 lime
1 cup confectioners' sugar
1 (8-ounce) can mild green chiles, rinsed, patted dry, and coarsely chopped
1½ cups whipped cream or vanilla ice cream
1 mint sprig, for garnish

Peel and slice the avocados. Transfer the avocado flesh to the bowl of an electric mixer bowl with the lime juice and confectioners' sugar. With the mixer on slow speed, beat the mixture until smooth. Add the green chiles and mix until incorporated. Add the whipped cream or ice cream and beat until thoroughly mixed.

Transfer the mixture to an ice cream machine and freeze according to the manufacturer's instructions. Serve garnished with mint.

triple-cherry cast-iron cobbler

While this recipe is for cherries, we also make a cast-iron cobbler with apples and peaches, depending on the season and what fruit is at its peak. Cherries are at their best in the middle of the summer and so you can be pretty sure of finding this on our menu in July or August. We call it a "cast-iron" cobbler to reference the rustic desserts made in Dutch ovens set over campfires by the settlers who traveled west. • *serves 4 to 6*

STREUSEL TOPPING

²/₃ cup all-purpose flour

¹/₃ cup old-fashioned oats

¹/₃ cup packed brown sugar

¹/₄ cup slivered almonds

¹/₄ teaspoon cinnamon

4 tablespoons cold, unsalted butter, cut into cubes

FILLING

1 (15.25-ounce) can pitted Bing Cherries in syrup (not pre-thickened), strained. Save the juice.

1 (14.5-ounce) can pitted tart cherries or fresh tart cherries (not pie filling), drained. Save the juice

¹/₂ cup black or red cherry nectar or juice

¹/₃ cup sugar

¹/₂ teaspoon salt

1 cup sun-dried cherries

¹/₄ cup cornstarch, mixed with water to a thin paste

To make the streusel topping: In a mixing bowl, stir together the flour, oats, sugar, almonds, and cinnamon. Using a pastry blender, cut the butter into the dry ingredients until the mixture resembles coarse crumbs. Cover and chill the streusel, until ready to use.

Preheat the oven to 375°F.

Mix the reserved juices, cherry nectar, sugar, and salt together in a medium saucepan and bring to a boil. Place the canned and dried cherries in an 8- to 9-inch cast-iron skillet or a 9-inch shallow baking dish. When the mixture comes to a boil, stir in the cornstarch mixture. Reduce the heat to medium and cook, stirring, for 3 to 5 minutes, until the juices thicken. Pour the juices over the cherries, and top with the streusel. Bake the cobbler for about 30 minutes or until golden brown. Let sit for 30 minutes before serving.

sarah's rosemary-infused panna cotta

This rosemary-kissed custard was created by our pastry chef Sarah Bailey who makes everything with love and passion. I particularly like to watch her work because her devotion and care are evident with every movement. One of my personal favorites is this light, creamy, and eggless Italian-style dessert. The texture of this dessert is best when it is served the same day you make it. • *serves 4 to 6*

1½ teaspoons unflavored gelatin
2 cups heavy cream
6 tablespoons sugar
2 sprigs fresh rosemary
6 ounces fresh huckleberries or blueberries
Lightly sweetened whipped cream

Soften the gelatin in 1 tablespoon of cold water.

In a medium saucepan, combine the cream and sugar. Add the rosemary sprigs and place over medium heat until the cream reaches a simmer. Remove the cream from the heat and allow to steep for 5 minutes. Remove and discard the rosemary, and stir in the gelatin. Stir until the gelatin is melted and well incorporated. Pour the mixture into wineglasses or ramekins and chill for 3 hours.

Top each panna cotta with fresh berries and whipped cream.

montana's wild huckleberry crème brûlée

This is another creation from our talented pastry chef Sarah Bailey, who makes smooth, creamy crème brûlée with its characteristic and irresistible crispy topping of caramelized sugar according to the season. We have put cinnamon, coffee, and pumpkin brûlée on the menu, but this wild huckleberry dessert is hands-down our customers' favorite.

• *serves 4 to 6*

2 cups (1 pint) heavy whipping cream
4 large eggs
½ cup sugar
1 teaspoon pure vanilla extract
Huckleberry preserves, page 241, or blueberry preserves
Raw sugar

Preheat the oven to 300°F.

Pour the cream into a large saucepan.

Separate the eggs. Place the yolks in a medium mixing bowl, and reserve the whites for another use. Add the sugar and vanilla to the yolks and whisk until the mixture turns pale yellow. Over medium heat, bring the cream just to a simmer. Gradually whisk the hot cream into the yolks.

Spread a thin layer of huckleberry preserves in the bottom of 4 to 6 ramekins. Fill the ramekins with the cream mixture. Place the ramekins in a shallow roasting pan and add enough hot water to come about halfway up the sides. Bake for 1 hour or until the custard is barely set. Place the ramekins in another shallow roasting pan and pour in enough cold water to come halfway up the sides. When cool, refrigerate the custards until completely set.

To serve, lightly sprinkle raw sugar over the top of each custard and place the custards under a hot broiler for a few seconds to caramelize the sugar.

Note: If you often make crème brûlée, you may want to invest in a special butane chef's torch made for caramelizing sugar.

capirotada or spotted dog bread pudding

This bread pudding evolved from the old Spanish dish called *capirotada* which, according to *Libro del Arte Cozina,* a cookbook compiled by Diego Granado in the late 1500s, began as a savory dish of layered bread, onions, cheese, and meat or poultry. It was topped with sweet meringue, an odd flourish to our modern sensibilities. My father conjectured that a dessert similar to this originated in New Mexico in the early nineteenth century.

"It is quite likely that the many apple orchards of New Mexico grew from seeds brought from Europe in the very early days by French and Spanish priests, when a supply wagon train came from Mexico to the missions every two years," Dad wrote. "Later, more frequent wagon trains continued to bring wines, fruit, grape shoots, chocolate, cheeses and delicacies north to New Mexico." He continued to explain that the dessert was considered a Lenten dish in New Mexico and further south in Mexico. "Onions in a dessert may seem strange," he conjectured, "but when cooked, they add to the pleasing apple flavor." As to its name, Dad said it was often called "spotted dog" because of the raisins, and also because the mountain men "had little patience with the Spanish language." • *serves 6*

1 ½ cups crushed piloncillo or brown sugar

1 cup water

½ medium sweet yellow onion, finely chopped

3 large eggs

1 ½ cups half-and-half or milk

4 cups toasted bread, cut or torn into
    approximately 1 ½-inch pieces

¾ cup raisins (plumped in hot water)

1 Gala or Granny Smith apple, peeled,
    cored, quartered, and sliced

4 tablespoons unsalted butter or margarine

1 ½ teaspoons ground cinnamon

½ teaspoon grated nutmeg

4 ounces yellow Cheddar cheese, grated (1 cup)

Heavy cream, for pouring on top

Preheat the oven to 350°F.

Boil the sugar and water to make the syrup approximately the consistency of maple syrup. Add the onion and continue boiling for 5 minutes.

In a separate bowl, stir together the eggs and half-and-half. Don't beat them!

In a 3-quart baking dish, layer the bread, raisins, apple, butter, cinnamon, and nutmeg. Pour the syrup-onion mixture on top, then the egg-milk mixture. Push down the filling with a spoon to make sure all the ingredients become moist.

Bake for 40 minutes, remove from the oven, and spread the grated cheese on top. Return the pudding to the oven for 5 minutes, or until the cheese is melted and well browned. The pudding should absorb all the liquid and be very moist, with a well-browned top. If it seems to be getting too brown, cover with foil for the remainder of the cooking time. Serve hot with a bit of cold heavy cream poured over each serving.

Note: Capirotada may be baked ahead of time, except for the cheese topping. Thirty minutes before serving, preheat the oven to 350°F. Cover the capirotada and heat for 20 minutes. Top with the cheese and return to the oven for 5 minutes to allow the cheese to melt and begin to brown.

bird's nest pudding

This recipe is one I remember from my childhood and to this day I make it every Easter with the kids from my neighborhood. It calls for dozens of empty eggshells to use as molds, so I suggest you start collecting them a few weeks before you want to make this, or plan on a lot of omelets. As with so many of the dishes I love, I learned this one from my father, Sam'l. Here is what he said about the pudding.

"Easter wasn't Easter at our house when I was a child without Bird's Nest Pudding. I have no idea where my mother learned the dish. It probably came from her mother's English Quaker ancestors, the Fox family. I found a similar recipe with the same name in *Brigg's Cookery,* published in London in 1788.

"It's basically a flavored blancmange molded in the shape of eggs and laid in a nest of candied orange and grapefruit strips on a bed of tasty wine gelatin. It's lots of fun for guests to choose which color egg they want. As a boy, I loved all of them, especially the green mint, blue almond, and pale vanilla." • *serves 6*

FOR EGGSHELLS
1 dozen large eggs

WINE GELATIN FOR THE NEST
2 tablespoons unflavored gelatin
½ cup cold water
1⅔ cups boiling water
1 cup sugar
⅓ cup orange juice
1 cup wine (sweet sherry or Madeira
   or any sweet wine)
3 tablespoons fresh lemon juice

BLANCMANGE FOR THE EGGS
(Makes 12 custard eggs)
2½ cups whole milk, scalded
1⅓ cups sugar
1 tablespoon cornstarch
1 teaspoon pure vanilla extract
Pinch of salt, to taste
2 tablespoons unflavored gelatin
½ cup cold water

FOUR FLAVORS
½ teaspoon pure vanilla extract
2 drops yellow food coloring
½ teaspoon mint extract
2 drops green food coloring
½ teaspoon almond extract
2 drops blue food coloring
1 teaspoon unsweetened cocoa

CANDIED ORANGE PEEL NEST
2 cups orange or grapefruit peel (no white pith),
   cut into thin strips
2¾ cups sugar
⅔ cup water

TOPPING
1 pint heavy cream

To prepare the eggshells: Pierce the eggs at the large end, carefully breaking a hole $1/2$ to $3/4$ inch in diameter. Gently shake the white and yolk out through the hole into a mixing bowl. Use the eggs for scrambled eggs, quiche, or another egg recipe. Rinse out the shells and invert them onto paper towels to dry.

To make the wine gelatin: Sprinkle the gelatin on the cold water and let it soften according to the package instructions. Add the boiling water, sugar, orange juice, wine, and lemon juice. Stir until the sugar is dissolved. Fill a large, shallow, serving bowl one-half to two-thirds full with the wine gelatin and chill for 3 to 5 hours, until set.

To make the blancmange: Whisk together the milk, sugar, cornstarch, vanilla, and salt in the top of a double boiler. Fill the bottom pot with enough hot water to almost reach the bottom of the top pot. Place the double boiler over medium heat and cook, stirring with a wooden spatula, until the mixture thickens enough to coat the back of the spatula.

Sprinkle the gelatin over the cold water and let it soften according to the package instructions. Add to the hot blancmange and stir well.

Divide the mixture equally among 4 bowls, and stir in the ingredients to make different colored and flavored eggs: In one bowl, add the vanilla and yellow food coloring. In another bowl, add the mint flavoring and green food coloring. In the third bowl, add the almond extract and blue food coloring. Add cocoa powder to the fourth bowl.

Rinse the eggshells with cold water to moisten and carefully pour in the colored and flavored blancmange. Return the eggshells to the carton with the open end up and chill until set, at least 3 hours.

To candy the peel: While the eggs and gelatin are chilling, prepare the candied peel. Place the peel in a saucepan with $1\frac{1}{3}$ cups cold water and bring to a boil. Simmer for 15 minutes, drain, and set aside.

Place 2 cups of sugar and $2/3$ cup water in a saucepan and bring to a boil, swirling the pan to melt the sugar. Boil, swirling, until the syrup reaches the firm-ball stage (244°F on a candy thermometer). Immediately drop the strips of peel into the syrup and boil for 1 to 2 minutes, until the syrup has thickened. Remove the citrus strips with a slotted spoon and allow them to cool; then roll them in the remaining $3/4$ cup sugar.

To serve: When the gelatin has set, build a "nest" of citrus strips around the edge of the bowl. When you're ready to serve, carefully crack and peel the custard eggs and set them on the wine gelatin so that they look as if they are in a nest.

Spoon the gelatin and candied peel into small dessert bowls and top each serving with 1 to 2 eggs. Serve with heavy cream.

beatriz's flan

Flans are as popular in Mexico as in their native Spain and have immigrated to New Mexico where a lot of the population is of Hispanic heritage. Made from easy-to-find and inexpensive ingredients (milk, eggs, sugar), the custards are soothingly smooth and pleasingly sweet. Flans must be cooked slowly at low heat because if not, they will bubble and turn spongy.

This amazing recipe comes from Beatriz Molina, who was our baker for a number of years. Beatriz and her husband Carlos came to work at the Fort in 1986 from Argentina and lived on the top floor of the building for more than twenty-five years. Carlos was our maintenance manager and when he died in 2009, he was laid to rest under the same pine tree next to our red rock as my father, mother, brother Keith, pet bear Sissy, and German shepherd Lobo.

• *serves 8*

6 large egg yolks
1 tablespoon pure vanilla extract
1 can (14-ounce) sweetened condensed milk
1 can (12-ounce) evaporated milk
1 cup whole milk
1½ cups sugar

Preheat the oven to 325°F. Mix together the egg yolks and vanilla, then add the condensed, evaporated, and fresh milk. Stir, don't beat, because beating will add air and result in a spongy flan.

Melt the sugar in a nonstick skillet, stirring almost constantly, until it becomes liquid and medium caramel in color. Watch it carefully! It will clump at first, then begin to melt. As the sugar melts, fill flan cups with very hot water. As soon as the sugar has caramelized, pour out the water from each cup one at a time and coat with caramel. Do this quickly. The syrup will harden almost instantly, and if it heats for even 30 seconds too long, it will turn to candy. Fill the cups with the flan mixture and place them in a shallow roasting pan. Pour in enough boiling water to come halfway up the sides of the cups. Bake on the middle rack of the oven for 45 minutes or until the custard is set.

Remove the cups of flan from the oven, cool in a pan of ice water, then refrigerate, preferably overnight, to allow the caramel to liquefy. When you're ready to serve it, run a knife around the edge of the cup, place a plate upside down on top of it, and invert it, so that the flan falls onto the plate topped with the caramel.

queso napolitano

We have served this flan at the Fort for years. It's not always on the menu, but is never absent for long. In the early 1950s, my father and mother read about a Mexico City restaurant in *Gourmet* magazine and when they traveled there, they also discovered this creamy dessert. Here is Dad's memory of what must have been a remarkable meal.

"*Gourmet* magazine published a story about a Yucatecán restaurant called *Circulo del Surest,* or Club Mayan, in the working class area of Mexico City. On our first trip to the restaurant we arrived to find young women patting out corn tortillas and chopping fresh roast chickens for soft tacos. We feasted on big, steaming roasts of young pork, mounds of shrimp salad in huge *cazuelas,* wonderful cold *congrejos moros* (stone crabs) with claws bulging with meat, and water-based hot chocolate, served in little *porrones,* which you sweetened to taste. For dessert there was *queso Napolitano,* a type of firm flan. It reposed on the counter like a great, circular, caramel-colored wedding cake. It cut and tasted like a soft cheese: sweet, rich, and glorious." • *serves 10 to 12*

²/₃ cup sugar
¼ cup water
1 can (14-ounce) sweetened condensed milk
1 can (12-ounce) evaporated milk
6 large eggs
1 tablespoon pure vanilla extract
8 ounces cream cheese

Preheat the oven to 325°F. Combine the sugar and water in a saucepan and cook over high heat, swirling the pot by the handle, to dissolve the sugar. When it comes to a boil, lower the heat to medium-low and simmer, swirling the pan often, until the sugar turns golden and caramelizes, 5 to 8 minutes. Once the sugar begins to caramelize, immediately pour the caramelized sugar into the flan mold and tilt so that it covers the bottom of the mold.

In the bowl of an electric mixer, combine the sweetened condensed milk, evaporated milk, eggs, vanilla, and cream cheese. Beat at medium speed until smooth.

Pour the mixture into the mold and cover with foil. Place the mold in another pan and pour in enough hot water to reach within an inch of the top.

Bake for 40 to 50 minutes, or until a knife inserted in the center of the custard comes out clean. Allow the flan to cool, then refrigerate overnight before unmolding and serving.

charlie carrillo's natillas

Natillas is a traditional dessert in Mexico and New Mexico at Christmastime and resembles the dessert some call floating island. The secret is to beat the egg whites until stiff, fold some into the custard, and then layer the rest with the custard for a light-as-air dessert. My friend Charlie Carrillo shared this recipe with me, and it's the best I have tasted.

While Charlie is a talented cook, his true gift is as a *santero,* a carver and painter of images of saints. He is recognized as one of the primary authorities on santero and also as the most accomplished artist practicing the regional tradition. He has won the Museum of International Folk Art's Hispanic Heritage Award, as well as numerous prizes (usually first place) at the Annual Traditional Spanish Market in Santa Fe. He helped me at the Tesoro Cultural Center create our juried annual Spanish market by bringing top, award-winning santeros as well as tin makers, potters, and jewelers to the event. I greatly admire Charlie for his humility, devotion, and great sense of humor. • *serves 6*

2½ cups whole milk

3 large egg yolks

⅓ cup sugar

1½ tablespoons cornstarch

1 teaspoon pure vanilla extract

Pinch of salt

3 pasteurized egg whites, see Note

¼ teaspoon cream of tartar

3 tablespoons confectioners' sugar

Cinnamon and/or nutmeg

Pour 2¼ cups of the milk into the top of a double boiler and whisk in the egg yolks and sugar.

In a small bowl, combine the remaining ¼ cup of milk and the cornstarch to make a thin paste.

Fill the lower half of the double boiler with enough hot water to almost touch the bottom of the top pot. Gently cook the custard over medium-low heat, stirring constantly. Just before it begins to simmer, stir in the cornstarch mixture. Continue to stir for 10 to 15 minutes until the custard thickens enough to thickly coat the back of a spatula. Remove the top pot from the heat, and stir in the vanilla and salt. Set aside.

Place the egg whites in the bowl of an electric mixer, and beat until soft peaks form. Add the cream of tartar and confectioners' sugar and continue to beat until the meringue is stiff and glossy.

Layer one-third of the meringue in a shallow serving bowl. Pour in half of the hot custard, then layer with one-third of the meringue, the remaining custard, and a top layer of meringue. Gently fold the entire mixture one or two times. Do not overmix the layers. Refrigerate for 1 hour.

Sprinkle with ground cinnamon and grated nutmeg, and serve chilled. The texture of this custard is best when it is eaten the day that you make it.

Note: Because of concerns about salmonella in some raw eggs, pasteurized egg whites are now sold at many supermarkets. We use them at the Fort when preparing uncooked meringue.

president andrew jackson's trifle

We first made this trifle in 1996 for the 150th anniversary celebration of Charles Bent's appointment as governor of New Mexico. Bent's Fort was built in 1833, during the last full year of Andrew Jackson's term as president. Jackson had a renowned sweet tooth and reportedly was extremely fond of this pudding made with sherry-soaked macaroons, sherry-flavored whipped cream, and orange marmalade. We serve this for private parties, and always to great acclaim.

• *serves 8 to 10*

2 cups whole milk

⅓ cup sugar

Pinch of salt

1 ½ tablespoons cornstarch

2 large eggs

½ teaspoon almond extract

½ pound almond macaroons

½ cup sweet sherry

1 cup orange or grapefruit marmalade

TOPPING

½ pint heavy whipping cream

2 teaspoons sugar

1 teaspoon sweet sherry

½ cup slivered almonds, toasted

In a saucepan over medium heat, bring the milk to a simmer.

Place the sugar, salt, cornstarch, and eggs in the top of a double boiler. Beat until smooth, then whisk in the hot milk a little at a time.

Fill the bottom pot with enough hot water to almost reach the bottom of the top pot.

Place the double boiler over medium heat, and cook, stirring with a wooden spatula, until the custard has the consistency of mayonnaise. Remove the custard from the heat and stir in the almond extract. Set aside to cool.

Arrange the macaroons on the bottom of a glass serving bowl. Pour the sherry over them, and then cover with the custard. Spread the marmalade on the top.

To make the topping, beat the heavy cream, sugar, and sherry until the cream stands in peaks. Top the trifle with the whipped cream and garnish with the almond slivers. Chill before serving.

sources: where to find it

Achiote Paste
La Perla Spice Company
555 N. Fairview St.
Santa Ana, California 92703
(800) 335-6292
 www.shop.delmayab.com

Aluminum Foil Smoking Bags
Hot Diggity Cajun
(888) 831-9674
www.hotdiggitycajun.com

My Secret Pantry
5135 E. Ingram Street
Mesa, Arizona 85205
(866) 440-2811
www.mysecretpantry.com

Buffalo Meat and Tongue
Altavista Bison
80 Hillside Road
Rutland, Massachusetts 01543
(508) 886-4365
www.altavistabison.com

Cushman Bison Farms
10225 W. 34 Road
Harrietta, Michigan 49638
www.CushmanBisonFarms.com

Great Range Bison
9757 Alton Way
Denver, Colorado 80640
(800) 327-2706
(303) 287-7100
(303) 287-7272 (fax)
www.greatrangebison.com

Liechty Buffalo Ranch
P.O. Box 36
Leo, Indiana 46765
(260) 627-0124
www.liechtybuffaloranch.com

Chiles and Ristras
The Chile Shop
109 East Water Street
Santa Fe, New Mexico 87501
(505) 983-6080
(505) 984-0737
www.thechileshop.com

Curry Bush Leaves
My Spice Sage
5774 Mosholu Avenue
Bronx, New York 10471
(877) 890-5244
www.myspicesage.com

Dried Damiana
EGarden Seed
(707) 733-3710
www.egardenseed.com

Quality Bulk Herbs
Deerfield Beach, Florida 33441
(619) 940-4516
www.QualityBulkHerbs.com

Grits
Agrirama
Georgia's Museum of Agriculture &
Historic Village
1392 Whiddon Mill Road
Tifton, Georgia 31793
(800) 776-1875
(229) 386-7289
www.agrirama.com

Local Harvest
P.O. Box 1292
Santa Cruz, California 95061
(831) 515-5602
www.localharvest.org

Southern Grace Farms
Rt.1 Box 28A
Enigma, Georgia 31749
(229) 533-8585
www.southerngracefarms.net

Heirloom Beans
Adobe Milling Company
P.O. Box 596
Dove Creek, Colorado 81324
(800) 542-3623
www.anasazibeans.com

Purcell Mountains Farms
Moyie Springs, Idaho 83845
(208) 267-0627
www.purcellmountainfarms.com

Rancho Gordo
1924 Yajome
Napa, California 94559
(707) 259-1935
www.RanchoGordo.com

Huckleberry Preserves
Eva Gates Homemade Preserves
PO Box 696
Bigfork, Montana 59911
(800) 682-4283
www.evagates.com

Huckleberry Morning
P.O. Box 190387
Hungry Horse, Montana 59919
(406) 387-4227
www.huckleberrymorning.com

The Huckleberry Patch Gift Shop
8868 US Highway 2 East
Hungry Horse, Montana 59919
(800) 527-7340
www.huckleberrypatch.com

Indian Garden Seeds
Museum of the Fur Trade
Highway 20
Chadron, Nebraska 69337
(308) 432-3843
www.furtrade.org
The museum saves enough of the precious seeds to replant, and any surplus is offered for sale to museum patrons.

Lamb Spareribs
Lava Lake Land & Livestock, L.L.C.
P.O. Box 2249
Hailey, Idaho 83333
(888) 528-5253
www.lavalakelamb.com/

U.S. Wellness Meats
P.O. Box 9
Monticello, Missouri 63457
(877) 383-0051
www.grasslandbeef.com

Mexican Jalapeños in Jars
Mex Grocer
(877) 463-9476
www.mexgrocer.com

Prickly Pear Syrup
Cheri's Desert Harvest
1840 E. Winsett
Tucson, Arizona 85719
(800) 743-1141
(520) 623-4141
www.cherisdesertharvest.com

Quail, Quail Eggs, and Other Game Birds
Manchester Farms, Inc.
P.O. Box 97
Dalzell, South Carolina 29040
(800) 845-0421
(803) 469-8637 (fax)
www.manchesterfarms.com

Lake Cumberland Game Bird Farm
7768 East Highway 90
Monticello Wayne, Kentucky 42633
(765) 381-3642
(606) 348-6370 (fax)
www.lakecumberlandgamebirds.com

Quinoa and San Luis Potatoes
White Mountain Farms
8890 Lane 4 North
Mosca, Colorado 81146
(800) 364-3019
(719) 378-2436
www.whitemountainfarms.com

Spanish Spices, Saffron, Sausages, and Cookware
The Spanish Table
109 North Guadalupe Street
Santa Fe, New Mexico 87501
(505) 986-0243
www.spanishtable.com

family fun-to-make recipes

Because I feel so strongly about cooking with kids and bringing them into the kitchen, I have designated a number of recipes as "Sissy Bear dishes." This means they are easy enough to make with your kids and appealing enough for the kids to want to cook: "Now, Mom! Please!"

The recipes do not contain alcohol (with the exception of the wine gelatin in the Bird's Nest Pudding on page 234). None is complicated or involves grilling or sautéing. As your children become more accomplished cooks, they will want to try more and more of the dishes on these pages. And that is how it should be.

I learned to cook from my mother and have included family recipes that we both cherished. Some are great fun around the holidays, such as Baked Stuffed Pumpkin on page 177 for Halloween, the Pumpkin-Walnut Muffins on page 146 at Thanksgiving, and the Bird's Nest Pudding at Easter. Others are good any old time.

a word to kids (and their parents):
Please be extra careful in the kitchen. Follow safety and hygiene rules as well as you can. This means tying up loose hair to keep it away from a flame, using oven mitts with hot pans, and letting your mom or dad wield the sharp knives. It also means washing your hands before you begin and several times during cooking. Take special care around boiling water, hot foods, and stove tops and grills. And always make sure an adult is supervising you.

index